Central Library
Y Llyfrgell Ganolog
☎ 02920 382116

ACC. No: 05113645

THE 100
BEST NOVELS
IN TRANSLATION

THE 100 BEST NOVELS IN TRANSLATION

BOYD TONKIN

G

Galileo Publishers
Cambridge UK

Galileo Publishers
16 Woodlands Road
Great Shelford
Cambridge CB22 5LW
UK

www.galileopublishing.co.uk

ISBN 978-1-903385-67-8

First published in the UK 2018

© 2018 Boyd Tonkin

All rights reserved.

This book is sold subject to the
condition that it shall not, by way of trade or
otherwise, be lent, resold, hired out or otherwise
circulated in any form of binding or cover other
than that in which it is published and without a similar
condition including this condition being imposed
on the subsequent purchaser.

1 2 3 4 5 6 7 8 9
Printed in the EU

"The only true voyage, the only bath in the Fountain of Youth, would be not to visit strange lands but to possess other eyes, to see the universe through the eyes of another, of a hundred others, to see the hundred universes that each of them sees, that each of them is."

Marcel Proust, from *The Captive (In Search of Lost Time V)*; translated by CK Scott Moncrieff and Terence Kilmartin, revised by DJ Enright.

"It seems to me that translating from one language to another, unless it is from Greek or Latin, the queens of all languages, is like looking at Flemish tapestries from the wrong side, for although the figures are visible, they are covered by threads that obscure them, and cannot be seen with the smoothness and colour of the right side... And I do not wish to infer from this that the practice of translating is not deserving of praise, because a man might engage in worse things that bring him even less benefit."

Miguel de Cervantes, *Don Quixote*, Part Two; translated by Edith Grossman.

"There is no greater service to literature than to transport from one language to another the masterpieces of the human mind. So few first-rate works exist; genius, in whatever genre, is such a rare phenomenon that if each modern nation were reduced to its own treasures, it would be forever poor. Moreover, the circulation of ideas is, of all the forms of trade, the one with the most certain benefits."

Anne-Louise-Germaine Necker, Madame de Staël, *On the Spirit of Translations*; translated by Boyd Tonkin.

"Hang up your hat/ in the halfway house."

WG Sebald, *Schattwald in Tyrol*; translated by Iain Galbraith.

CONTENTS:

INTRODUCTION

I

On a grey February day towards the end of the last millennium, I went to interview the writer WG Sebald at the university in eastern England where he taught. His book *Die Ausgewanderten* (*The Emigrants*) had appeared a couple of years previously in Michael Hulse's outstanding English translation. Self-exiled from Germany, the author-professor had begun to enjoy in the English-speaking world the early whispers of an acclaim that, after his death in 2001, would rise into a global roar. During his career, and then as a posthumous presence, Max Sebald embodied for many readers the meanings of translation in much more than a strictly linguistic sense.

After he came to England in 1966, he had taught German literature in Manchester. That city supplies the drizzly backdrop to one of the quartet of stories in *The Emigrants*, and also, incidentally, the sodden setting for another experimental work by a former foreign-language teacher at Manchester University: Michel Butor's *L'Emploi du Temps* (*Passing Time*). In 1970, after a spell in Switzerland, Sebald had moved to the University of East Anglia outside Norwich, where he settled for the rest of his career. As UEA's Professor of European Literature, then the first director of the British Centre for Literary Translation, he led a long-overdue drive to create for the translator's art a solid institutional niche in UK higher education.

Beyond this professional role, his chosen passage from Germany to England, his mesmeric prose and his personal authority – quizzical, ironic, self-deprecating, but no less real for all that – marked him out as someone who lived, thought and wrote in between; in between languages, cultures, sensibilities. Yet he was the opposite of the rootless cosmopolitan pilloried through two centuries of nativist calumny, from the blood-and-soil rhetoric of the Third Reich, whose victims his books so magnificently mourn, to the foolish sneers at "citizens of the world" heard today from politicians with a shaky grasp of history. The German Sebald wholly contained the English Sebald, and the other way around. Far from rootless, he seemed doubly grounded. He never wrote books directly in English but collaborated intensively with fellow artists who transformed the voice of his first language into his second: above all, Michael Hulse and Anthea Bell. Millions of people, in all ages and places, have also lived completely in that space where tongues and worlds converge. Occasionally as artists, always as citizens, they have not been diminished but enriched by an intimate, life-long traffic between different expressions of the same, shared human experience.

Translation not only takes place between tongues, a formal dialogue of one lexicon with another. On that dour late winter day, wandering through the UEA grounds or sitting in the hi-tech aircraft hangar of its arts centre, Sebald explored – but never quite defined – the uncanny transits between biography and fiction, present and past, that lend his books their liminal potency. To write, and to read, is forever to cross thresholds. Or, perhaps, to wish that they might be crossed. Max Sebald used to scour market stalls for the vintage postcards which, uncaptioned, cast their ghostly spell across his books. "Like all the dead," he told me, they have "a sense of grievance. They say, 'Please, can you try and do something about it?'"

Reading books from the past, even the recent past, is one thing we can do to overcome the barriers that time, language and environment erect. Read them in translations from languages we do not know and we can hope to leap over several hurdles in one bound. Globally-minded critics salute literary translation as a privileged means of passing border-posts, a sort of universal passport issued by that Utopian state, the Republic of Letters. Since the ages of Enlightenment and Romanticism, the champions of translation – such as Goethe and Madame De Staël – have urged its necessity, if only as an inferior substitute for the true polyglot's command of several tongues. That case still needs to be made, especially in English, whose position as a planet-spanning *lingua franca* may trick native speakers into the delusion that their language, or any language, may encompass the whole world of thought and art. The example of Max Sebald, with his works that glide like melancholy spectres around the frontiers of fact and fiction, memory and history, suggests too that translation might be no more than a special instance of the need to understand other minds, and other lives, that drives all human interchange.

I first encountered this argument as an awestruck undergraduate reader of George Steiner's book *After Babel*. For Steiner, "When we read or hear any language statement from the past, be it Leviticus or last year's bestseller, we translate". We are always translating, even if we have never learned a single word of any other tongue. Regions and dialects have to translate one another; so do classes, communities and sub-cultures. Women, of course, have to translate men and vice versa, although usually with less success. Supremely, the present must always translate the past, even if that past began only yesterday. Steiner insists that "a human being performs an act of translation, in the full sense of the word, when receiving a speech-message from any other human being. Time, distance, disparities in outlook or assumed reference, make this act more or less difficult." Only when the perceived distance between sender and receiver grows wide enough, as in the gap between written languages, does this universal activity pass "from reflex to conscious technique".

Thinking of translation in this light may help to demystify, but not downgrade, the process. On the one hand, literary translators sometimes appear as hierophants or psychopomps, lofty priests of a cult of the crossroads and the threshold whose esoteric mysteries outsiders can never hope to fathom. Much of what counts as "translation theory" appears to be designed as a kind of arcane compensation for the very real neglect, financial and intellectual, that translators often suffer in the course of their working lives. It succeeds best, at least in my experience, when it frankly embraces the mystical rather than technical aspects of the craft. In his famous essay "The Task of the Translator", for example, Walter Benjamin suspends the usual battles between "literal" and "creative", "nativising" and "foreignising" schools to imagine translation as transcendence; as a movement up into a celestial sphere where minds and tongues finally touch. "In translation the original rises into a higher and purer linguistic air... It cannot live there permanently, to be sure; neither can it reach that level in every aspect of the work. Yet in a singularly impressive manner, it at least points the way to this region: the predestined, hitherto inaccessible realm of reconciliation and fulfilment of languages." In a more practical register, the writer and translator Kate Briggs quotes her distinguished fellow practitioner Anthea Bell as saying that, between her immersion in the source book and starting work on its translation, "the translator's mind dwells somewhere, for a little while, where there isn't any language at all". Or where, perhaps, the Biblical curse of Babel has lifted, and consciousness can glimpse a paradise of friction-free mutual understanding.

On the other hand, translation sceptics have for centuries followed the lead of Cervantes' *Don Quixote*. During his conversation in a

Barcelona printshop, the Don dismisses translations from modern languages as like "looking at Flemish tapestries from the wrong side", their figures "covered by threads that obscure them". The Don later drops the small change of faint praise in the translator's cap: "a man might engage in worse things". Yet his simile had done its work, for all that Cervantes presents his novel as no more than a translation from the Arabic original of a Muslim historian "Cide Hamete Benengeli", picked up for a song in the Toledo marketplace. That faded tapestry would unroll across centuries of translator-bashing disdain.

If the mystagogues of translation theory may deter non-specialists, then so do the purists – let's call them the "Untranslatables" – who dwell on the ineffable uniqueness of the source text and the language it employs. In their world view, a tough task becomes an impossible one. The inevitable loss of some signal in the conversion of a complex work of art from one verbal code to another becomes a reason either for never doing it all, or for pouring scorn on any poor bodger rash enough to try. Needless to say, this book would not exist if its author shared that attitude.

Read the polemics of the "Untranslatables" and a variety of motives appear. Most nobly, lovers and scholars of a major author – Gogol, perhaps, or SY Agnon, or Cao Xueqin, three figures whose alleged untranslatability often arises in discussion of their fiction – may simply see the obstacles to successful translation so clearly that they conclude that no amount of skill and learning will ever surmount them. Then again, translation does not take place, and never has, on anything like a level playing-field – itself a first-world, Anglocentric image. Historically, since the Renaissance at least, the West has translated the Rest. Even more, the dominant language-powers – in large part, English and French over the past three hundred years – have employed selective, unequal translation as a weapon in the armoury of imperial power. Examine Pascale Casanova's trail-blazing study *The World Republic of Letters* and you will see how closely the geography of translation fits the map of colonial and commercial control. Metropolitan centres such as Paris, London and later, New York, have acted as the publishing Vaticans that "consecrate" foreign authors from less-favoured parts. In the unbalanced global economy of literature, doubts about the accuracy or artistry of translation may belong with a stubborn resistance to outside plunder and abuse.

Less wholesomely, the cult of the untranslatable author or work may ratify a sort of nebulous nationalism; the sort that locates the soul of a people in the words of a beloved author. The guardians of such a sacred text assume that they have unimpeded access to its secrets – but that outsiders to some imagined community never will. At its most innocent, this is just cultural one-upmanship. You think you can appreciate Proust, or Chekhov, or Tanizaki, not just without French, Russian or Japanese, but a without thorough grounding in the ways of life embedded in their prose? What a ridiculous delusion… Snobbery aside, belief in the occult qualities of a language or writer may bolster ideologies of communal identity and special destiny. Such doctrines partnered the growth of literary nationalism from Britain to Russia, France to China. As the critic Franco Moretti puts it, the 19th-century nation-state "found the novel. And vice versa: the novel found the nation-state. And being the only symbolic form that could represent it, it became an essential component of our modern culture". Alexander Pushkin's novel-in-verse *Eugene Onegin* is perhaps the best-known example of a work deemed "untranslatable": the ironclad flagship of Russian cultural exceptionalism. Yet even this "essentially untranslatable" work has generated several persuasive renderings – most recently, in English, Stanley Mitchell's splendid version. In this context, I would translate "untranslatable" as "incredibly hard to translate well", and shift attention from the theology to the pragmatics of the job.

Some distinguished writers, and translators, have no patience for the hocus-pocus of untranslatability. Javier Marías, not only the author of many accomplished novels in his native Spanish but a gifted translator from English who has channelled works by Sterne, Stevenson, Conrad, Kipling and Faulkner, gives shockingly short shrift to the metaphysics of language. Heretically, he snaps the numinous bond between great authors and their mother tongue. For Marías, "The writer knows that the country in which he was born and the language in which he wrote, while important, are only secondary, even, up to a point, accidental, fortuitous and reversible. He knows that Proust could have existed in Italian or English, Lampedusa in Spanish or German, Thomas Mann in Czech or Swedish, or Cervantes, even, in French or Portuguese: he knows that language is just a vehicle, a tool, never an end in itself or something sacred, and not in any way superior to those who use it."

Marías cites Conrad, Nabokov and Wittgenstein as authors who swapped languages and flourished in their linguistic second homes. I would add both Samuel Beckett, another inspired self-translator who like Nabokov appears in this book, and also a leading novelist of the past half-century who has reverted to his mother tongue. Ngũgĩ wa Thiong'o, from Kenya, ceased to write fiction in English and returned to Gikuyu as part of a mission to promote the decolonisation of African culture. His work in Gikuyu culminated in the masterly epic satire *Wizard of the Crow*, published in 2006 and so just beyond the chronological confines of this work. Ngũgĩ also translated it, formidably, into the English he had quit. From ancient Rome and Renaissance England and France to post-colonial Africa today, the ability of so many writers of distinction to code-switch among languages, on the highest level of complexity, suggests that the Untranslatables may be worshipping a mirage.

II

The works of fiction discussed in this book represent both a kind of reader's autobiography, and the record of a professional path. As with many teenagers in the Great Britain of the late 1960s and 1970s, a blessed combination of well-stocked public libraries and the widespread availability at low prices of the Penguin Classics and Penguin Modern Classics series offered me a parallel education. Whatever might happen in school and, later, university classrooms, the local library shelves and those black- or grey-uniformed ranks of Penguins opened the doors onto a global literary landscape. Only translation could unlock them. At that stage I had no idea that, in the 1820s and 1830s, Johann Wolfgang von Goethe had theorised, and idealised, the notion of "world literature". He maintained that "National literature is now a rather unmeaning term; the epoch of world literature is at hand, and everyone must strive to hasten its approach. But, while we thus value what is foreign, we must not bind ourselves to some particular thing, and regard it as a model." In a project such as the twin Penguin lists, created in large part by veterans of the Second World War and by publishers and editors affected in some way by the chauvinistic madness of the Third Reich, Goethe's flame of transnational Enlightenment still burned bright.

It did not illuminate every culture equally. In my case, the journey began with the Russian classics that – often in Constance Garnett's still-attractive versions – had done so much to shape English fiction in the era of Woolf and Lawrence. Then came, like some bitter caffeine jolt, the Western European modernism of the first half of the twentieth century. For me, the novels of Kafka, Camus, Mann or Sartre are still affixed to memories of the art-works paired with them on Penguin covers, chosen by a graphic designer of genius (and anti-Fascist exile), Germano Facetti. A little later, the Latin American "boom" exploded overseas – detonated, in English, by Gabriel García Márquez. Against the permafrost of the Cold War, Central and East European fiction blossomed abroad in the work of Milan Kundera, Ismail Kadare and others. With the "post-modernist" and meta-fictional vogues of the 1980s came an appreciation of deadly serious pranksters like Georges Perec and Italo Calvino, and of restless innovators such as Clarice Lispector, Julio Cortázar and Marguerite Duras.

That still left, and leaves, huge gaps on the map. Especially in English, which has tended to give a tardy and tepid welcome to fiction from elsewhere, the topography of translation still resembles the late 19th-century atlas we had at home. In it, vast expanses of non-European land were no longer filled with quaint doodles of monsters but simply left blank. Piece by piece, translation of works from outside the European and American heartlands of traditional publishing has begun to widen the horizons Anglophone readers. Many absences and silences persist. Put like that, though, and curiosity about global fiction may begin to mimic the absurd conceit of European explorers in the ages of Columbus or Cook, when intrepid voyagers "discovered" human cultures that had got on perfectly well without them for millennia.

So let's tweak the metaphor. Rather, eager readers in the English-speaking world can feel like star-gazers. Light from distant suns may reach them in fitful flickers, decades or even centuries late. Sometimes, a major author's star may shine briefly in translation and then go dark again. Take the Swedish Nobel laureate Selma Lagerlöf. Strong modern English versions exist of her (somewhat untypical) debut *Gösta Berling's Saga*, and (as of 2017) her delightful children's story *The Wonderful Adventures of Nils*. Other, admirable, new translations have begun to appear from Norvik Press. Yet her landmark novel of Swedish migration to the Holy Land, *Jerusalem* (1901-2), has no accessible modern edition in English. The ageing of translations and the absence of accessible editions can, for English-language readers, extinguish the brightest of lights. A century ago, DH Lawrence acclaimed the work of the Sardinian novelist Grazia Deledda – another Nobel Prize winner. She was widely translated (always by women translators) but then, like many of her peers, vanished from the Anglophone's view. Only thanks to recent re-translations, notably by Martha King, can she occupy the place that she deserves in this book. In English, even a novel as important as Hermann Broch's *The Death of Virgil* – arguably, the equal of Mann's *The Magic Mountain* or Musil's *The Man Without Qualities* – has almost disappeared, except in the online market for second-hand titles. I had hesitated over the inclusion of another German Modernist masterwork, Alfred Döblin's *Berlin Alexanderplatz*, because that heady whirlwind tour of metropolitan life existed in English only in a flavoursome but dated translation. Then, in the nick of time, Michael Hofmann's sharp and spruce renovation arrived to save the day.

Some summits of fiction have been quite invisible to Anglophone readers. During the preparation of this book, for example, I began to glimpse the brilliant peak of Ahmad Fāris al-Shidyāq's *Leg Over Leg*. First published in Arabic in 1855, *Leg Over Leg* is the eccentric, satirical, picaresque story of a nomadic hero whose exploits reflect the life of its maverick Lebanese author. Like many rule-busting works of fiction, it stretches to breaking point any definition of the "novel". However you classify it, al-Shidyāq's merry masterpiece re-draws the orthodox map of Arabic literature in Western criticism. Yet it took 160 years for "the Fariyāq's" *Tristram Shandy*-esque adventures, in Humphrey Davies's virtuoso translation, to travel into English. In his rhapsodic defence of art's power to teleport us into other human galaxies, Proust in *The Captive* writes that great creators let us "fly from star to star". Without translation those stars – like *Leg Over Leg*, which should perhaps count as the honorary 101st entry in this book – may be forever hidden from us.

Although I read fiction in translation with scattergun voracity from my teenage years, it was only much later that an opportunity arose to think in a formal framework about the translator's art. In 2001, when I was literary editor of *The Independent*, vital support from Arts Council England allowed us to revive and develop the annual *Independent* Foreign Fiction Prize – first won in 1990 by Orhan Pamuk and his translator Victoria Holbrook, but in abeyance for five years. Arts Council backing gave me the precious opportunity to showcase, in a national newspaper which took pride in its cultural coverage, a range of translated fiction often overlooked elsewhere. The annual cycle of the prize anchored the international perspectives of a literary section that sought to offer readers an alternative to the mid-Atlantic bias of so much orthodox publishing. As well as editing those pages, I was one of the award's five co-judges from 2001 to 2015. Winning authors and translators included Javier Cercas and Anne McLean; Per Petterson and Anne Born; José Eduardo Agualusa and Daniel Hahn. The prize's longlists and shortlists also became a guide for publishers in various languages seeking to translate the best in new international fiction.

As an honour for a newly-translated book, the *Independent* prize mostly rewarded recent publications – although the belatedness of English translation meant that some contenders had originally appeared decades previously. Year after year, however, I found that many of the most memorable novels engaged in a dialogue with their forebears. My reader's journey into the more remote past recommenced. I tried to chart at least fragments of the literary hinterland that lay behind new fiction in German, Norwegian, Spanish, French or Turkish. One novelist winner of the *Independent* prize features in this book: WG Sebald himself, whose *Austerlitz* – in Anthea Bell's beautiful translation – appeared in English shortly before his death. So do two translator winners: Edith Grossman and Tiina Nunnally.

The Independent Foreign Fiction Prize split its £10,000 award equally between author and translator. That uncommon equality aimed to honour, and to spotlight, the art of the performers who transpose works of fiction from one language-key into another. The principle of parity survived when, in 2016, the *Independent* award merged with the Man Booker International Prize. Founded in 2005 to complement the Man Booker Prize, as a biennial award for a writer's entire body of work, the Man Booker International now adopted the *Independent* prize's guidelines. It became an annual honour for a single novel in English translation. I chaired the first jury of the re-configured prize, which garlanded Han Kang from South Korea, and her translator Deborah Smith, for her novel *The Vegetarian*. Within a few months of winning, it had sold 140,000 copies in the UK alone.

Gradually, a passion for fiction from beyond the "Anglosphere" ceased to feel like such an eccentric pursuit. Growing interest in translated literature among artisan publishers and independent bookshops joined robust campaigns by translators themselves, and a welcome widening of horizons in other media outlets, to echo and amplify my work with the paper and its prize. In 2016, the Man Booker International Prize commissioned a study into translation statistics from the market-research company Nielsen Book. It found that UK sales by volume of translated fiction had grown by 96 per cent since the millennium. Even more heartening, the report stated that "On average, translated fiction books sell better than books originally written in English, particularly in literary fiction." Literary fiction in translation accounted for around 3.5 per cent of fiction titles, but 7 per cent of total sales.

Still, the pious truism that translators seldom receive their just desserts – from publishers, editors, critics, bookshops and so on – bears repeating. More than that: historically, the translation of key works of fiction – at any rate, into English – has proved a random, haphazard and accident-prone business. The mere existence of so many glorious interpretations of foreign novels still feels almost like a miracle. For every *Don Quixote*, translated both early and often since the diplomat and (perhaps) spy Thomas Shelton published his version of Part One in 1612, there are many more tales of blocked channels and crossed wires. Cao Xueqin's *Dream of the Red Chamber*, the latest of China's canonical "Four Great Novels", was known to Chinese-speaking Western missionaries from the early 19th-century. It only broke into English in nuggets, extracts and abridgements until David Hawkes and John Minford undertook their wonderfully readable edition in the 1970s. Love, greed, fashion, rivalry, vanity, politics, diplomacy, and sheer obsession, have all played their part in the zigzag passage into English undergone by many of the titles discussed in this work. Besides, every translator – however experienced – must start from scratch with each book, pushing the rock back up the hill like Sisyphus in the myth that (in the same year he published *The Outsider*) Albert Camus chose as the very emblem of human striving. As Kate Briggs writes, "Books don't come with designated translators; they don't have built-in protocols, accepted codes of behaviour which can be followed (success) or ignored (failure). Our manners of translating have to be each time improvised and invented in new response to the book in hand." Any compilation such as this one represents not the chronicle of an orderly progress, but an inventory of some of the nippier vehicles that have survived the pile-ups, road-blocks and dead-ends on the highway of cultural transmission.

III

In literature, prescriptive canons have rightly lost much of their lustre. This book has no wish to polish up a tarnished genre. However, the "hundred best books" formula has a deeper, less authoritarian background than critics might presume. In Britain, the business began more than a century before the advent of the internet-friendly "listicle", with the eminent Victorian Sir John Lubbock. A banker, reformer, educator and Liberal politician, Lubbock in 1886 delivered a lecture about his ideal hundred-volume library to the Working Men's College in London. Founded by Christian Socialists in the 1850s, the College (still going strong as WMC: The Camden College) was and is an adult-education institution with a proud role in working-class history. In the aftermath of the Education Acts that enforced universal state schooling, and during the era that witnessed the birth of a mass-circulation popular press, the College (which, despite its name, supported courses for women as well) stood for an alternative ideal of independent-minded, self-directed education for emancipation.

Lubbock's list, then, did not intend to batter cowed students into submissive obedience. It aspired to raise horizons, and to initiate debate. "No list can be more than a suggestion," he modestly wrote when his "Hundred Best" had become a popular phenomenon, with even the Prince of Wales joining in the fun. "Whether they are the 'best' books or not, no one will deny that they are very good ones." Exactly. His choice, by the way, still looks impressively eclectic. It includes the *Analects of Confucius*, the *Qur'an*, the *Mahabharata*, the *Ramayana*, Ferdowsi's Persian epic poem *The Shahnameh* and the Sanskrit drama *Shakuntala* by Kālidāsa. Lubbock sought to cover every genre and every period. "Novels" in the modern sense only account for a dozen or so items. We agree on *Don Quixote*, although from Voltaire's satires he picks *Zadig* and *Micromégas* in preference to *Candide*. Rather than chuckling smugly over his inclusion of Edward Bulwer-Lytton's Roman potboiler *The Last Days of Pompeii*, contemporary list-makers should pause to ask which of their cherished touchstones will crumble into laughable kitsch over the decades to come. Framed within the progressive politics of late-Victorian self-organisation and self-improvement, Lubbock's "Hundred Best" sought not to lay down the law but point a way and, above all, open a conversation. This book shares those goals.

Of course, any such selection has its arbitrary and subjective elements. This one offers a personal roadmap that will, I hope, guide readers towards its proposed destinations, but might also stir them to take other routes. On one side of this map stand the limits of my own knowledge; on the other, the constraints imposed by the translations available in English-language publishing today. To hijack *Don Quixote*'s evergreen simile, I have had to choose not from an intact, comprehensive tapestry of global fiction, but from a ragged patchwork pitted with holes. Even so, the task proved predictably daunting. My initial list included well over 200 items. After pitiless pruning, around 140 candidates were still pressing their claims. This book's groundrules, though no doubt whimsical, have at least helped to finish the job. These one hundred books have one hundred authors. Another set of criteria might have delivered four novels by Dostoyevsky alone (*The Brothers Karamazov*, *Crime and Punishment*, *The Idiot, The Possessed*), plus multiple entries from Tolstoy, Kafka, Balzac, Zola, Mann, Duras, Lispector, García Márquez and many others.

My eligibility period – the four centuries between 1600 and 2000 – excludes a whole continent of pre-modern fiction at one pole, and a narrower peninsula of 21st-century works at the other. Learned literary histories, in particular by Steven Moore and Margaret Anne Doody, have lately stretched the origins of "the novel" back and out from the European age of Cervantes towards the ancient narrative traditions of India, China, the Middle East, Greece and Rome. For Doody, even within "the West", "The novel as a form of literature… has a continuous history of about two thousand years". Practicality rather than principle keeps this book within comparatively traditional channels, although I have tried to reflect the slightly wider availability in English of fiction from outside that "Western" sphere. I do not agree with Milan Kundera when he argues that "The novel is Europe's creation; its discoveries, though made in various languages, belong to the whole of Europe." However, this selection does seek to respect another of his ideas. Sceptical about the claims of "establishment modernism", with its pseudo-scientific model of fiction as one game-changing breakthrough after another, Kundera detects in this view "a residue of an ingenuous eschatological belief: that one History ends and another (better) one begins, founded on an entirely new basis". I hope, on the contrary, that this book conveys something of the parallel, multiple histories of fiction; histories which often meet, cross or fuse, but have never wholly converged.

Novels have always served as the vectors of impurity and contamination; dubious locales where peoples, stories, forms and ideas promiscuously mix. For Doody, "Novels are the hangout of slaves and lowlifes – of servant girls and delinquent picaresque boys, of strollers and the homeless, of people down on their luck or stuck in a strange environment." These marginal types care little for aesthetic norms and laws. From Daniel Defoe to WG Sebald, fiction has digested, incorporated and transformed the facts of journalism, history and biography. It may also devour poetry, philosophy, memoir, and a dozen other genres. This absorbency presents a challenge for a guide such as this one. Should I, for instance, have classified as a "novel" a hybrid masterpiece such as Fernando Pessoa's *The Book of Disquiet*, that fragmentary encyclopaedia of dream and fable, poem and essay, that the Portuguese writer presents as the notebooks of a fictional character, one "Bernardo Soares"? With some reluctance, I decided to leave *The Book of Disquiet* in a class of its own. At least its spirit enters this book in the guise of José Saramago's extraordinary novel in the vein and the wake of Pessoa, *The Year of the Death of Ricardo Reis*.

The length of "the novel" posed another problem. At one end, I found no reason to exclude multi-volume sequences – whether by Marcel Proust, Naguib Mahfouz or Pramoedya Ananta Toer – when they traced a single arc of narrative, however lengthy. For all the internal bonds and echoes between individual books, in contrast, the architecture of a multi-part series, such as Zola's *Rougon-Macquart* cycle, surely belongs to a different order. Great short works, however, proved even more troublesome than great long ones. My "novel" embraces the two forms designated in French as the "*roman*" and the fictional "*récit*", a distinction also active in other language traditions. This selection also has few qualms about inviting through its gate works that in English tend to be called "novellas". As a result I have slipped in – smuggled in, perhaps – masters such as Kleist and Chekhov. At what length, however, does the novella become a short story? These demarcations have little solid grounding in the history and practice of fiction. In any case, they often come couched in a parochial English-language terminology that ignores other literary landscapes.

That said, short fiction deserves a companion volume of its own. From Bruno Schulz in Poland to Lu Xun in China, Jorge-Luis Borges in Argentina and Saadat Hasan Manto in India and Pakistan, several giants of modern narrative throve in confined spaces. (Schulz's lost novel *The Messiah*, a recurring motif in David Grossman's *See Under: LOVE*, has become the phantom masterpiece that haunts his admirers.) Then there are the indisputably first-rank writers that, in my opinion, translators into English have served better with their shorter than their longer works. For me, this group includes Danilo Kiš in Serbo-Croatian, Eileen Chang in Chinese and Roberto Bolaño in Spanish. The absence from this selection of these – and other – compelling voices reflects a judgment, no doubt partisan and provisional, not on their stature but the current state of their English translations.

It seems that the adjective "quixotic", to mean a fanciful and eccentric mission or adventure, first appeared in English in 1718, although "quixotical" dates from the 1650s. On any reading this book must rate as a quixotic – though not, I hope, a hubristic – project. Although his friends and fellow-travellers, from the village priest and barber and the kindly graduate Sansón Carrasco to Sancho Panza himself, agree that Don Quixote has gone crazy, most accept that he means well. And, of course, it is reading old novels that has driven the scrawny gent of La Mancha out of his wits. Beloved tales of chivalry and romance have befuddled his brain with their "combats, battles, challenges, wounds, courtings, loves, torments, and other impossible foolishness". Yet his adventures, which take in characters and narratives from many different backgrounds, will paradoxically allow Cervantes to champion the truth, and dignity, of fiction. I hope that this book captures that quixotic spirit, forever curious and open, and that readers will enjoy following some of the paths down which it leads. Through the next wood, across the next plain, another encounter, another story, always beckons. The Don and the Squire only have to take a nap beneath a cork-oak for two mysterious horsemen to ride along. "Brother Sancho, we have an adventure!" "May God make it a good one…".

Works Cited:

Marcel Proust, *The Captive/ The Fugitive* (*In Search of Lost Time* V); translated by CK Scott Moncrieff and Terence Kilmartin, revised by DJ Enright (London: Chatto & Windus, 1992)

Miguel de Cervantes, *Don Quixote* Part Two; translated by Edith Grossman (London: Secker & Warburg, 2004)

Madame de Staël, *Oeuvres complètes de Mme la baronne de Staël*, Tome 17; Mélanges (Paris: Treuttel & Würtz, 1821)

WG Sebald, *Across the Land and the Water: Selected Poems 1964–2001*; translated by Iain Galbraith (London: Hamish Hamilton, 2011)
George Steiner, *After Babel: Aspects of Language and Translation* (Oxford: Oxford University Press, 1975)

Walter Benjamin, "The Task of the Translator", in Marcus Bullock and Michael W Jennings (eds.), *Walter Benjamin*: *Selected Writings Volume 1, 1913–1926*; translated by Harry Zohn (Cambridge, Mass. & London: Harvard University Press, 1996)

Kate Briggs, *This Little Art* (London: Fitzcarraldo Editions, 2017)

Pascale Casanova, *The World Republic of Letters*; translated by Malcolm DeBevoise (Cambridge, Mass. & London: Harvard University Press, 2004)

Franco Moretti, *Atlas of the European Novel, 1800-1900* (London: Verso, 1998)

Javier Marías, "The Isolated Writer", in *Between Eternities & Other Writings;* translated by Margaret Jull Costa (London: Hamish Hamilton, 2017)

Johann Wolfgang von Goethe, from Johann Peter Eckermann, *Gespräche mit Goethe (*1836*)*; quoted in David Damrosch, *What Is World Literature*? (Princeton, New Jersey: Princeton University Press, 2003)

Ahmad Fāris al-Shidyāq, *Leg Over Leg*; translated by Humphrey T Davies (New York: Library of Arabic Literature/ New York University Press, 2015)

Horace G Hutchinson, *Life of Sir John Lubbock*, Lord Avebury (London: Macmillan, 1914)

Margaret Anne Doody, *The True Story of the Novel* (New Brunswick, New Jersey: Rutgers University Press, 1996)

Steven Moore, *The Novel: An Alternative History – Beginnings to 1600* (London: Continuum, 2010)

Milan Kundera, *The Art of the Novel*; translated by Linda Asher (London: Faber & Faber, 1988)

Milan Kundera, *The Curtain*; translated by Linda Asher (London: Faber & Faber, 2007)

Fernando Pessoa, *The Book of Disquiet*; translated and edited by Richard Zenith (Harmondsworth: Penguin Classics, 2001)

A Note on the Entries.

To fix the date of a novel's first publication is not as straightforward a task as it might appear. Several of these books, from Gogol's *Dead Souls* to Bulgakov's *The Master and Margarita*, were either never completed to their authors' satisfaction or else never published in full, or at all, during their lifetimes. Others went through one or more revisions and re-workings, or appeared in more than one part. In general, my chronological arrangement chooses the year of the first substantive (if not definitive) volume or edition in the original language. With novels published only posthumously, I have given the year in which the writer's work on it ceased. In a couple of cases (such as Némirovsky's *Suite Française*), publication came only long after the author's death.

The relationship between a writer's language, culture and nationality can also be complicated. Where the original language of a novel does not by itself indicate an author's country or countries of origin and/or long-term residence, I have tried to elaborate. For writers who habitually used pen-names, I have also given birth-names. So, for instance, "Marguerite Yourcenar (Marguerite de Crayencour), *Memoirs of Hadrian* (1951); French (Belgium/France/United States)".

Each entry gives, at its head, a recommended translation that will normally be readily available to Anglophone readers. On a few occasions I have quoted from other translations as well; if so, they are mentioned. In some cases, the best may not be the most accessible. But I have almost always tried to suggest translations that are both excellent and straightforward to find. Once or twice, I have departed from this rule, for instance by preferring the Penguin Modern Classics India edition of Tagore's *Home and the World* to the older text still published by Penguin Classics in the UK. Translations, notoriously, age faster than their originals. Some antique accounts of foreign classics – such as Tobias Smollett's 1750s *Don Quixote* – are works of genius in themselves. They merit a book of their own. This one errs on the side of modernity.

Acknowledgements.

Warm thanks to all those editors and colleagues whose support, at *The Independent,* the *New Statesman* and elsewhere, gave me the opportunity to explore the planet of fiction. They include Tony Gould, Harriett Gilbert, Malcolm Imrie, Nicci Gerrard, Andrew Marr, John Walsh, Simon Kelner, Christina Patterson, Katy Guest, Arifa Akbar, Lorien Kite and Sam Leith. The staff and officers of Arts Council England and the Man Booker International Prize eased this journey in many ways: among them, Gary McKeone, Amanda Hopkinson, Antonia Byatt, Fiammetta Rocco. Year by year, my fellow-judges of *The Independent* Foreign Fiction Prize and, in 2016, the Man Booker International Prize opened my eyes and widened my horizons with their erudition and enthusiasm. Innumerable conversations have fed these choices – for which I'm solely responsible. Respect to everyone who nourished my curiosity. The resources, and expertise, of the London Library made researching this book a pleasure. Rebecca Morrison helped find it a home. For Maya Jaggi's unflagging insight, wisdom and encouragement: all my love and gratitude.

1 | Don Quixote (1605 and 1615) by Miguel de Cervantes.

Spanish

Translated by Edith Grossman (Vintage)

In *Don Quixote*, dawn breaks at twilight. Over the four centuries

since the Knight of the Doleful Countenance first set out from his home in La Mancha "to wander the world righting wrongs and rectifying injuries", the two volumes of Cervantes' novel have become the acknowledged pattern-book or seed-bank which germinates every branch of Western fiction. If so, then the novel in the West begins at the end of days. Most obviously, the threadbare gentleman Señor Alonso Quixano has gone crazy from reading antiquated books. Thanks to obsessive consumption of old romances of chivalry about legendary heroes and their far-fetched exploits, he imagines himself as "Don Quixote" and embarks on his – yes, "quixotic" – mission to revive "the lost and dying order of knight errantry". He has even sold "acres of arable land" to buy these silly yarns. The priest and barber forever try to talk, or trick, the Don out of his madcap "sallies" with the peasant farmer Sancho Panza, who consents to act as his "squire". They seal his library and burn the noxious books.

So, as its founding premise, *Don Quixote* tells of a nostalgic fixation with a worn-out genre which prompts a delusional countryman to dream of restoring a defunct medieval honour-code: "I have redressed grievances, righted wrongs, punished insolence, vanquished giants, and trampled monsters." Even the manuscript that recounts his fantastical forays, Cervantes tells us, is a translation from the Arabic of the Moorish author Cide Hamete Benengeli, "flower of all historians", found in the market-place in Toledo. Later, we hear that reading translations is, in any case, "like looking at Flemish tapestries from the wrong side". Besides, this retro tale supposedly composed in a half-forgotten language, now taboo in Catholic Spain, unfolds over a landscape of decline.

Hunger, strife, decay and dislocation dog the steps of Quixote and Sancho – one on the bony nag Rocinante, the latter on his accident-prone donkey – across La Mancha, Aragon and Catalonia. Starved villages, chained prisoners, hunted fugitives, squalid inns (which the ever-innocent Don takes for castles with "spires of gleaming silver"): their adventures unroll amid "detestable times". The peerless comedy of his feats and follies, recounted with a sympathetic irony that never slips into mere burlesque, leads us into the darkest corners of Cervantes' world. From the tales of sea battles with Muslim pirates and slavery in Algiers (both of which the author had experienced) to the plight of ethnically-cleansed "Moriscos" (Muslims who had converted to Christianity), *Don Quixote* plants its stories of "enchantment" in the soil of history. On these stony plains, the "golden age" of "peace, harmony and friendship" – conjured by the novel's interpolated tales of well-born, love-lorn swains and damsels disguised as goatherds or shepherdesses – has long vanished. Only in his visions can the Don enter his paradise of chivalry: as when he descends into the Cave of Montesinos and witnesses an idyllic fairyland,"reserved only for thy invincible heart and wondrous courage", or in his tireless devotion to the flawless Dulcinea of Toboso (in truth, a warty peasant wench). Or, perhaps, that courtly Utopia lies in his friendship with Sancho: those complementary archetypes of imagination and reality that every novel, like every mind, must learn to balance.

Yet it only takes another ragged traveller to meet them on the road and "Brother Sancho, we have an adventure!" "May God make it a good one…". Just as the hard-headed Sancho intermittently shares the fantasies of his "master" and so connives in his dreamworld, so Cervantes sweeps his reader into a realm of invention while keeping one foot securely planted on this dusty earth. *Don Quixote* abounds with debates about the virtues and vices of fiction: a literary canon the duo meets argues that worthy tales must, "by restraining exaggeration and moderating implausibility", "enthrall the spirit and thereby astonish, captivate, delight and entertain". Reality should tame fancy. From the forty windmills of La Mancha charged by the gangly Don ("these are giants!") to his sword-fight with an ogre in the guise of tavern wine-skins; from his frenzied attack on the "pasteboard figures" of Master Pedro's puppet show to that descent into the spellbound Cave, the Don's escapades thrust him – and us – into the hazy borderlands between myth and truth. Cervantes folds the ancient into the modern, romance into realism. By presuming to mock the "lunatic actions" provoked by "perverse books" of chivalry, he proves by example the authentic nobility of the storyteller's art. For these days, as the canon claims, "the epic can be written in prose as well as verse".

Proud of his artistry, scornful of his imitators, jealous of his fame (Part Two echoes to the sound of the author crowing about the success of Part One: "Thirty thousand copies of my history have been printed"), Cervantes tilts at his detractors much as the Don gallops at his own – actual or imagined – foes. *Don Quixote*, which pioneers so many of the novel's classic tropes, even becomes in Part Two a thoroughly "postmodern" jaunt through metafictional terrain. In these later "sallies" his own celebrity becomes one of the fiercest giants he must fight. Meanwhile, his old friends from the village, and the friendly graduate Sansón, try to return the Don to his home and his wits. Intrigued by the renown of this eccentric vagabond who inspired a bestseller, aristocratic patrons subject the Don and Sancho to cruel stunts. Only a well-intentioned deception, when Sansón defeats the Don in a joust while disguised as the Knight of the White Moon, will guide him back "from madness to sanity", and into a peaceful death. Those "enchanters" the Don blamed for his mishaps have ceased to plague him. The grounded magic of his story remains. Cervantes, as much the chivalric hero as his scatty hidalgo, has championed the honour of the old-new novel, his own Dulcinea, and released it from its mystifying bonds. Knight-errantry may be extinct, but fiction's armour shines. As an inn landlady says, recalling how her weary customers love to hear a tale after a long day's harvesting, "I never have any peace in the house except when you're listening to someone read".

Translation: Faithful, readable, creative, festive, contemporary: Edith Grossman's version (2003) now takes pride of place among its many, often distinguished, peers.

See also: Diderot, *Jacques the Fatalist* (1796); Dostoyevsky, *The Brothers Karamazov* (1880); Mann, *The Magic Mountain* (1924); Garciá Márquez, *One Hundred Years of Solitude* (1967)

Selected works by the same author: *Exemplary Novels* (1613); *Journey to Parnassus* (1614); *The Labors of Persiles and Sigismunda* (1617)

2 | The Princesse de Clèves (1678) by Madame de La Fayette (Marie-Madeleine Pioche de la Vergne).

French

Translated by Robin Buss (Penguin Classics)

Small worlds breed grand passions. Today, much of genre fiction, film and television turns on the pressure cooker intrigues of life in workplaces and institutions, from university campuses to hospitals and police stations. Crucially, the presence of women in these professional milieux, holding positions of responsibility, drives plots in which the need for respect and autonomy can fall foul not only of overt discrimination but of individual desire. "There were so many different factions and parties," *The Princesse de Clèves* informs us, "and the women played so great a role in them, that love was always allied to politics and politics to love".

It may sound strange to consider a sort of fictional chamber-drama, set within a narrow circle of nobles in and around the French court of the late 1550s, as a prototype of modern stories about the entanglement of private and public life in societies that pay at least formal tribute to equality between the sexes. In contrast, the engineer's daughter who became Madame de La Fayette on her marriage to a much older widower in 1655 survived – and managed to thrive – at a court that only granted power to non-royal women strictly behind the scenes. In Renaissance or Baroque palaces, the personal was invariably political.

Covert female power, however, might be decisive. Women at court who armoured themselves carefully enough against compromise or disgrace could hope to sway kings and steer policy. Yet love beyond the bounds of marital convention would still expose a woman, however grand her title, to risks far beyond those run by any male paramour. At the same time, only outside marriage – a dynastic and commercial contract among the aristocracy – could "passion" be found. Towards this novel's end, the widowed Princess baldly tells the admirer she rejects that her late husband "was perhaps the only man in the world able to preserve something of love within marriage".

Madame de La Fayette's pioneering novel of passion and power in a gilded crucible of suspicion and betrayal ostensibly takes place during the last years of the reign of Henri II (1547-1559). Since its first, anonymous appearance, readers have dissected it as a veiled picture of the treacherous cockpit that the author knew as a super-observant insider at the court of Louis XIV in Paris and then Versailles. She had become a confidante of Henriette of England, wife to Louis's brother Philippe, Duke of Orleans, and perhaps projects this friendship back onto the bond in her third novel between the Princess and the gifted, beautiful but scheming "Dauphine": Mary Stuart, Queen of Scots. She does take care to make her story work as a period piece rather than a topical exposé in thin disguise, drawing lavishly on histories of the earlier age. Anglophone fans of Tudor fiction and drama will find plenty of familiar characters and incidents here, from Mary herself to the early struggles of Elizabeth I, and a flashback to the already-legendary rise and fall of Anne Boleyn.

Married well at a tender age to the virtuous and devoted M de Clèves, the former Mlle de Chartres enjoys the devotion of a husband she respects, but cannot love. He only once suspects her of infidelity. When he does, it kills him. Despite herself, the Princess falls for the serial seducer the Duc de Nemours, described as "nature's masterpiece" and a charming narcissist who glories in his erotic allure. Yet she refuses to begin an affair with him. This is, above all, a tale of wrenching self-denial, control and renunciation. In the hothouse of the court, rumours and confidences serve as currency that – hint by hint, drip by drip – link the princess and the duke. Breaking all the conventions of discreet liaisons, she tells her husband of this unfulfilled passion for another. Why, he wails, could she not have left him "in that untroubled blindness so many husbands enjoy"?

In an extraordinary scene, he sends a gentleman to spy on Nemours while Nemours, voyeuristically, spies on the half-naked princess with her hair down, in her pretty "pavilion" in the forest. She, in turn, gazes at a picture of the suitor she has never touched, "with the intensity of mediation that only passionate love can induce". This fatal chain of looks will lock them all into the final crisis that ends with her husband's death in near-despair, and the bereaved heroine's refusal of Nemours – even though no barrier of law or custom now forbids their union. The serial predator, she fears, will devour and discard her, for all the evidence of true love that he shows. Meanwhile, she accepts that "I am sacrificing much to an idea of duty that exists only in my mind". Subtle, acute and startlingly modern, this novel of whispered secrets and stifled yearnings allows its heroine to glimpse a form of freedom she can never reach. Only solitude, and the lonely virtues of the convent where she will spend part of every year, lies ahead in her "somewhat brief" life.

Translation: *The Princesse de Clèves* had its first English translation in 1679. Lively and engaging, Nancy Mitford's rendering (1950) shows one novelist of thwarted love responding to another. Robin Buss's version (2004) blends scholarship and readability.

See also: Laclos: *Dangerous Liaisons* (1782); Sand, *Indiana* (1832); Flaubert, *Madame Bovary* (1857); Duras, *The Lover* (1984)

Selected works by the same author: *The Princess of Montpensier* (1662); *Zaïde, a Spanish Romance* (1670)

3 | Candide, or Optimism (1759) by Voltaire (François-Marie Arouet).

French

Translated by Theo Cuffe (Penguin Classics)

Within the brief compass of *Candide*, Voltaire spares no sacred cow the lash of his mocking wit. That includes the canonisation of literary works as "classics" to be foisted on sullen students. "Fools admire everything in an established classic" scoffs the hard-to-please Venetian nobleman Pococurante while he, in short order, trashes the epics of Virgil, Homer ("it bores me to distraction") and Milton ("that barbarian"). Our gormless young hero is astonished at these heresies, for "he had been brought up never to exercise his own judgment". The rapid ascent of Voltaire's scattershot satire into the pantheon of Western civilisation began with multiple editions launched secretly, like underwater missiles, across Europe in 1759. In its own way, *Candide*'s status confirms that slavish craving for

authority, and the surrender of independent thought, that Voltaire laments in all human affairs. Yes, the naïve *Candide*'s picaresque jaunt through the societies, the creeds and the ideologies of 18th-century Europe and America richly merits its enduring place on the syllabus, and in books like this one. But its prime targets change with the tenor of the times. Everyone can now nod in dutiful consent as Voltaire flays the hypocrisies and superstitions of organised religion, the wickedness of war and colonialism, or the commercial greed that lays waste the earth and curses its peoples. As a mutilated slave in Surinam says as he explains how punishments in the factory where he toils have robbed him of his limbs, "That's the price of your eating sugar in Europe."

Voltaire, though, pushes his all-weather scepticism even into the self-satisfied circles where enlightened minds congratulate one another on their superiority to the common herd. Although he might share Voltaire's opinions on Homer and Milton, the carping Pococurante becomes a figure of fun, narcissistically in thrall to his "pleasure in not being pleased". In Paris, quarrelsome capital of "this absurd nation", Candide runs into fault-finding "men of taste" whose slash-and-burn criticism exposes envy rather than rigour, "just as eunuchs hate successful lovers". Voltaire sees that the forces of Enlightenment, whose power he did so much to promote as satirist, historian and polemicist, might also be an army of the night. No one escapes whipping – not even the weary pessimist Martin, hedged against suffering by a conviction that "a man is badly off wherever he is".

Suffering and misery in every form burn at the molten core of this skipping, skittish work. Voltaire's "philosophical tales", with *Candide* foremost among them, ditch any pretence to plausibility in favour of effervescent, ideas-driven fantasy. Today, *Candide* might remind us of an animated film, a graphic novel, or a high-end TV satire. It feels like a stylised game, a lark, a romp; but one that takes aim through its cartoonish episodes and quick-fire shifts of scenery at the weightiest institutions and ideas. Voltaire, though, seeks to tickle rather than bludgeon them to death.

Candide is a Westphalian adventurer, both scamp and innocent, expelled from the "earthly paradise" of his estate, and separated from the Baron's daughter, his beloved Cunégonde. He and his tutor Dr Pangloss endure battle, flogging, disease, prison, torture, enslavement and robbery as they bounce from Germany to Lisbon, Buenos Aires to Paraguay, Paris to Constantinople. Misfortune by misfortune, atrocity by atrocity, from earthquake to syphilis to plague to rape to massacre, Voltaire skewers in deadpan prose the folly of Panglossian optimism, with its belief that "all is for the best in the best of all possible worlds". The dogmatic rationalism of Leibniz, his principal bugbear, has sunk into oblivion, along with other fads *Candide* also crushes. However, the evidence-proof faith in human perfectibility, either within radical politics or in brands of "new age" uplift, remains a favourite illusion of our century, as of Voltaire's. We may have exchanged old models of sentimentality for new ones; *Candide* remains a sovereign purgative for all. On the brink of ecological catastrophe, still menaced by nuclear annihilation, beset by conflict and oppression, we hope with Pangloss that "everything would turn out right in some marvellous way".

Although he endorses no system, Voltaire saves many of the best lines for heretics, freethinkers and non-Christians. The Anabaptist James concludes that men "were not born wolves, yet they have become wolves". At rest on a little plot outside Constantinople, Candide and his companions learn from an old Turkish farmer that honest work "banishes those three great evils: boredom, vice and poverty". All ambition and theory discarded, "We must cultivate our garden". So *Candide* ironises its own irony, and capsizes its cynicism. Its wide-eyed hero does return to the pastoral idyll of his Westphalian boyhood. Allergic to all absolutes, Voltaire makes sure that his critique of irrational optimism gives little succour to the doctrinaire gloom of the Manichean sage Martin, who fears that "Man's origin is evil". Such lofty notions hardly befit "such a strange animal as man", a frail vessel for fitful dreams and desires. So get digging in the garden, and console yourself with a coffee – Voltaire, something of a connoisseur himself, recommends "pure Mocha… unmixed".

Translation: Both Theo Cuffe (2006) and John Butt (1947) hit the right Voltairean note: sly, waggish, and droll, but also wholly invested in the thrills and upsets of these fantastic adventures.

See also: Diderot, *Jacques the Fatalist* (1796); Sand, *Indiana* (1832); Hugo, *Les Misérables* (1862); Hašek, *The Good Soldier Švejk* (1923)

Selected works by the same author: *Letters Concerning the English Nation* (1734); *Zadig* (1747); *Micromégas* (1752); *Philosophical Dictionary* (1764).

4 | Dangerous Liaisons (1782) by Choderlos de Laclos (Pierre-Ambroise-François Choderlos de Laclos).

French

Translated by Douglas Parmée (Oxford World's Classics)

Like Hugo's *Les Misérables, Dangerous Liaisons* sometimes appears

in English translation under its French name [*Les Liaisons Dangereuses*]. As with so much else on this brutal epistolary battleground of seduction and revenge, deception and betrayal, we may read that fact two ways. Does the original title safely confine Laclos's novel-in-letters to the gowned and wigged degenerates of a parasitic elite, on the eve of its annihilation in the French Revolution? Even the "publisher's preface", which pretends that these are real letters printed with the moralistic aim of alerting readers to the wages of sin and vice, recoils in mock disgust from the idea that such monsters of depravity may exist in this "philosophical" century of "universal enlightenment". Or, on the contrary, does the familiarity of Laclos's title hint that the worldview of the Marquise de Merteuil and the Vicomte de Valmont – his pair of cynically debauched aristocrats, who deploy sex as their weapon of choice in the social and emotional downfall of their victims – still flourishes under other skies? Valmont, the rakish egotist and conniving misogynist who believes that "to bring a woman to heel anything goes", certainly thrives far from the boudoirs of the Ancient Regime.

Ever since it scandalised audiences in the 1780s, this only novel by an artillery officer and military engineer who would serve the Revolution and die as a general under Napoleon's command has divided its titillated, horrified readers. Does it diagnose a local infection, or a general malaise? The 175 letters scarcely move in their settings beyond a handful of noble households in and around Paris. Only a few walk-on parts for servants or priests interrupt the claustrophobic clash by correspondence of will and desire, pride and principle, among a half-dozen titled characters. The odd glimpse of ordinary life startles by its rarity, as when the high-minded target of his campaign of seduction glimpses Valmont in a traffic jam of carriages outside the Paris opera house with a "notorious prostitute" by his side (he has arranged the sighting to make her jealous). Yet at the same time, the narrow arena of these vicious manoeuvres appears as a test ground for general ideas about the nature of men and women in love, in lust, in hope and in despair. The mother of another of Valmont's victims insists that "his despicable behaviour is a matter of principle", not instinct or passion. With nerveless expertise, Laclos rides the twin steeds of eroticism and philosophy.

Through its swift, often suspenseful transitions from viewpoint to viewpoint, with the same episodes seen through different eyes, *Dangerous Liaisons* lets us piece together the past as well as the present of its protagonists. Merteuil, a voracious if not merry widow, and the notorious libertine Valmont have been lovers; they still care more for each other than any other objects of desire. Challenged by Merteuil, Valmont sets out to seduce the gentle, pious judge's wife, Madame de Tourvel, "an adversary worthy of my steel". As a sub-plot, he also schemes to bed the fifteen-year-old Cécile Volanges and so shatter her affections for her naïve suitor, the Chevalier Danceny. This supreme sexual tactician succeeds on both fronts of his heart-breaking mission, thanks to "the classic purity of my methods", but seems genuinely to fall in love with Tourvel. Worse – or better – he and Merteuil skirmish, then brawl: "It's war". Sentiment, even devotion, disrupts the stratagems of both arch-seducers. Love is the ghost in their machine of desire. Arguably, not ice-hearted lust but authentic passion pushes each principal into misery and shame: Valmont improbably slain duelling with Danceny (perhaps a passive suicide), Tourvel broken, and killed, by a depressive collapse; Cécile self-sentenced to life in a convent; Merteuil ostracised by her class when the awful truth emerges, bankrupted by a lawsuit, then "terribly disfigured" by smallpox. The "wicked" and pure suffer alike.

His rationalistic mind overthrown by the mutiny of his heart, Valmont develops in his letters from libertine villain to stricken, proto-romantic hero. According to Merteuil, he can never be "a woman's friend or lover, but always her tyrant or her slave". The Marquise, though, is Laclos's most remarkable creation. From her youth, when she "took accurate note of the pain and the pleasure" while losing her virginity, she has by force of will and intellect sought to overcome the subordination endured by even the most privileged women. Widowhood and wealth grant a certain freedom. To survive in society she needs "a writer's wit and the gifts of an actor": she wields both. She reminds Valmont that in the "highly unfair contest" of the sex war, the struggle is forever unequal. And she commends the autonomy of mature women who prove "capable of creating a life of their own when nature begins to desert them". Merteuil's insatiable drive for mastery over others (especially younger and weaker women) disqualifies her as any kind of feminist heroine. She does, though, touch the heights, or depths, of tragedy. Elegant and ruthless, graphic and gnomic, Laclos lays bare these bodies and souls. But his cunningly engineered epistolary fortifications mean that the author himself never breaks cover. Like the invisible, fugitive God of the 18th-century Deists, he vanishes to leave us quarrelling, or weeping, over the ruin of his proud but pitiful creatures.

Translation: With pace and wit, Douglas Parmée (1995) conveys both the euphemistic refinement of the letters and the sheer savagery of what lies beneath.

See also: La Fayette, *The Princesse de Clèves* (1678); Goethe, *The Sorrows of Young Werther* (1787); Kundera, *The Book of Laughter and Forgetting* (1978); Duras, *The Lover* (1984)

Selected works by the same author: *On the Education of Women* (1783), *On War and Peace* (1795)

5 | The Sorrows of Young Werther (1774, revised 1787) by Johann Wolfgang von Goethe.

German

Translated by David Constantine (Oxford World's Classics)

Unrequited love, pursued through obsession to the point of death, has become such a staple commodity among the stories the world tells that it takes effort to imagine a time when such consuming passions felt fresh, heady – and dangerous. The European literature of the Middle Ages and Renaissance had spread the cult of "courtly love". Poets had worshipped their muses and knights fought for their damsels – a motif already ripe for parody by the time of *Don Quixote*. Only with the 18th-century mania for "sensibility" and the arrival of styles of expression that we can label as "Romantic" – in both the artistic and emotional senses – does love conquer the world of feeling. As Goethe's stricken hero sighs, "my feeling for her devours everything", and "without her everything is nothing".

Prompted in part by his own, losing role in a romantic triangle and the suicide of a love-lorn colleague in the German city of Wetzlar, the youthful Goethe first wrote his explosive, epistolary novel of a passion that leads to suicide, in 1774. Already, the young prodigy had also started work on the themes of *Faust* and found his early voice as a poet. A transnational bestseller, Werther caused a sensation across Europe. Wannabe Werthers dressed in his protagonist's garb of blue coat and yellow waistcoat. Sequels and parodies multiplied. Napoleon adored the book. Male tears fashionably fell across the Continent in homage to the hero who "weeps inconsolably". As with the rock star suicides of two centuries later, the death of any depressed youngster who took their own life would be laid at Werther's door.

Unlike other novels in the form of letters, Goethe gives us only Werther's side of the correspondence with his shadowy friend Wilhelm. His hopeless passion for Lotte, who is engaged and then married to the stalwart, phlegmatic Albert, rises towards its peak with only brief glimpses of her plight as this storm of wild longing bursts around her. An all-round Romantic as well as a romantic,

Werther gushes with sympathy for the poor countryfolk, for the birds and beasts of the springtime fields, above all for children, who are "closest to my heart". Later readers have wondered why this universal compassion cannot extend as far as leaving Lotte and Albert in peace. That, as Goethe taught and Europe avidly agreed, is not how true, mad love can ever work.

When she does have a speaking role, as Werther's frenzy nears its fatal climax, Lotte reproaches him for "this uncontrollable clinging passion". Earlier, she has indulged and – if we can believe his letters – encouraged him. This one-sided report gives the story ambiguity and suspense – how far can the hero sanely hope for a requital of his feelings? – as the seasons turn and Werther tumbles towards despair. Later, a seemingly objective "editor" intervenes to add an element of omniscient narration to the novel. This editor sounds rather like a forensic psychiatrist and, under Goethe's guidance, later Romantic fiction would dissect unruly passions as much as celebrate them.

At their final encounter, Werther and Lotte read, in Goethe's own versions, poems by "Ossian": the ancient Gaelic bard whom James Macpherson fabricated in the 1760s as the alleged author of the folk-poems that he collected, re-invented and then transformed into an international Romantic cult. In one light, "Ossian" looks like an utter fake; in another, an authentic voice of profound feeling.

Werther's own self-annihilating fixation has just that double aspect: both a narcissistic fantasy, and the noblest expression of his true self. Creative and destructive, this ideal of passion enthralled Goethe's age, with its new faith that "nothing on earth but love makes a person necessary". This can feel like a male stalker's love – controlling, paranoid, even misogynistic. Evidently, it held the power to overwhelm all other beliefs. Werther comes to despise the hierarchies of the provincial court that employs him. Love alone commands his loyalty. After he shoots himself, at the furtive funeral, rank and religion dissolve: "Working-men carried him. No priest attended."

Goethe never disowned *The Sorrows of Young Werther*, his calling-card to European renown. His revision of the novel in 1787 does nod in the direction of the ironic distance and perspective that the older, more "classical" polymath would often seek. Still, the mood of feverish delirium never abates. The reckless excitement of Werther's story stems not only from its erotic intensity but the growing realisation that suicide may offer the only exit from his anguish. Before the final act, Werther tells Wilhelm about a "noble breed of horses" that bite their own veins: "Often I feel like that: I'll open a vein and get myself a freedom that will last for ever." In the event, a bullet does the job.

Passion and suicide would – as in Madame Bovary's fate – waltz through the next century as inseparable partners. Later, as obsessive romance loosened its literary grip, self-destruction retained its glamour as the ultimate guarantor of human freedom. To Albert Camus, in *The Myth of Sisyphus*, suicide stood as "the one truly serious philosophical problem". The heirs of Werther dance down the history of European culture in a tight embrace where love and death entwine.

Translation: First translated in 1779, *Werther* went through many – not always faithful – incarnations in English. Oxford's compelling edition comes from a Goethe scholar who is also a first-rate novelist and poet.

See also: La Fayette, *The Princesse de Clèves* (1678); Choderlos de Laclos, *Dangerous Liaisons* (1782); Flaubert, *Madame Bovary* (1857); Duras, *The Lover* (1984)

Selected works by the same author: *Wilhelm Meister's Apprenticeship* (1796); *Faust, Part One* (1808); *Elective Affinities* (1809); *West-Eastern Divan* (1819)

6 | Dream of the Red Chamber (The Story of the Stone) (1750s–1763; published 1792) by Cao Xueqin.

Chinese

Translated by David Hawkes and John Minford (Penguin Classics, five volumes)

At the end of this vast, lively and endlessly entertaining fresco of 18th-century Chinese social and domestic life, our scatty young hero disappears after – at long last – sitting his exams to enter the imperial civil service. During the hunt for the missing Jia Baoyu, a hermit tells the searchers that, "The Legend of Illusion and the Paradise of Truth are one and the same". That idea, that fiction and reality, dream and fact, always intertwine and will never separate, snakes like a golden thread across the stories of family, love, friendship, snobbery, economics, politics and faith that scroll in such vigorous profusion through this enormous but never boring work. Like its greatest counterparts in the West, Cao Xueqin's gargantuan saga-cum-romance stands up for the dignity of fiction itself, insisting that "Truth becomes fiction, when the fiction's true". At the finale, the stone that has descended from heaven to sample mortal life returns to its celestial home, with the record of its adventures passed on to Cao Xueqin himself. With mock-modesty, he reckons that it might be fun to share this tale with some friends, "to help the wine down after a meal or to while away the solitude of a rainy evening by a lamplit window". After all, as Jane Austen once ironically wrote, it's "only a novel".

The comparison is not quite as far-fetched as it might seem. In its date of composition, *Dream of the Red Chamber* (also known as *The Story of the Stone*) ranks as the latest among China's "Four Great Classical Novels". Scholars of "Redology" still argue over the status of the text; above all, whether its first editor, Gao E, himself wrote most (or some) of the final forty of its 120 chapters. But for all its bulk, its excursions and digressions, and its proliferating cast of characters (three dozen major figures; around 400 minor ones), the *Dream* never moves far from a pair of high officials' households in the Qing Dynasty-era Beijing of the mid 18th-century. In spite of its supernatural interludes, and the poetry contests that allow Cao to show off his virtuosity in traditional verse-forms, the mood and tone remain for the most part sociable, domestic, intimate, genial and high-spirited. Austen's heroines might (almost) feel at home with the Jia clan in its decades of decline.

Baoyu, the romantic, feckless heir to one branch of the noble Jias, loves and pursues his equally dreamy cousin Lin Daiyu. She is a frail, imaginative outsider in this sprawling tribe who feels like "a refugee… living here as a hanger-on". After her heart-breaking, drawn-out death from consumption that out-Dickenses Dickens, Baoyu must marry the more practical, and wealthier, Xue Baochai, "a lady with a destiny of gold". For all the pride of their ancient lineage, and the status of one family member as an imperial concubine, the Jias will fall on hard times. Bribery, corruption and usury scandals – even the brazen attempt to dodge a capital charge – spread from the family of the conniving Jia She to ruin the fortunes of Jia Zheng himself: Baoyu's father, and the model of the "incorrigibly upright" Confucian mandarin. Grandmother Jia, the fearsome and all-knowing matriarch, has always sought to defend "our family tradition, our family honour" above all else: "Families like ours simply do not dabble in such things". Yet when the emperor and court turn against them, the Jias learn that "Prosperity may crumble in the twinkling of an eye, like the passing of a spring cloud or the falling of an autumn leaf".

As Baoyu's romance with Daiyu ends in shattering grief, as the noble clan founders in disgrace, the Buddhist theme of escape from worldly matters sounds more strongly: "All is insubstantial, doomed to pass". Yet even as he lauds the virtue of release from "the quagmire of greed, hatred, folly and passion", Cao never loses his delight in the merry ups and downs of life among the Jias: the feasts, the debts, the gossip, the affairs. Baoyu loves to dally with "the girls": not only well-born young ladies, but the bondservants whose clever, witty, down-to-earth voices sound through the novel with a zest and candour, even cheek, beyond anything in Western fiction. "We're just maids," Oriole says ruefully, "Being lucky or not doesn't really enter into it for us". Without the maids, though, *Dream of the Red Chamber* would lose half of its drive, and most of its charm.

Meanwhile, Cao's ravishing evocations of domestic life steep every scene in vibrant colours. Critics who somehow imagine that stereoscopic realism in fiction only began in 19th-century Europe have never met (say) Aroma, Baoyu's favourite maid and confidante, whom we encounter dressed (on this occasion) in an "ermine-lined tapestry dress of peach-pink satin", along with her "leek-green padded skirt embroidered in couched gold thread", the whole ensemble topped off with "a black satin jacket lined with squirrel". Cao never slackens in his sheer delight in the visible world; in his relish both for the saucy below-stairs badinage of the servants and the elegiac wistfulness of poems recited under plum-blossoms on a moonlit spring evening in the beloved family "Garden". The novel's valedictory retreat from worldly things has a profound poignancy for its readers, as for its characters. Its Buddhist teaching (with a Taoist tinge) lauds renunciation, as Baoyu – that "very strange creature" – vanishes from the earth he has briefly graced. Yet his story will endure: "just so much ink splashed for fun", but still immortal in its own, entirely human way.

Translation: In the buoyant, colloquial prose of David Hawkes (volumes one to three) and John Minford (four and five), Cao's epic speeds and skips along, both a perpetual pleasure – and a heroic feat of scholarship (1973-86).

See also: Sōseki, *The Gate* (1910); Proust, *In Search of Lost Time* (1913-27); Qian, *Fortress Besieged* (1947); Lampedusa, *The Leopard* (1958)

7 | Jacques the Fatalist (1778–1786; fully published 1796) by Denis Diderot.

French

Translated by David Coward (Oxford World's Classics)

"I don't care for novels," the narrator of Diderot's most revolutionary novel tells us – unless they're by Samuel Richardson, whose psychological realism in works such as *Clarissa* had, during the mid 18th-century, held literary Europe, Diderot included, in its spell. "I'm writing a chronicle here," he tetchily asserts. *Jacques the Fatalist* purports to be, not one of those fanciful made-up stories packed with sensations, revelations and coincidences ("there's nothing easier than churning out a novel"), but a record of events with all the blind alleys, repetitions and digressions of real life dutifully noted.

Not long after Richardson, Defoe and their counterparts in France had established the novel as a mainstream form of mass entertainment – even of moral argument – radical critics began to mock its laws. To sceptical thinkers of the Enlightenment, it made little sense to question the subject's dumb obedience to a king, or the believer's to a god, only to worship some all-knowing deity of a storyteller who artfully manipulates both an outlandish plot and the reader's emotions. Early in Diderot's wonderfully entertaining and provoking philosophical shaggy-dog story, the servant Jacques and his Master quit one of the many inns where they have adventures, hear fellow guests' tall stories, or recount their own. Diderot takes care to tell us that "I've no idea what happened at the inn after they left." Next, Jacques, with his bullet-damaged knee, goes under the surgeon's knife – but "let's skip the operation". No more absolute monarchs for Diderot, and no more omniscient narrators.

Polymathic editor of the *Encyclopédie*, the mischievous gadfly of the French Enlightenment whose free-thinking candour landed him in jail, Diderot was not quite the first author to deconstruct the despotic conventions of fiction. Laurence Sterne's *Tristram Shandy* – beyond doubt, the most globally influential of all English-language novels – gave him a model. Several episodes in *Jacques the Fatalist* borrow from his "brother-maverick" across the Channel. Smart, cunning, thoughtful, Jacques and his somewhat slow-witted Master meander from hostelry to hostelry, forever trying to tell the story of their romantic liaisons while exposure to the lives, and yarns, of others interrupts their thread. Whiplash dialogue, droll and quick, speeds us from tale to tale, punctuated by economical visual clues that draw on Diderot's command of the methods not only of drama but of painting. Sex, with its usual baggage of delusion and deceit, drives most of the yarns they spin or learn – often served with a side-order of religious hypocrisy and snobbish vanity. Desire unpeels the skin of rank and piety from lascivious prelates and predatory aristocrats. Diderot, meanwhile, claims the right to speak of it to his outraged but two-faced audience: "Carry on fucking like rabbits, but you've got to let me say fuck". If the joking, quarrelling master-servant pair at first recalls *Don Quixote*, we soon learn who is really in charge. In a richly symbolic scene, Jacques consents to accept his nominally inferior status only after the Master has bowed to his superiority in mind: "It was decreed that you would have the name and that I should have the thing". Like a more cerebral colleague of the canny Figaro in the plays of Beaumarchais, Jacques in his playful, teasing way voices not just the irony of the critical free-thinker but the active insolence of the revolutionary.

As Diderot exposes the mechanics of fiction, a merry gale of liberation blows through the book. The reader feels unshackled, emancipated, by this "tasteless mishmash" of anecdotes and incidents, "written without style and served up like a dog's breakfast". Here lies the key paradox of *Jacques the Fatalist*. As a philosophical novel, it relentlessly insists that human beings are unfree, determined in every wish and deed by chains of causation that elude our comprehension, let alone control. Jacques quotes his Captain, a follower of the radical materialism of Spinoza (as was Diderot): "Everything good or bad that happens to us here below is written on high." Jacques asks, "Do we control our destiny, or does destiny control us?" His adventures answer that rhetorical question. That "great ledger in the sky" decrees not only the chances that befall us but the will-driven choices that we make. "We stumble along in the dark between what is written on high, as crazily yoked to our desires as to our joys and sorrows." Yet for Jacques, as for Diderot, the embrace of destiny – social, biological, psychological, certainly not divine – breeds not passive resignation but a cheerful zeal to improve whatever can be improved. If Diderot unmasks the illusions of free will conjured by faith, by philosophy, by fiction itself, the result exhilarates rather than seeding despair. Around destiny's next corner there will always be another inn, another amour, another glass of wine – above all, another story to enjoy. "Most of the time we act without volition," Jacques tells his nice-but-dim "Master". "Haven't you been a puppet…?" "You mean that was all a game?" "Just a game." Its rules both dictate our every move – and set us free.

Translation: David Coward's 1999 version has a bright-minded swing and zest that honours both Diderot's playfulness and his profundity.

See also: Cervantes, *Don Quixote* (1605-1615); Voltaire, *Candide* (1759); Laclos, *Dangerous Liaisons* (1782); Kundera, *The Book of Laughter and Forgetting* (1978)

Selected works by the same author: *The Indiscreet Jewels* (1748); *Rameau's Nephew* (1761); *D'Alembert's Dream* (1769); *The Nun* (1780)

8 | Corinne, or Italy (1807) by Madame de Staël (Anne-Louise-Germaine Necker).

French (France/ Switzerland)

Translated by Sylvia Raphael (Oxford World's Classics)

Sent back from Rome to stay on her English father's estate in

damp and foggy Northumberland, the adolescent Corinne profits from her boredom and isolation to study English literature. Its "depth of thought and feeling" makes up for the lack of the "lively imagination" found in Italy, her birthplace and her mother's homeland. As Corinne later writes, her "dual education" has lent her "particular advantages". She possesses, "if I may put it that way, two different nationalities". "If I may put it that way", because no one ever had: the word "*nationalité*" enters literature with Madame de Staël's astonishingly original novel, at once a romance, a treatise, a manifesto – and a sort of fairy-tale.

Anne-Louise-Germaine de Staël (who took her surname from her first husband, the Swedish ambassador to France) was the daughter of Jacques Necker: the Swiss Protestant banker who served as Louis XVI of France's reforming Minister of Finance. Her prestige and influence as a polymathic arbiter of taste, as novelist, dramatist, pioneer sociologist and top-level diplomatic activist, made her former ally and arch-enemy Napoleon exile her for a decade. In 1814, one wit claimed that Europe had three great powers: England, Russia and Madame de Staël. She wrote *Corinne*, her second novel, after her travels there had added Italy to England, Germany and France as nations and peoples she knew at first hand, studied and sought to define.

Corinne breaks new ground on different fronts, but endures above all as a wildly romantic cross-cultural love story. It traces the passion of the high-minded, generous-spirited Scottish nobleman Oswald for the multi-talented poet, actor and singer Corinne – daughter of a Roman mother, and a beloved people's artist in that city. She commands every gift but never loses her unaffected kindness, "a wonderful genius but… a sensitive and reserved nature". Alongside its forthright, feminist portrait of an independent artist-heroine who insists that "I suffer, I enjoy, I feel, in my own way" – trail-blazing in itself – *Corinne* defends the culture and customs of Italy. Now fragmented, occupied and cherishing the arts as its "only glory", the country suffers the patronising slights of French and English observers. ("One must be proud like them [the English], or brilliant like us," says the French chauvinist Count d'Erfeuil. "All the others are only imitators.") In Corinne and Oswald's intense, doomed liaison, Staël seeks to analyse the cultural factors that shape character and so may divide lovers who share "similar natures" and have "an all-powerful fellow-feeling". Through the woes of both partners, she explores the effects of depression, loss and mourning at a time when "in our cold, oppressive society, grief is our noblest emotion". She fervently champions both women's creativity and autonomy, and the Romantic imagination across every art-form. A child of the Enlightenment but also a torch-bearer for Romantic values, Staël both traces the frontiers of temperament and history that separate people, and looks for their common attributes: "The world, this vast theatre, does not change actors. It is always man who comes on stage."

Along the way, Corinne and Oswald's travels in Rome, Florence, Venice, Naples and elsewhere allow Staël to depict the monuments, art-works, cities and landscapes of Italy with such rapt prose and lively learning that libraries used to catalogue *Corinne* as a guide-book. Corinne herself, the improvising poet and performer "lovable for ordinary virtues, quite apart from her brilliance", becomes the embodiment of Italy itself. That proud home of "feminine" imagination, artistry and spontaneity is now both ruled and scorned by the cold intellect of the "masculine" north.

Yet Staël's story complicates those national stereotypes, or archetypes, that she did so much to fix. Corinne is half-English herself. For all her adolescent misery in patriarchal, philistine Northumberland, and her impatience with its "petty opinions", she admires the balance, reason and quiet integrity of Oswald's life. He is the true English gentleman; indeed, a European model for that concept. (Oswald, Lord Nelvil, actually holds a Scottish peerage: Staël mostly ignores that particular border.) As for Oswald, Italy ignites his senses and unlocks his soul. He is torn between his love for Corinne and the dutiful commitment made to his dead father to marry the ultra-English rose Lucile Edgermond – whom we belatedly learn, in a Gothic twist, is Corinne's own half-sister.

In one picturesque spot after another, from the Roman Forum to the slopes of Vesuvius, often accompanied by her own rhapsodic improvisations, Corinne and Oswald affirm their love, but shrink from marriage. As the Napoleonic wars convulse Europe, and harden borders, Oswald retreats in anguish to England, to Lucile, and to self-sacrificial combat against the French in the West Indies. Distant from "the intoxicating wave of the arts", Corinne and Italy fade for him into a "brilliant apparition", now departed. "Human destiny," he tells Corinne, "is disturbed by a thousand different ties which disturb the heart's constancy." She languishes, abandons poetry, settles in Florence in silent seclusion: "Genuine grief is by nature infertile". In another Gothic touch, Corinne, before expiring, begins to tutor little Juliet, Oswald and Lucile's daughter. (Shakespeare's Juliet has been one of her stellar roles). Her free and creative spirit, like that of Italy itself, will never die.

Translation: Sylvia Raphael (1998) commands all the novel's registers, from sublime nature-writing and romantic rhapsody to philosophical debate, cultural sociology and colourful travelogue.

See also: Goethe, *The Sorrows of Young Werther* (1787); Stendhal, *The Red and the Black* (1830); Manzoni, *The Betrothed* (1827-1842); Lispector, *Near to the Wild Heart* (1943)

Selected works by the same author: *Delphine* (1802); *Germany* (1810); *On Suicide* (1813)

9 | Michael Kohlhaas (1810) by Heinrich von Kleist.

German

Translated by David Luke (in *The Marquise of O and Other Stories*; Penguin Classics)

Much like his rebel hero, Heinrich von Kleist spent his short, fitful creative career smashing rules in pursuit of a higher but elusive ideal. For his future followers, the wayward example of this great German iconoclast – dubbed by Thomas Mann a genius "too wild and elemental ever to conform to any aesthetic convention" – spurred them to rewrite the laws of fiction. *Michael Kohlhaas*, his relentlessly gripping tale of a 16th-century horse dealer whose implacable quest for justice leads to terror, chaos and catastrophe, occupies the space of a succinct novella. But it has the style of an epic and the aura of a myth. Its lapidary grandeur and eerie resonance push the folk tale genre cultivated by the German Romantic writers towards the unsettling domain of the modern fable of identity. Franz Kafka revered this story, and once read aloud from it in Prague.

If *Michael Kohlhaas* ranks as a parable of the human quest for justice and recognition, forever deferred or denied, it also sports the features of an antique shaggy-dog story. It has the stop-start motion of a fireside anecdote in a country inn. Taken from "an old chronicle", and inspired by a historical figure, Kleist's yarn tells of a travelling trader outraged when a high-handed nobleman confiscates two black horses at a borderpost between Brandenburg and Saxony. Against the ruling class arrogance and contempt of Junker Tronka, Kohlhaas appeals, as he will again, to the fair-minded majesty of the law. Thwarted by social prejudice and cronyism in local courts, with his wife fatally wounded when she tries to petition the Elector of Saxony, he soon loses faith in any state that fails "to protect me in my rights". As the injustices multiply, the pursuit of his claim escalates into a "righteous war" on a cruel social order. He becomes the chieftain of an impromptu guerrilla campaign: an "angel of judgment" who rampages across Germany. Aghast, the palaces of Saxony and Brandenburg – destabilised by this spontaneous revolt, and torn between hardliners and conciliators – feel as if "a foreign power had attacked our country".

Wittenberg burns, and the authorities panic. With the intercession of Martin Luther himself as peacemaker, for a while Kohlhaas regains his faith in the powers that be. After the appearance of a copycat rebel, however, the rulers seize the chance to frame him. A death sentence ensues. Once again he languishes "in the fist of arbitrary power". The literary ancestor of every asymmetric warrior, Kohlhaas can turn defeat into victory and humiliation into triumph. He exults in his ability "to wound his enemy mortal in the heel" just when that heel "was treading him in the dust". Somehow, this wretched and absurd outcast becomes the arbiter of princes' destinies. A gypsy prophecy of doom, which deepens the uncanny shadows of this story, comes into his possession to strengthen his hand. Now fat and sleek, the horses are returned, but "the business of his revenge" will cost him his life. Even at the moment of execution, this avenging angel can deliver a judgement on the Elector of Saxony that leaves the overlord "shattered in body and soul".

Both ancient and modern, this flint-hard saga of grievance, protest and vindication has led readers to view the horse-dealer's baffled hunt for right and justice through many lenses: theology; law; politics; psychology. We might even interpret Kohlhaas as a pocket Napoleon, breaking down the petty hierarchies and snobberies of the small German states just as Bonaparte's invading armies did as Kleist wrote this work. More of a millenarian rebel than a post-Enlightenment idealist, Kohlhaas titles himself "Viceroy of the Archangel Michael", and issues proclamations from the headquarters of his "provisional world government". The pure justice he seeks has a folkloric, even child-like, quality. It lies closer to the realm of magic than of reason. Meanwhile, a mist of superstition and rumour swirls around the disputed facts of his insurgency.

His nightmarish setbacks and betrayals in courtrooms and throne rooms feel more like the material of modern psycho-drama than late-Gothic melodrama. This naïve rebel, "one of the most upright and at the same time one of the most terrible men of his day", can sound like a prototype both of the existential pilgrim, and the Third World revolutionary, of ages yet to come. Austere, laconic, yet ferociously compelling, Kleist's narration never robs Kohlhaas of his dignity – or his mystery.

Translation: Kleist must sound timeless and sinister, not quaintly archaic: Martin Greenberg's 1963 translation finds that tone; even more so, David Luke's 1978 rendering.

See also: Voltaire, *Candide* (1759); Stendhal, *The Red and the Black* (1830); Zola, *Germinal* (1885); Camus, *The Outsider* (1942)

Selected works by the same author: *The Broken Jug* (1806); *The Marquise of O* (1808); *Penthesilea* (1808); *The Prince of Homburg* (1810)

10 | The Betrothed (1827; revised 1842) by Alessandro Manzoni.

Italian

Translated by Bruce Penman (Penguin Classics)

As wedding-gift and compulsory school text, the ark of Italy's language and icon of its nationhood, Manzoni's romantic adventure story has met a monumental fate that no book should have to endure. Even in 2015, Pope Francis could recommend it as inspirational reading for engaged couples: the closest thing to canonisation that can happen to a work of fiction. Its modest and self-critical author – who had trouble finishing any book, and did not complete another novel after *The Betrothed* – never sought such literary sanctity. He might have noted that, for all the institutional pomp that later smothered his story, the hope voiced by its heroine's mother feels as distant now as it ever did: "There's justice in this world in the long run."

The Betrothed begins and continues as a novel of justice thwarted by coercive elite power. Read it not as some mothballed classic but an exciting, radical yarn of colonial oppression and the quest for integrity – in love and in life – in combat with a wicked system. Then the cobwebs soon start to disperse. In effect, its plot traces a vast parenthesis. This marathon saga of escapes, disasters, perils and rescues lights up every corner of a corrupt state. It spans the two years between the day, in a village near Lake Como in 1628, when a thuggish local aristocrat wrecks the planned wedding of a poor and loving couple because he wants the bride, and their belated union. Although he drew on 17th-century chroniclers of Milan, Manzoni's period setting – in Lombardy, under the brutal but ramshackle control of the Spanish royal house – was easy to decode. From the first, readers treated his novel as a thinly veiled exposé of Austrian domination in post-Napoleonic Italy. It became a sacred scripture of his nation's reunification movement: the Risorgimento.

Under the regime that divides the long-suffering silk weaver Renzo and his beloved Lucia, "impunity was organised". "Little oligarchies" – among the landowners, the clergy, the lawyers, the merchants – fix the rules in their selfish interests. Negligent authority takes a cut and looks the other way. Manzoni's critique of shambolic colonial power as a cloak for sectional greed and violence has echoed down the decades within Italian literature. It still resonates far beyond its local circumstances. His vision, however, finds expression in a series of thrilling, mysterious and often comic episodes. Manzoni adopts the template for dramatic historical fiction first forged by Walter Scott. He uses it, arguably, to shape a finer work that the Scottish pioneer ever himself composed.

After their separation and escape from the villainous squire Don Rodrigo, Lucia finds refuge in a Monza convent. Hear we learn the sad tale of the lovelorn nun Gertrude, forced against her will into seclusion. A youthful sceptic, Manzoni wrote *The Betrothed* after his return to committed Catholicism. Yet even his saintliest clerics have their inner demons to wrestle: the benevolent Fra Cristoforo, both a moral lodestone and a crucial agent of the plot, is a penitent killer. With tormented Gertrude, even the pious author makes us feel "the chill, dead shadow of the cloister".

Renzo, meanwhile, finds himself caught up in bread-riots in Milan – depicted with cinematic clamour and colour – after inept governance has wrecked the economy. On the run after a seditious, drunken rant, he finds his own sanctuary with a weaver cousin in Bergamo. Now Manzoni engineers an epic encounter between the good and evil faces of authority. On one side stands Cardinal-Archbishop Federigo Borromeo of Milan: a historical figure, reformer, philanthropist and patron of learning, whom the novel elevates into the ideal Christian prince. To secure the safety of kidnapped Lucia, his example must prevail against "The Unnamed". This provincial "super-tyrant" spreads mayhem and misery from his "blood-stained nest" of a castle on a crag. The embodiment of depraved injustice, the nameless godfather – based on a notorious member of the Visconti dynasty – aims "to be arbiter and dictator of the affairs of others, from no other motive than a pleasure in power".

Swayed by Borromeo's virtue, the melodramatic ogre reforms and releases Lucia. Gothic horror yields to immersive realism. The devastating plague of 1630 sweeps through Milan and our protagonists meet again – along with 16,000 other citizens – at the fever hospital, the *lazaretto*. Manzoni's masterly narrative of the psychic as well as medical progress of the epidemic moves through the stages of denial ("the very word was taboo"), hysteria, paranoia, social collapse and moral breakdown, as "the virulence of the disaster brutalised men's minds". At length, the survivors resurface "like people risen from the dead". Manzoni clears the ground for a happy ending that emphasises the simple – and yet revolutionary – ordinariness of his bride and groom. After all her dangers and mishaps, the villagers find the radiant Lucia to be "Just a peasant girl like lots of others". That, of course, is the entire point. Manzoni has ennobled his common folk, validated their needs and passions, and cut their abusive "superiors" down to size. His lavish, romantic and picturesque storytelling will open the way for a century and more of everyday heroes.

Translation: *The Betrothed* had to wait until Archibald Colquhoun's spirited and learned version of 1951 for an English text worthy of its achievement. Bruce Penman's 1972 text has an admirable freshness of its own.

See also: Stendhal, *The Red and the Black* (1830); Hugo, *Les Misérables* (1862); Lampedusa, *The Leopard* (1958); Vargas Llosa, *The Feast of the Goat* (2000)

Selected works by the same author: *The Count of Carmagnola* (1820); *Adelchi* (1822)

11 | The Red and the Black (1830) by Stendhal (Marie-Henri Beyle).

French

Translated by Roger Gard (Penguin Classics)

In a moment of triumph, a young social climber from the rural backwaters of Franche-Comté walks through a forest to scan the plains below. A sparrowhawk wheeling overhead serves as a sublime emblem of his strength and solitude. "It was the destiny of Napoleon – would it one day be his?" In reality, this titan-in-waiting has just got a small pay rise as tutor to the children of a local bigwig whose wife he fancies. One of the many reasons why the fiction of the writer, soldier, bureaucrat, traveller and small-time diplomat who called himself "Stendhal" feels so contemporary is that each heroic or romantic scene undermines, satirises and even parodies itself. Duels, salons, assignations, seductions, trials, jails – from the boudoir to the guillotine, each step on Julien Sorel's progress through *The Red and the Black* risks stumbling into bathos, pantomime or farce.

Often enough, it does. Meanwhile, Stendhal's freestyle narration, urbane and confidential, glides with quicksilver ease between one narrative angle and another. It can speed up or slow down the story, veer off into epigrams or anecdotes, or plunge into inner monologues that catch the glint of thought in a startlingly "modern" way. At the end of his adventures (though still only twenty-three), Julien in the condemned cell at Besançon is reunited with his peasant father. He experiences "a sharp pang of guilt" for his unloving conduct towards the tight-fisted old carpenter. Julien hints that he has savings to bequeath – whereupon his father starts to tot up the cost of the kid's upbringing. Almost no one, in this story of pretences and performances, can ever quite keep up the dignity of their allotted part. Even the hyper-ambitious Julien, who laments that "My life is just a succession of hypocritical poses", regularly backslides into sincerity, candour and even innocence. You might say that he's masquerading as an impostor. A unique tincture of pathos and comedy colours every episode in Julien's spectacular rise and fall through the rotten ranks of French society.

Stendhal wrote *The Red and the Black* just as frustration with the reactionary, Royalist order of France-after-Napoleon climaxed in the Liberal revolution of 1830. Obsessed with Bonaparte's exploits (as was Stendhal himself), Julien seeks to carve out a similarly splendid path to renown. But in this age of mediocrity, he can play the tunes of glory only in a minor, mock-heroic key. Hypocrisy, "the only weapon I have", will serve as his sabre on the civilian battlefields of Church and State. As a tutor to the Renals, this bright but gauche son of the sawmill at Verrières, with his "beautiful complexion" and "manner of a shy young girl", wins the heart of the affectionate, vulnerable Madame de Renal: the novel's long-suffering touchstone for true feeling. After the threat of scandal shatters their idyll, his ambition sends Julien into the seminary at Besançon.

He has no religious vocation, but hankers after the sort of elite position an ecclesiastical rank may bring. Priestly black rather than military scarlet counts as "the uniform of my century" in an era of pious conservatism. With the help of his wily mentor Abbé Pirard, Julien secures a job in Paris as secretary to the influential aristocrat Marquis de La Mole. Now he can "figure on the stage of great events" – but not before an encounter with Madame de Renal ends with this blundering "cold schemer" expelled from Verrières at gunpoint. In artificial Paris, stuck in the numbing routine of a household where "the slightest vital idea would seem glaringly vulgar", Julien turns his charms on Mathilde: daughter of the Marquis, and more than Julien's equal as both strategist and fantasist. Stendhal depicts their liaison, a dance of mutual desire and delusion, with a trenchant hilarity. In this zero-sum game of passion, authentic emotion hands a winning card to your opponent: "Mathilde, certain that she was loved, despised him utterly." As much a cerebral thrill-seeker as Julien himself, Mathilde does "allow her heart to feel", but only "when she has reasoned herself into thinking it should". Julien, still hungry for advancement, becomes embroiled in a complicated ultra-reactionary plot of clerics and aristocrats, even though Stendhal has dismissed politics in fiction as "like a shot in the middle of the concert. The noise is deafening but it imparts no energy."

One of the joys of *The Red and the Black* is the author's free-wheeling commentary, shrewd and witty, on the course of his own tale. After an elaborate ploy by Julien to make Mathilde jealous, Stendhal airily dismisses this section as "the flatlands of our journey". Soon, though, we regain the dramatic heights. Back in the Franche-Comté, Julien, in a "moment of madness", shoots and wounds Madame de Renal in church. Almost like some existential hero who commits a freedom-defining crime, he embraces his guilt as a premeditated would-be murderer (although, typically, he has botched the job). He refuses to appeal. Is this cult of willed doom just another fashionable pose, and do we credit his defiant apologia to the middle-class jury as "a peasant… in rebellion against the baseness of his lot"? In this time of masks and acts, courage and integrity confer the ultimate starring role. Even in the shadow of the guillotine, the Julien Sorel show goes on: "Alone, talking to myself, two steps away from death, I am still a hypocrite… Oh, Nineteenth Century!"

Translation: Nimble, mercurial, quizzical, intimate: the tone of Roger Gard's translation (2002) delivers all the wit, and poignancy, of Stendhal's storytelling.

See also: Diderot, *Jacques the Fatalist* (1796); Sand, *Indiana* (1832); Hugo, *Les Misérables* (1862); Kundera, *The Book of Laughter and Forgetting* (1978)

Selected works by the same author: *On Love* (1822); *Lucien Leuwen* (1835); *The Life of Henri Brulard* (1836); *The Charterhouse of Parma* (1839)

12 | INDIANA (1832) by George Sand (Amantine-Aurore-Lucile Dupin).

French

Translated by Sylvia Raphael (Oxford World's Classics)

Naïve, fanciful, shackled as a teenaged bride to a controlling husband within a society that treats married women as children and as chattels, young Indiana Delmare has "turned life into a tragic novel". Like her successor Emma Bovary, Indiana – her given name hints at the colonial origins that matter so much in this story – takes too much account of the "optimistic, childish fictions" found in "novels written for ladies' maids". Throughout *Indiana*, George Sand warns against the lure of fantasy, romance and rhetoric: of words and poses that mimic true feeling so artfully that they beguile not just audience but author. Raymon, the caddish, aristocratic serial seducer with whom Indiana falls catastrophically in love, "enacted passion so well that he deceived himself". Unlike Flaubert or Balzac, however, Sand sets Indiana's arduous journey through the wreckage left by broken dreams within a novel that itself leaps from one splendid scene of passion and peril to the next. First Gothic twilight, then tropical sunshine, frame Indiana's yearning and suffering. Along with its fiercely argued critique of women's woes, men's impunities and the gross injustices of post-Napoleonic France and its slave-worked colonies, *Indiana* bounces along with the almost skittish delight of a young writer who has insolently snatched the reins of authorship. She will drive her vehicle just how and where she chooses.

In collaboration with a lover, the unhappily married Aurore Dupin – at that point "Madame Dudevant" – had already published two books. *Indiana* announced the birth of "George Sand", and began an independent career she would sustain over sixty novels. It still reads as a work of spellbinding confidence, candour and ambition. In a later preface, Sand recalled the fuel of outrage that impelled her to dramatise through fiction "the injustice and barbarity of the laws which still govern the existence of women" in marriage, family and society. Through her misfortunes, Indiana rails with forthright fluency against the chains that bind women, and the selfish edifice of patriarchal power in law, society and religion: "You think yourselves masters of the world; I think you are only its tyrants." *Indiana*, though, owes its enduring appeal to a spectacular tug-of-war between feminist tract and thrill-seeking melodrama; between reason and imagination, realism and romance.

We meet Indiana in the eerie chiaroscuro of a pictorial tableau. She is the captive "trophy wife" of the infirm warrior Colonel Delmare in his gloomy manorhouse near Paris, with the enigmatic figure of Sir Ralph Brown – a stolid, phlegmatic English kinsman of hers, raised like Indiana in the colonies – in residence as permanent guest, mentor, protector and friend. The first calamity to strike this tense ménage occurs when the suave and vain playboy, Raymon de Ramière, seduces, then discards, Indiana's foster-sister and companion, Noun. The two young women had grown up as "Creoles" among the planters of Bourbon Island (now Réunion) in the Indian Ocean; we surmise that Noun is mixed-race, if not black. The injuries of race as well as gender preoccupy Sand. As a child, Indiana can "help and console" the island's slaves "only with her pity and her tears".

When Noun commits suicide, her death does not prevent the innocent Indiana from succumbing to Raymon's phoney charms. Ever the idealist, she will not be his mistress but chastely returns his love; her resistance has "the charm of the unusual" for him. Their liaison ebbs and flows through separations and scandals. "You can tie up my body," Indiana tells the furious Colonel, "but over my will, Monsieur, you have no power". Sand broadens her social critique to indict the faction-ridden political landscape of France under the restored monarchy, in an "age of scepticism and ranting oratory". When the Colonel's factory fails, the couple retreats to Bourbon Island with the ever-faithful Ralph still as Indiana's guardian angel. Bewitched again by Raymon's words, in flight from her husband after his cruelties have moved from words to kicks, Indiana makes an intrepid escape from the island. Penniless, she almost dies in Paris, only to discover that Raymon has married a hard-headed heiress motivated not by love but "stoical calculation". They now occupy the manor.

In despair, Indiana agrees to return to the island with Ralph (who at last admits his eternal love) and they apparently die in a suicide-pact by leaping from the top of a misty waterfall: Sand can turn on a coin from incisive realism to florid fantasy. After Ralph's heartfelt peroration induces a joint state of "exaltation and ecstasy", they jump… but a coda tells us that they survived to live out a tropical idyll, devoted to caring for freed slaves. ("If only we were rich enough to free all who live in slavery!") Sand has defended the "egotism" of the liberated woman "as a human right and not as a vice", but in this Hollywood-style postscript, Indiana loses her voice. Only loyal, kindly Brown – the brother-turned-lover – speaks. To the last, *Indiana* skids and darts between the modes of treatise and fairytale, psychological case study and exotic adventure. With unflagging dash and daring, it performs all the divisions, all the ambivalences, of the clever, fearless, painfully gullible young woman at its heart.

Translation: Too much neglected by modern translators, Sand recovered her English voice in all its shades – fantastic, romantic, satirical, intellectual – thanks to Sylvia Raphael (1994).

See also: Laclos, *Dangerous Liaisons* (1782); Stendhal, *The Red and the Black* (1830); Flaubert, *Madame Bovary* (1857); Lispector, *Near to the Wild Heart* (1943)

Selected works by the same author; *Mauprat* (1837); *Consuelo* (1843); *The Devil's Pool* (1846); *La Petite Fadette* (1849)

13 | Old Goriot (1835) by Honoré de Balzac.

French

Translated by Olivia McCannon (as *Old Man Goriot*; Penguin Classics)

Long before the age of Don Corleone, a cunning and cynical master criminal tells a young man on the make that "I'm going to make you an offer that no one could refuse". In the Paris of 1819, our Godfather goes by the name of Vautrin. The scheme suggested by this "fallen archangel" – the plot that prompts Balzac to coin the phrase that Mario Puzo, and Marlon Brando, borrowed – truly comes from hell. With the help of a friendly assassin, Vautrin will arrange for a rich young heir to be slain in a duel. The heir's sister, currently penniless and rejected, will return to her father's favour with a whopping dowry. She has fallen in love with Vautrin's dashing but penurious collaborator, who will then scoop up his newly-wealthy bride and pass over a twenty per cent commission to the mastermind. Vautrin then plans to emigrate to America and set himself up as a slave owner, "because I want two hundred Negroes to satisfy my appetite for the patriarchal life". In *Old Goriot*, patriarchs come in various shapes and forms – all of them thoroughly dubious.

Clinging to the tattered remnants of his conscience, our young adventurer – Eugène de Rastignac – spurns Vautrin's indecent proposal. A well-born law student from southern France, Rastignac is avid to rise in Parisian society but still dependent on family hand-outs. Vautrin likens the treacherous city to "a forest in the New World, crawling with... savage tribes". Here, might equals right. "Strike hard, and you will be respected," advises Rastignac's aristocratic cousin, Madame de Beauséant – holder of his entry-ticket into the *beau monde*. He must lodge, though, in Madame Vauquer's smeared and whiffy guesthouse. At Vauquer's, the seamy side of Paris lies exposed in all its shabbiness, poverty and despair. Here, amid the symbolic mould, grime and dust evoked with a hallucinatory power that feels more surrealistic than naturalistic, "everything is sliding into decay". The eighteen disputatious tenants, rising or falling in the world or simply stuck in a threadbare routine of bare survival, "present in microcosm the elements that make up society as a whole".

Among the lodgers, in the cheapest garret, is the aged Goriot, once a dealer in the grains used for making pasta. As Rastignac gropes his way through "each twist and turn of the Parisian labyrinth", he learns that this broken down old buffer, this mangy "dark horse" who inspires "general loathing", has two fashionable daughters. Both have married into the top echelons of Parisian society. Anastasie has wed a Count, and Delphine a banker. In a time and place that fatally confuses "money and feelings", they have carried with them the bulk of their doting father's fortune as dowries. Paris, in the scrambled aftermath of Napoleon's downfall, is a "battlefield" where "bundles of banknotes" permit new money to break down every defence raised by the snobs and nobs.

Besotted with the spoiled children who have become "ashamed of him", willing to sacrifice everything for them ("Fathers must always be giving to be happy"), Goriot emerges as the King Lear of the down-at-heel Left Bank. The defeat of this tragic figure intertwines with Rastignac's first efforts to navigate through the murky "ocean" of Paris: "Heave in the lead as often as you like, you'll never sound its depths." He will win the lonely Delphine's affection but not secure her, or his own, happiness. Rastignac's prowess as a "chancer", a gambler and seducer, opens the doors of the elite. Yet he feels that "I myself am in hell and I must stay there."

Balzac's "Human Comedy", his panoramic survey in fiction and essays of French society and morality, amounts to more than ninety items. His investigations have a scientific flavour, with the France of his time studied as a single, interdependent eco-system. The novelist acts as the intrepid explorer who connects the peak and the abyss, the apex predator and the bottom-feeding parasite. In *Old Goriot*, which introduces several major characters who will reappear in later volumes, Rastignac befriends the zealous young doctor Brianchon. When Goriot, shattered by his daughters' ingratitude, sickens, Brianchon insists that "we're going to follow the progress of the illness". Balzac does just that for Paris as a whole. This forest of savages, this "ocean of mud", breeds monsters. Their delusions and deformities give a face to the virus in the bloodstream of a system where "wealth equals virtue", while "laws and morality have no power over the rich".

A giant, even heroic, shark in these poisoned waters, Vautrin – a criminal paterfamilias himself – mirrors with his clear-eyed ruthlessness the ruinous self-sacrifice of Goriot. In a great crook's credo, he tells Rastignac that a man can advance only "through the brilliance of his genius or the skill of his corruption". Since "Honesty will get you nowhere", the ambitious newcomer must either court or dodge corruption, that ubiquitous "weapon of mediocrity". For Vautrin, "there are no principles, only events; there are no laws, only circumstances". No work before *Old Goriot* had with such tonic clarity charted this proto-Darwinian jungle, with human nature red in tooth and claw. Vauquer's seedy boarding-house became the power station that generated a century of grainy social realism. But the tragic, mythic dimensions of its lodgers' fates belong to Balzac alone.

Translation: Olivia McCannon (2011) scrubs off the gloomy patina of the "classic" to reveal the colours of Balzac's prose in all their brilliance.

See also: Stendhal, *Scarlet and Black* (1830); Hugo, *Les Misérables* (1862); Zola, *Germinal* (1885); Arlt, *The Seven Madmen* (1929)

Selected works by the same author: *The Wild Ass's Skin* (1831); *Eugénie Grandet* (1833); *Lost Illusions* (1843); *Cousin Bette* (1846)

14 | A Hero of Our Time (1840) by Mikhail Lermontov.

Russian

Translated by Natasha Randall (Penguin Classics)

Grigory Alexandrovich Pechorin, that bitter, twisted root of the great tree of Russian fiction, thinks of himself as a fatally divided soul. "Two people" coexist within Lermontov's scandalous and melancholy anti-hero, "one who lives in the full sense of the word, and the other who reasons and judges him". For Pechorin's creator, still in his twenties, that judgment took the form of the idiotic duel that killed him in 1841. Eerily, Pechorin himself survives such a duel near the same Caucasian spa resort where Lermontov died. A comrade of the fellow officer he kills consoles the future victim with the thought that "Everything on earth is nonsense… Nature is a fool, fate is a turkey".

With its fractured protagonist, who thinks his life amounts to "a chain of sad and unsuccessful contradictions", and its self-destructive episodes of erotic and military derring-do, Lermontov's novel became a handbook for alienated wanderers – in literature and society. Its author revered Lord Byron, and Pechorin inherits a Byronic mantle of intertwined self-conceit and self-disgust. The English, not the French, we hear, set the "fashion of boredom", while the feckless, reckless officer understands that egotism and abjection show two sides of the same medal: "I sometimes despise myself… is that not why I despise others?" With his urge to "destroy the hopes of others", above all the unfortunate young women he charms and then spurns, Pechorin can look not only like the forerunner of the broken selves who drift though modern fiction but the sociopathic rogue male who, in life and art alike, long ago lost his meretricious allure. He describes happiness as "sated pride", and confesses that passion's crucible has tempered him into a being "as hard and cold as iron".

Yet the experience of reading *A Hero of Our Time* delivers much more than cynicism and disenchantment, or the gloomy frisson of Romantic fatalism and self-loathing misogyny. To begin with, the teasing, shifting ambiguities heralded by the title ripple across every page. The narrator imagines that readers will react to that title by proclaiming "What vicious irony!" Many still do. As for him, "I don't know." Fittingly, Lermontov depicts his torn hero, a man in pieces, by composing a story in pieces. No book could read less like the textbook stereotype of a 19th-century novel, all rock-solid characters, complacent moralism and omniscient narration, than *A Hero of Our Time*. It consists not of a continuous action but a clutch of Pechorin yarns, told in different ways. Always brisk, lively and supple, the narrative begins in remote Georgia with a travel writer who passes on the tall tales of an outlandish young warrior, relayed by a staff captain met at an inn. Further north, the narrator himself – who insists that "I am not writing a novel, but travel-notes" – has a fleeting encounter with Pechorin. The latter leaves behind some journals of his "sojourn in the Caucasus", which form the remainder of the book. "We almost always forgive those we understand," the narrator opines. Lermontov assembles the raw materials for that verdict. The reader must decide.

Throughout, the rugged, stirring landscapes of mountain, valley and torrent counterpoint human frailty and folly with scenes of the Romantic sublime. As with many authors, from Pushkin onwards, the cultural otherness of Russia's own Deep South in the Caucasus sets the stage for danger, daring and desire. Here flourishes an exotic sensuality unimaginable in Moscow. In this "oriental" playground, as with the British fiction of India, simple racism ("What awful rogues, these Asiatics!") shades into fascination, wonder and longing. None of which disrupts the crude imbalance of power that sees Pechorin seduce the Muslim teenager Bela, "with black eyes like a hill chamois", break her heart, and watch her die from injuries during a botched kidnap: "she suffered for a long time".

Although "Pechorin was unwell for a long while" after Bela's death, his lady-killing ways revive in the more genteel milieu of the Pyatigorsk spa. As Pechorin strings along the innocent Princess Mary and wrecks the married Vera's peace of mind, Lermontov never sanitises his rascal-hero. Narcissism sliding into sadism, the diary admits that "there is an unbounded pleasure to be had in the possession of a young, newly blossoming soul!" But as he sets out for the duelling ground – and probable death at the hands of the cadet Grushnitsky – the scoundrel has already indicted himself. "The loss to the world won't be great. Yes, and I'm fairly bored with myself already." Pechorin lives. Within a year of publication, his maker would – in the same region, in the same fashion – die. "We are no longer able to be great martyrs," reflects Pechorin after another pointless death. The vision of life as absurdity still demands sacrifices. Lermontov offered his work, even his life, to that idea.

Translation: Much translated (with one English text by Vladimir and Dimitri Nabokov), Lermontov's seductive monster found a compelling modern voice in 2009 thanks to Natasha Randall.

See also: Laclos, *Dangerous Liaisons* (1782); Dostoyevsky, *The Brothers Karamazov* (1880); Chekhov, *The Duel* (1891); Camus, *The Outsider* (1942)

Selected works by the same author: *Vadim (1832); Princess Ligovskaya (1836)*

15 | Dead Souls: an Epic Poem (1842/1855) by Nikolai Gogol.

Russian

Translated by Donald Rayfield (New York Review Books)

Midway through his uproarious, tragi-comic journey around the circles of a provincial Russian hell, Gogol's narrator laments that he cannot be one of those happy writers "who transcends dreary, loathsome characters", hides "the miseries of life" from sight, and simply shows his readers "human beauty". Alas, instead he must chronicle "the frightful, shocking swamp of trivia that traps our lives" and depict the "fragmented, squalid creatures which swarm over our earth". At least his instruments of satire, mockery and grotesque mirth ought to command respect, he claims, since "lofty ecstatic laughter deserves equal status with lofty lyrical impulses".

Ever since its only completed part appeared in 1842, *Dead Souls* has rocked both Russia and the fiction-reading world with "ecstatic laughter" that always borders on fury, or on tears. Ideological chasms separate those interpreters who see it as a reformer's manifesto for social progress, a religious allegory of sin and redemption – or a bizarre, even surreal, vision of individual and collective life as a crazy circus filled with masks, mountebanks and marionettes; as a great stage of fools. Each lens captures some of the colours in Gogol's dazzling spectrum, but not all.

Indeed, the meaning of this fable exercises the leading citizens of the forlorn provincial backwater, where a certain Pavel Ivanovich Chichikov arrives with a strange mission. He wishes, for some reason, to purchase "dead souls": in other words, serfs still listed on the last census return as belonging to their owners, but since deceased. For a negotiable fee, which in an assortment of ramshackle manor houses becomes a subject of tricky discussions, Chichikov will take this taxable expense off the hard-up gentry's hands and recruit a ghostly serf legion of his own. "What sort of parable was it then, this parable of the dead souls?" In the ballrooms, salons, taverns and offices of the dull town of "N–", the baffled beneficiaries of Chichikov's largesse hunt for an answer. So does the reader, buttonholed by a self-chastising storyteller who complains that he has to deal with the sordid wrangles of these "dreary and unprepossessing" types, while aspiring to write some uplifting tale with a "majestic lyrical flow".

In truth, Gogol – and the reader – has a delirious, a hilarious ball. For Vladimir Nabokov, the glorious satire of *Dead Souls* skewered the very essence of "poshlust": that peculiarly Russian amalgam of snobbery, kitsch, vulgarity and self-delusion. From the swaggering bully Nozdriov to the shabby Plyushkin, these backwater big shots reveal their selfishness and foolishness in scene after bustling, sparkling scene. Gogol's style boasts a Dickensian brio and a Swiftian violence as the indecent serf-purchase proposal tempts this greedy gaggle of squires, widows, soldiers and bureaucrats. Anyone else "would cheat you and sell you rubbish, not real souls," wheedles the bear-like landowner Sobakevich, "but my lot are like top-grade produce, all prime quality".

Like the government inspector of Gogol's own classic play, or the devil who descends on Moscow in Bulgakov's *The Master and Margarita*, the opaque Chichikov draws out the sins, desires and fears of all he meets. Behind the vitriolic merriment, a refrain of sorrow and compassion keeps the real lives of these lost souls in view: the porters, the cobblers, the servants, the barge haulers bought and sold, abused or protected, all stained by "toil and sweat" and singing "the same song, as endless as Russia". Only at the end of the finished section does the demonic, or maybe angelic, visitor collect a realistic back story. Chichikov emerges as a banal, corrupt chiseller and swindler much like his victims, a "scoundrel" hero for a scoundrel time. He's not strong, not brave enough for outright villainy: "The fairest thing would be to call him an owner, an acquirer."

In the second, fragmentary portion, this ignoble "acquirer" begins to reform. Inferno gives way to mere purgatory. Gogol's gorgeous lyricism, never absent as Chichikov rides from scam to scam, swells into rhapsody as he evokes the estates of the well-meaning but idle landowner Tentetnikov. On this soil, *Dead Souls* draws closer to the overtly reformist strand of Russian fiction. The squire has neglected practical improvement in favour of intellectual dilettantism. He plans a pretentious volume meant "to encompass all Russia" rather than getting his hands dirty. Even Chichikov, now in this vicinity, learns to feel respect for hard, honest graft on the farm. The narrator, meanwhile, dreams of a national leader "capable of uttering that all-powerful word, 'Onwards!', in a language the Russian should understand".

Scandal, disgrace and a spell in jail redirect Chichikov, and Gogol, back on the path of satire. The manuscript ends with the public-spirited governor calling on the nation to rise up "against injustice and lies". Yet the emblematic Russian Chichhikov still possesses an "inner soul" that resembles "a dismantled building". Reconstruction has not started "because the architect has not delivered the final plans". Russian literature, and politics, would soon abound with "final plans". None would ever match the savage joy of Gogol's wrecking ball.

Translation: More than a dozen English versions of Chichikov's adventures exist, but Donald Rayfield's (2008) commands both stylistic grace and a rollicking, colloquial panache.

See also: Turgenev, *Fathers and Sons* (1862); Bulgakov, *The Master and Margarita* (1940); Qian, *Fortress Besieged* (1947); Saramago, *The Year of the Death of Ricardo Reis* (1984)

Selected works by the same author: *Village Evenings near Dikanka and Mirgorod* (1832); *The Government Inspector* (1835); *The Nose* (1836); *The Overcoat* (1842)

16 | MADAME BOVARY (1857) by Gustave Flaubert.

French

Translated by Adam Thorpe (Vintage)

What shade are Emma Bovary's eyes? In the novel that, throughout

Europe and beyond, raised the bar for standards of verbal finesse and observational precision in prose fiction, Gustave Flaubert remains artfully vague. When the gauche, second-rate country doctor Charles Bovary first meets the glance of "guileless daring" flung at him by the quick-witted but dreamy daughter of a well-off widowed farmer, he sees eyes that, "although they were brown, her lashes made them appear black". A little later, though, they look to Charles "black in shadow and deep blue in daylight". However painfully Flaubert toiled to whittle every sentence into a jewel-like nugget of controlled colour, texture and rhythm, wayward human beings rather than camera-like machines propel his story. And where there are humans, there is ambivalence and doubt, confusion and delusion. In the filigree artifice of its prose, as much as the convulsive emotions of its people, *Madame Bovary* lays bare the dual, or the multiple, nature of human things. Famously, after Emma has taken two lovers, she "found in adultery all the same dullnesses of marriage". "Everything lied" in Emma's life. Every emotion, sensation or idea flips into its antithesis: "Each smile concealed a yawn of tedium, each joy a curse, every pleasure its disgust". Even in the pivotal scene when Emma and Rodolphe, her first lover, consummate their affair in a wood, the forensically exact Flaubert mixes up his bodily fluids so that she feels "the blood circling through her flesh like a river of milk". When, after one of literature's most harrowing, most cruelly spotlit, deathbed scenes, the pharmacist Homais concocts a cover story to conceal the truth of Emma's suicide, he makes sure that the townsfolk "all heard his story of the arsenic which she had mistaken for sugar, when making vanilla custard". With Flaubert, tragedy and farce, the sublime and the ridiculous, can also swap places in a heartbeat.

No novel has so masterfully guided the eyes and pens of future writers as *Madame Bovary*. So familiar has its narrative method become, with its "free indirect speech" that opens the characters' minds and its simultaneous command of an impersonal voice that registers everything, later readers can miss the revolutionary craft in this most sensational of debuts. (Flaubert was tried – and acquitted – on immorality charges.) Early on, when we meet Charles as an ungainly, rustic schoolboy in a silly hat (another "composite" entity that resembles both "bearskin" and "cotton bonnet"), the narrator sounds like some gossipy classmate. But this narrator figure soon vanishes. Then we gaze into Emma's inner and outer worlds with an objective, microscopic clarity of focus that makes Flaubert akin to the various experimental physicians who turn up through the book.

These "progressive" types, with the pompous secularist Homais as their champion, do battle with conservative priests and landowners in the semi-industrialised corner of Normandy that serves Flaubert as his microcosm of bourgeois France. As a daughter, as a wife, as a fitfully affectionate mother to little Berthe, Emma cannot fight as an equal in either camp. A woman, she knows, "is continually impeded". From girlhood, her thwarted energy mutates into fantasy. Boredom is the "silent spider" that spins its "shadowy web" in her heart. The passionate love she learns from the romantic fiction she devours must strike like "a hurricane from heaven"; she detests "commonplace heroes and mild feelings". Her lovers, the wealthy, cynical *roué* Rodolphe and the affected legal clerk Léon, play their part in her melodramatic theatre of desire. Léon, but not Rodolphe, shares her dreams: "She was the lover from every novel, the heroine of every play". Even her spells of remorse turn into a romantic performance: "She wanted to become a saint".

As her debts mount up, the bills fall due and the hideous finale nears, it would be easy – but glib – to conclude that reality takes its revenge on fantasy. In fact, Flaubert takes care to show that the "respectable" forces ranged against Emma dwell in illusory wonderlands of their own. Emma's shopping sprees and mania for luxury display a pioneering grasp of consumer culture's drive to sell material possessions as the tokens of our innermost desires. When, in the virtuoso contrapuntal scene at the agricultural show, Rodolphe sweet-talks Emma in the town hall while a local bigwig drones on about hogs, flax and "decent manure" in the square beneath, both seducer and politician utter a string of manipulative clichés. Radicals and royalists, clergymen and journalists (Homais is a loquacious hack): in this landscape of docks and factories as well as châteaux and cathedrals, persuasive words are "a rolling-mill that always stretch out one's feelings". Emma succumbs to the romantic and erotic product ground out by that mill. Homais, smugly triumphant at the close, enlists medical and political jargons as footholds for his ascent. So often tongue-tied, Charles himself – a dolt as the novel begins, a martyr as it ends – never finds a form of speech to call his own. As for their author, despite the tireless refinements of style that lends *Madame Bovary* its imperishable power to shock, to move and to delight, he sensed that reality would always escape even the most keenly engineered of verbal instruments. "Human utterance," he writes, "is like a cracked kettle on which we beat out tunes to make the bears dance, when we would like to move the stars to pity."

Translation: among recent versions, those by Lydia Davis and Geoffrey Wall both excel, but the novelist Adam Thorpe (2011) – who, brilliantly, employs only the English vocabulary of Flaubert's time – achieves a flavour that approaches the dream-like strangeness of Flaubert's hyper-realism.

See also: Goethe, *The Sorrows of Young Werther* (1787); Stendhal, *The Red and the Black* (1830); Eça de Queiroz, *The Crime of Father Amaro* (1875); Colette, *Chéri/The Last of Chéri* (1920–26).

Selected works by the same author: *Salammbô* (1862); *Sentimental Education* (1869); *The Temptation of St. Anthony* (1874); *Bouvard and Pécuchet* (1881)

17 | Les Misérables (1862) by Victor Hugo.

French

Translated by Julie Rose (Vintage)

"Victor Hugo, alas!" André Gide's retort, when asked to name France's greatest poet, might also answer a question about the most influential novelist of the 19th-century. A popular triumph from the moment of its well-orchestrated launch, Hugo's epic arguably altered social history more than literary history. "As long as social damnation exists through laws and customs creating an artificial hell at the heart of civilisation," Hugo's preface claims, such a book will be "not entirely useless". As he wished, his encyclopaedic epic of rebellion and redemption in post-Napoleonic France spurred movements of reform: from the rehabilitation of ex-offenders to the care of street children. *Les Misérables* travelled the world and it changed the world, as desired by an author who shunned both "despotism and terrorism": "We want progress that has a gentle incline." After the stalled revolution of 1848, which Hugo greeted with the qualified sympathy evident in his political asides, he fled the repressive regime of Napoleon III for exile in the Channel Islands. The mammoth project he then set aside resumed in 1860. So firm is the spine of Jean Valjean's quest for justice and rebirth that his story can also be read at intervals. Valjean and his tribe of helpers – and hinderers – will patiently await your return.

Yet this grand but never oppressive voyage through soul and a society, with its five parts and 365 chapters, endures as much more than a foundation stone of liberal values. For all its bulk, and the essay-like reflections that interrupt the action, we never lose the thread. Released from the prison hulks in the year of Waterloo (subject of a digression on the day "the perspective of the human race shifted" that trumps Tolstoy's clumsier battlefield philosophy in *War and Peace*), our convict-hero Jean Valjean seeks renewal in a society that has stacked all odds against the poor, the helpless and the outcast. "Human society had only ever done him harm." Yet through prosperity in business under an alias, exposure, capture, escape and near-mythical acts of compassion, he will attain his journey's end: "To be a just man." Along his winding way, Hugo melds every species of unfortunate – the sad, the mad, even the bad – into the single portmanteau term, *Les Misérables.* With his insistence that "there is a point where the poor and the wicked become mixed up", and his defiant challenge to privilege ("Whose fault is that?"), Hugo cuts through the moralising cant that divided the worthy pauper from the criminal chancer.

"When it comes to probing a wound," Hugo insists, "since when has it been a crime to go too far, to descend to the very depths?" In jails, convents and mansions, or in the Parisian rookeries and hovels, the likes of the street girl Fantine and the urchin Petit Gavroche fight to survive under the weight of law and prejudice imposed by "that prodigious pyramid we call civilisation". Valjean encounters the instantly legendary characters whose trials excite, move and fascinate. From Fantine and her daughter Cosette, whom he adopts and protects, to the remorseless, conscience-stricken police chief Javert, with "his superhuman bestiality of a bloodthirsty archangel", via the saintly cleric Myriel, the rascally innkeeper Thénardier, the idealistic student Marius and the uncrushable Gavroche, the cast of *Les Misérables* leapt off the page and into global folklore. For all the novel's sprawl and heft, Hugo knits their fates with a commanding strategic vision especially powerful in the final two parts. Here Cosette's sweetheart Marius and his fellow-revolutionaries mount the Paris barricades in the foiled Parisian uprising of June 1832; that outbreak of the fratricidal class warfare Hugo treats as "a disease of progress".

Both literally and figuratively, Hugo guides us through that "honeycomb of underground tunnels" that snake just under the surface of respectable society. Not for nothing does the entire epic reach its climax in the sewers of Paris, where Valjean rescues Marius after the insurrection. The sewer is "the conscience of the city. A heap of crap has this going for it: it does not lie." In this abyss of truth, Javert will acknowledge the greatness of Valjean, and salute "the sublimeness of that poor miserable bastard".

Its prodigal endowment of high drama and big ideas mean that the novel will never bore the open-minded reader. Between the life of a man, the history of a nation and the fate of humankind, it forever shifts focus and scale. The microcosm and macrocosm swap places: "A patch of mould is a Pleiade of flowers, a nebula is an anthill of stars". Likewise, the naked, startling realism of its streetlife scenes always lead, at the end of fetid alleyways, into the glorious literary vistas of the epic, the fairy tale, and the vision of civic enlightenment. On the barricades of Saint Antoine, the militant Enjolras declaims that "the nineteenth century is great but the twentieth century will be happy". Among the multiple registers that *Les Misérables* deploys, from street slang to thunderous rhetoric, weary irony never finds a place. We end in myth, even pantomime, with Cosette and Marius wed and Valjean, triumphantly redeemed, blessing the couple. "To love or to have loved is enough. Don't ask for more."

Flaubert scorned the swarming profusion of *Les Misérables*. Its brand of torrential, mythic melodrama fell out of favour among critics. Readers, though, have never lost the taste for such gloriously impure blockbusters. Its molten amalgam of pilgrimage and panorama has lent a model to writers in many societies shaken by bewildering change. David Bellos entitled his incisive study of *Les Misérables* and its world "The Novel of the Century". That century, however, might be Russia's or Latin America's 20th – or China's 21st.

Translation: Most early translations into English cut or shuffled entire sections. It took until 2008 for a complete version in the right order to appear, from the tirelessly energetic and creative Julie Rose.

See also: Stendhal, *The Red and the Black* (1830); Tolstoy, *War and Peace* (1869); Dostoyevsky, *The Brothers Karamazov* (1880); Vasily Grossman, *Life and Fate* (1959)

Selected works by the same author: *The Hunchback of Notre Dame* (1831); *The Contemplations* (1856); *Toilers of the Sea* (1866); *Ninety-Three* (1874)

18 | Fathers and Sons (1862) by Ivan Turgenev.

Russian

Translated by Peter Carson (Penguin Classics)

At the end of *Fathers and Sons*, the liberal landowner Nikolay Petrovich Kirsanov takes up a new role as an "arbitrator", managing relations between emancipated serfs and their former masters. "Both sides," we learn, "found him too soft." Turgenev, too, had to dodge heavy crossfire when his long-awaited novel of provincial Russia on the eve of the peasants' liberation failed to gratify the partisans in any camp. The author's own loathing of serfdom and Tsarist autocracy – despite, or because of, his own propertied family – sent him into self-imposed West European exile for much of his adult life. Always a principled reformer, he never made the customary switch from youthful radicalism to middle-aged reaction: a source of wry observation in *Fathers and Sons.*

But the finesse of his art complicates every ideal, every assertion. This never makes his exquisitely nuanced prose sound like the work of some bland, middle-of-the-road fence-sitter – although he draws that character type superbly. Rather, it allows him to mine the contradictions within his figures rather than merely record the antagonism between them, and haul up treasure from their conflicts. About the independent-minded widow Anna Sergeyevna Odintsova, Turgenev writes that, although she saw many things clearly, "nothing fully satisfied her: she probably didn't want complete satisfaction". Arguably, neither did her creator – or the restless seekers in his book. In this novel, so rooted in questions of the Russian soil – who owns it; who works it; who cares for its tillers – almost everyone seeks an ideal home. Peace of mind eludes the pack of them.

The title (strictly, *Fathers and Children*, but the early rendering has stuck) announces a debate, or dispute, between Russian generations. On the side of the "fathers" stand the amiable Nikolay Petrovich, a moderate reformer whose estate has by 1859 begun the shift from feudalism to tenant farming, and his brother Pavel Petrovich: a melancholy dandy, aesthete, and romantic "European". Back to the estate at Marino comes Nikoly's son Arkady, accompanied by his firebrand friend Bazarov. A scientist and physician who believes that "A decent chemist is worth twenty times any poet," Bazarov self-consciously shocks Marino with his materialism and his stance as a "nihilist": one "who bows down to no authority, who takes no single principle on trust". "We've had our day," the shocked Nikolay frets: "the young are clearly cleverer than we are". In witty, theatrical scenes of quarrelling and badinage, Bazarov scorns not only Pavel's "decadence and frivolity" and the "aristocratic trash" of the serf-owning elite, but the useless "nonsense" of high-minded do-gooders and "so-called progressives". Pavel, in contrast, rates the pleasure given by any "cheap pianist" who plays for a handful of kopecks higher than the nihilist's righteous fury and "crude Mongol force".

Thanks to the rippling grace and charm of Turgenev's narrative, these clashes never descend into dualistic tit-for-tat. Each of the contenders wrangles with himself as much as his opponents. The womenfolk of the household and neighbourhood soon expose these inner rifts. Nikolay, the widowed patriarch, has had an illegitimate son with the old housekeeper's daughter Fedechka, who lives under his roof. Anna Odintsova offers a proud model of self-sufficiency beyond the grip of any dogma, while her shyer sister Katya will win Arkady's heart. Bazarov's visit to his pious, contented parents – his father a former army doctor, his mother an old-fashioned but kind-hearted gentlewoman – helps turn him away from amateur botanising and salon rhetoric. He starts to give medical aid to the poor. By the time arch-enemies Pavel and Bazarov fight a ridiculous duel (no one dies), the abstract clash of slogans has yielded to a focus on step-by-step improvement.

Comically, Bazarov goes out to canvass popular opinion only to be told that "the stricter the master's demands, the dearer they are to his muzhik [peasant]". But this woeful shortfall in political consciousness hardly matters; there are illnesses to treat, injuries to tend. During an autopsy on a typhus victim, Bazarov picks up a cut – and the septicaemia that will kill him. The nihilist whose "almost Satanic pride" has shocked the timid gentry dies not a scoffer or a wrecker, but a helper and a friend. On his deathbed, he even accepts that "To be happy is never a bad thing". Now the bold rebel's challenge, "the giant's whole task", is "how to die a decent death". As so often in Russian literature, the windbags and dreamers must yield to the doers, the toilers, even though the disorganised post-feudal estates "squeaked like a wheel that hadn't been oiled". At least, thanks to the labour of both parents and children, that wheel is starting to turn.

Translation: Much translated over 150 years, Turgenev's poised wit and gentle wisdom find a new and trustworthy modern voice thanks to Peter Carson (2009).

See also: Lermontov, *A Hero of Our Time* (1840); Gogol, *Dead Souls* (1842); Tolstoy, *War and Peace* (1869); Lampedusa, *The Leopard* (1958)

Selected works by the same author: *The Diary of a Superfluous Man* (1850); *A Sportsman's Sketches* (1852); *On the Eve* (1860); *Virgin Soil* (1877)

19 | War and Peace (1869) by Leo Tolstoy.

Russian

Translated by Anthony Briggs (Penguin Classics)

In August 1812, with Napoleon's invading army marching fast towards Moscow, Prince Andrey Bolkonsky leaves his regiment to visit his family estate at Bald Hills. There he spots two girls scrumping plums from the summer's bumper crop. The sight of the little thieves fills him with "a lovely, heart-warming sensation": the recognition "that there were such things as other human interests, a million miles from his own but no less legitimate".

Time and again, across the vast narrative steppe of *War and Peace*, Tolstoy startles – and uplifts – us with scrumped plums. Ordinary life, cherished and celebrated as no writer ever had and, arguably, ever would again, blooms and ripens. It defies the grand designs pursued by the principal characters – not to mention the preposterous delusions of control harboured by statesmen, commanders and so-called "heroes". Almost since publication, readers who revere Tolstoy's huge yet microscopically precise cyclorama of Russian private and public life between 1805 and 1820 have also grumbled that his ruminative excursions into the philosophy of history interrupt their delight. They drag, for some, like a baggage cart stuck in a muddy rut during one of the many episodes that show "millions of men in movement" across war-ravaged Europe. Tolstoy, however, always insists that if we want to grasp "laws of historical movement" then we must dump all abstractions and aggregates to focus on "an infinitely small unit of observation". As in some fictional foreshadowing of chaos theory, every closely observed act plays its part in fulfilling an "ultimate purpose" that remains "beyond comprehension". Each well-wrought human knot in the gigantic carpet that is *War and Peace* contributes to the pattern of the whole.

Because of his speculative sermons, almost absent in the first two of four volumes but rising in frequency as Napoleon's campaign in Russia comes to dominate the action, Tolstoy denied that *War and Peace* even counted as a novel rather than an investigation into the meanings of history. Aptly enough, given his argument that the outcome of battles depends not on top-down commands but "the interplay of infinitely varied and arbitrary twists and turns", readers have always countermanded his orders. For millions, *War and Peace* remains not just a novel but *the* novel: the summit of the art and a supreme reading experience that rivals the moments of vision and ecstasy that punctuate this story. There is Natasha Rostov at the ball, touching "the very peak of happiness", or throwing off her Frenchified airs to dance like a peasant in a hut; her brother Nikolay during a wolf-hunt, "the happiest moment of his whole life"; and questing Pierre Bezukhov, released by his sufferings to look for "decency, happiness and peace in everything he saw".

Yet because of its granular, even pointillist method – step by step, scene by scene, plum by plum – *War and Peace* never intimidates, never overwhelms. This novel, which salutes each small deed of hospitality and solidarity in the face of war, grief and ruin, welcomes every reader as a beloved guest. Precisely because "no one who takes part in any historical drama can ever understand its significance", every chat, every ride, every thought, above all every gesture of kindness and sympathy, may mean as much – more, probably – than the megalomaniac plans of a Napoleon. That delusional "butcher of nations" dreams of absolute power – but "Kings are the slaves of history".

In summary, Tolstoy's world-historical epic can sound like a family saga played out among three intersecting aristocratic clans. At a Petersburg salon in 1805, the Russian elite responds to Napoleon's conquests. We glimpse the ties which bind the cash-strapped but merry Rostovs, the upright, idealistic Bolkonskys, the flashy, sensual Kuragins, and Pierre Bezukhov himself – that lumbering bear of a count's bastard son,"over-sized and out of place", but super-wealthy when his father dies. Catastrophically, Pierre weds flighty Helene Kuragin; tormented Andrey Bolkonsky and dashing, feckless Nikolay Rostov go to war. After Napoleon's victory at Austerlitz – the first of two extraordinary set-piece battle scenes that break down history's big pictures into a cellular ferment of "disparate and senseless eventualities" – Andrey falls for the blooming Natasha Rostov, but delays marriage. Natasha – vital, fallible, a singing, dancing work-in-progress as impossible to fix as history itself – courts disgrace when the caddish seducer Anatole Kuragin plots to abduct her.

As do-gooding Pierre lurches from one philanthropic project to another, from freeing serfs in Ukraine to "the reformation of the human race" via mystical freemasonry, he is plagued by "the constant search for purpose in life". Napoleon's fateful invasion of 1812 fast-forwards every destiny. After the bloody stalemate at Borodino, that "long drawn-out massacre" that nonetheless saves Russia, Moscow falls and burns. Natasha and Pierre, a prisoner of war, grow up fast. Nikolay rescues, and will wed, the long-suffering Marya, sister to the mortally wounded Andrey. Liberated, Pierre bonds with Natasha after his life-changing encounter with the saintly peasant Platon Karatayev, that stoic "epitome of kind-heartedness and all things rounded and Russian". Napoleon retreats, his defeat overseen by the phlegmatic, enigmatic Marshal Kutuzov. The epilogue hints that public-spirited Pierre will leave his domestic bliss with Natasha to join Russia's reformers, and revolutionaries, of the 1820s.

Each of these turning points has an "incalculable multiplicity" of causes. Lunatics and historians, with Napoleon and his "maniacal self-adulation" at their head, try to impose a "fictitious" order on events. As a novelist, Tolstoy acts not like Bonaparte but Kutuzov – that wise procrastinator, so "nondescript" to his detractors, whose "amazingly intuitive insight into the significance of events" stems from his "feeling for the people".

If *War and Peace* is a national epic, which sets organic Russian virtues against the arid, schematic ideologies of "Europe", then it develops not by pitting one Big Idea against another but by the cultivation of meaning in each grain, each cell, each fruit, of respect, fellowship and love. On a lovely spring day, Andrey balks at a gnarled, ancient oak tree, a "sneering monster" which seems to say: "I don't believe in any of your hopes and shams." *War and Peace* strips hopes and shams away like a winter gale. On his deathbed, though, Andrey will share Pierre's epiphany to grasp that "Everything is bound up with love, and love alone". That love, that truth, lies in doing good through minute particulars. The epilogue refers to acts of free will as an "unexplainable leftover" that the laws of history reject. Out of a thousand residues, the scourings of an unknowable necessity, Tolstoy builds his luminous castle of choice and of change.

Translation: Napoleonic battle lines divide the partisans of *War and Peace*'s translators. Anthony Briggs (2005) is sturdy, readable, reliable, colloquial. The more radical Richard Pevear and Larissa Volokhonsky (2007) have many champions – as do Louise and Aylmer Maude, who worked with Tolstoy.

See also: Stendhal, *The Red and the Black* (1830); Hugo, *Les Misérables* (1862); Némirovsky, *Suite Française* (1942–2004) Grossman, *Life and Fate* (1959)

Selected works by the same author: *Anna Karenina* (1877); *The Death of Ivan Ilyich* (1886); *Resurrection* (1899); *Hadji Murad* (1912)

20 | The Crime of Father Amaro: Scenes from the Religious Life (1875; revised 1880) by Eça de Quieroz (José Maria de Eça de Queiroz).

Portuguese

Translated by Margaret Jull Costa (Dedalus)

"If a man has no religion, he has no morality." Much of literature – and politics – in Europe during the century after the French Revolution aimed to test, and to contest, that belief. In Eça de Queiroz's captivating, exuberant but finally harrowing novel of hypocrisy, repression and revolt in 19th-century Portugal, the abuses committed both by priests and pious laypeople shred the pretensions of organised religion. Those words, for instance, are intoned by the lustful, deceitful Father Amaro to the vulnerable young woman, Amelia, whom he plans to seduce. His "brutal longing to possess her" will succeed. He wins her love, and takes acute "pleasure in this domination", while his besotted lover becomes "an inert accessory to his person". Amaro feels "neither compassion nor charity" towards the disabled teenager – daughter of the cathedral sexton – whom he pretends to visit in order to secure a safe room for their trysts. Amelia, and their son, will die, although Amaro uselessly repents of his decision to send the baby to a wet-nurse known as a "weaver of angels" – in other words, the killer of unwanted infants entrusted to her "care".

In bald summary, *The Crime of Father Amaro* sounds like exactly the sort of anti-clerical shocker that would have gladdened the godless hearts of the "atheists and republicans" who run the newspaper in Leiria, the novel's setting. After its first edition, the Brazilian writer Machado de Assis reproached Eça for publishing just such a lurid, anti-Catholic tract. The revised version does remove a few sensational touches. However, Eça never writes as a liberal propagandist or a secularist preacher. Much of his novel hums with joyous energy; with a big-hearted, broad-minded relish for the oddities and quiddities of its small-town milieu.

In a manner that might put Anglophone readers in mind of Trollope as much as Dickens, he converts the follies and foibles of Leiria's priests, aristocrats and liberal progressives into sumptuous, richly observant social comedy. Eça treats his weak-willed backsliders and hot-headed fools with more sympathy than disdain: from the furtive affair of worldly Canon Dias and São Joaneira, Amaro's landlady and Amelia's mother, to the bar room bravado of the young revolutionaries at the District Voice, who after three litres of red proclaim that, "Everything must be torn down, everything!" Mixed motives and self-delusion give rise to wry chuckles rather than irate scorn, as when Amelia channels her taste for melodramatic emotion into histrionic piety: "The Cathedral became her Opera House; God was her luxury." Much of the book feels as genial, generous, and satisfying as the pastoral landscapes that Eça lavishly evokes.

Within this comedy of provincial manners, though, a tragedy of passion and obsession begins to swell. Selfish, sensual, Amaro has joined the priesthood against his will. A protegé of the local aristocracy, he endures the seminary although it combines "the humiliations of prison with the tedium of school". He tolerates his parish duties chiefly for the access it brings to devoted women who serve, flatter – and excite – him. However, as the narrator reminds us, we can "dodge everything except love". First his fleshly prey, Amelia, becomes his fixation. Her own "intense desire" for the handsome priest, and guilty bliss in its fulfilment, drag the novel far away from being some Portuguese equivalent to Trollope's *Chronicles of Barsetshire*. Rather, we enter the domain of Flaubert's *Madame Bovary*. As Amelia's worthy, and secular, suitor João Eduardo threatens to expose the liaison, the clergy closes ranks. Eça has ripe satirical fun with the vested interests of Church and State. The civil governor defends free speech in this enlightened "century of electricity" while, for the Canon, "what matters is upholding the honour of the priesthood". Amid this parade of hypocrites, Eça takes care to single out rare examples of virtue either in cassocks and frock-coats: with the public-spirited non-believer Dr Gouveia, "the very model of kindness" who knows that the Church deems him a "rogue" bound for Hell; or with compassionate Father Ferrão, whose God is "an indulgent, caring father", and who supports Amelia as her pregnancy – and her panic – develops.

Expertly, Eça frames one novel inside the other. The fervid, frankly erotic chamber drama of Amaro and Amelia burns towards its agonising end. A delicious social dance of ambition, snobbery and disguise plays on around it. After the catastrophe, the armour-plated Amaro merely lies low for a while. We glimpse him in Lisbon, deploring the radical excesses of the Paris Commune of 1871 with his spiritual and secular patrons, the Canon and the Count. This band of charlatans agree that "faith... is the very basis of order". Portugal, they claim, remains "the envy of Europe". All around we see the signs of poverty, backwardness and vice, while the citizens of this earthly paradise display "the anaemic pallor of a degenerate race". The crimes of this society – of this age – hardly begin or end with a single vain priest's lust.

Translation: Margaret Jull Costa's new translations of Eça's masterpieces – with *Father Amaro* published in 2002 – have restored the sparkle, freshness and mischief of his style.

See also: Voltaire, *Candide* (1759); Flaubert, *Madame Bovary* (1857); Machado de Assis, *Epitaph of a Small Winner* (1880); Saramago, *The Year of the Death of Ricardo Reis* (1984)

Selected works by the same author: *Cousin Bazilio* (1878); *The Relic* (1887); *The Maias* (1888)

21 | Epitaph of a Small Winner (The Posthumous Memoirs of Bras Cubas) (1880) by Machado de Assis (Joaquim Maria Machado de Assis).

Portuguese (Brazil)

Translated by William L Grossman (Bloomsbury)

According to the bare facts of his life, Machado de Assis should rank

as literature's quintessential outsider. A Brazilian of mixed race, epileptic and unwell, his father a house-painter and his step-mother a cook, he worked in Rio de Janeiro – thousands of miles from the sacred citadels of 19th-century culture. He made a living as a lowly government pen-pusher. So much, as the deceased narrator of *Epitaph of a Small Winner* would argue, for conventional ideas and rigid systems of cause-and-effect. On the page, and above all in this extraordinary novel, Machado thought and wrote with a breathtaking, indeed aristocratic, freedom, grace and mischief. Bras Cubas, the drifting dilettante who has just died and addresses us from beyond the grave, pursues "a spirit of looseness and informality". His unbuttoned, ad hoc philosophy is to be expounded "in one's short-sleeves and suspenders". Life, for all the Schopenhauer-influenced pessimism that critics find in Machado's outlook, feels more like a joke or farce – if, sometimes, a sad and perplexing one – than a solemn tragedy. Besides, "what the devil is absolute in this world?" In his, as in every human brain, "Thoughts of every kind and of every caste mixed with one another."

These "posthumous memoirs" break every rule of orthodox fiction from the very first page, which merrily informs us of "the death of the author". There follow 160 short chapters that wittily dismantle the architecture of the 19th-century novel, brick by dusty, dreary brick. After all, "long chapters are better suited to ponderous readers". In fragments, often out of sequence, Bras Cubas – "good-looking, elegant, rich", so unlike his insecure creator – recounts his pampered childhood, his student days in Portugal, his misadventures in love and politics, and the shipwreck of all his hopes for a glittering, respectable career. "I did not achieve celebrity, I did not become a minister of state, I did not really become a caliph, I did not marry." These reminiscences, composed "with the pen of Mirth and the ink of Melancholy", treat life as a losing game of chance. If Bras Cubas comes out fractionally ahead, it is because he "had no progeny" (although he does, briefly, hint at sorrow over his lover's stillborn child): "I transmitted to no one the legacy of our misery".

For a while, Bras Cubas joins his friend Quincas Borba, a philosophical poseur, as an apostle of the creed of "Humanitism": a biting parody of 19th-century doctrines of optimism and progress. Yet the errant, frivolous dandy can never play the "caliph" sidekick to Quincas Borba's prophet. Life strikes him as much too provisional and arbitrary for any such grand theory. His writing matches his outlook: "you like straight, solid narrative and smooth style, but this book and my style are like a pair of drunks: they stagger to the right and to the left, they start and they stop… they slip and fall." Machado, an Anglophile in his literary taste, draws on the antic textual gambits of Swift and, above all, Sterne. One chapter of dialogue consists solely of punctuation ("!…?…!"); chapter 136 merely informs the reader that "I have just written an utterly unnecessary chapter".

Bras Cubas does clutch on to a few signposts as he weaves and stumbles through his memories. A love for unattainable women, fitful but recurrent, threads his days. The nearest he comes to stable domesticity is a secret long-term affair with the married Virgilia. Her husband Lobo Neves becomes Bras Cubas's political patron – our defunct narrator does like to complicate things – so even this approximation to a settled relationship calls for "the furtiveness and cunning of snakes". For the most part, however, Machado gleefully trashes the bourgeois decor of the Romantic novel. No more villain than hero, Bras Cubas accepts that he contains multitudes: the spirit of "the eagle and the hummingbird", but also "the frog and the snail". Any life demands understanding as an exercise in "spiritual geology". A core, or bedrock, of personality may persist. But nearer the surface, "loose earth and sand" will be blown around by the "eternal torrent" of chance events.

Hilarious, original and bracingly fresh, the "posthumous memoirs" record an astonishing feat of imaginative daring. Perhaps Machado's marginality did help him to untie so many of the mental and formal knots that bound his peers in Europe. In any case, this prophetic book, which opened new horizons to the writers of the next century, couches its vision of freedom and mutation in highly literary terms. Bras Cubas conceives of man as a "thinking erratum". Each "new edition" of his life "corrects the preceding one", until the definitive imprint, "which the publisher donates to the worms". Those worms, and Machado's readers, have a timeless treat in store.

Translation: William Grossman's droll and robust 1952 version has powerful competition from Gregory Rabassa (1997) in the Library of Latin America series.

See also: Svevo, *Zeno's Conscience* (1923); Sartre, *Nausea* (1938); Beckett, *Trilogy* (1951-52); Tanpinar, *The Time Regulation Institute* (1962)

Selected works by the same author: *Helena* (1876); *The Alienist* (1881); *Quincas Borba* (1891); *Dom Casmurro* (1899)

22 | Niels Lyhne (1880) by Jens Peter Jacobsen.

Danish

Translated by Tiina Nunnally (Penguin Classics)

In one of his many dark hours of the soul, the hero of Jens Peter Jacobsen's trail-blazing tale of faith, doubt and love inspects the modern alternatives to religious belief. "Atheism, the New, truth's holy cause – what purpose did they all serve?" These lofty principles rank no higher than "names of tinsel for the one simple idea: to endure life as it was!"

Niels Lyhne has plenty to endure. The archetypal post-Christian wanderer of late 19th-century European fiction, he spurns the stolid conventions of his family in provincial Denmark. Crucially, he also rejects the Christian God: not as a liberated soul, but as "a vassal who takes up arms against his rightful master". A poet, idealist and spiritual seeker of the kind that Ibsen and Strindberg (who owed a heavy debt to Jacobsen) would soon bring to the Scandinavian and world stage, Niels tries to find a substitute for religion in romantic love. In rapturous prose lit by the kind of radiant anguish also found in the work of his compatriot Søren Kierkegaard, Jacobsen traces his unhappy history of serial passion and separation. The objects of his consuming love range from the free-spirited Fru Boye to the tender and vulnerable Fennimore, who marries Niels's sculptor friend Erik.

For Niels, so much a child of his time, love becomes another god that fails. Fennimore comes to see that his voracious, high-minded devotion destroys more than it creates: "you came along with your poetry and your filth, and your lies dragged me down into the dirt with you". Fennimore, at least, survives to leave Niels. Otherwise, heart-breaking deaths punctuate the plot, from Niels's beloved, adventurous Aunt Edele to – at the wrenching finale – his own little son.

Jacobsen studied natural science before turning to fiction. In the 1870s, he had translated the work of Charles Darwin into Danish: both *The Origin of Species* and *The Descent of Man*. His articles propagated evolutionary ideas among the Danish public. Yet no more than Darwin could Jacobsen feel content with the pitiless neutrality of Nature, stripped of any divine design. The flight from belief leaves free-thinkers like Niels bereft and helpless at a period when practical medicine – as opposed to scientific theory – can still do little to mitigate suffering and grief.

One Christmas in Copenhagen, Niels wrangles about religion with the shrewd Dr Hjerrild: another non-believer, but one who respects outward piety as a social bond. Hjerrild tells Niels that he must have an "amazing faith" in humanity, for "atheism will make greater demands on people than Christianity does". Later, in bereavement and despair, Niels will fall to his knees again before a God "from whom no escape is possible, not to the farthest ocean nor down into the abyss".

Few other novels convey with such compact force the loss of supernatural faith not as a leap into freedom but a well-nigh insupportable ordeal. Niels and his peers strive to live out Romantic ideals in a severely Realistic landscape of risk, pain and isolation. Artistic skill, erotic desire, spiritual enlightenment: no surrogate can properly fill that God-shaped chasm of emptiness. As Hjerrild insists, with chilly wisdom, "Will you help a single human being if you die with one idea instead of another?" Even natural beauty, which Jacobsen summons in some splendidly sensuous passages, serves mainly to offset human woe. Niels takes his dying mother to Switzerland to relish one final "festival of spring". But even amid the loveliness of Rousseau's beloved Clarens, beside Lake Geneva, Niels sees her "withering in all that lushness of renewal".

The thwarted idealist, adrift in a godforsaken universe, hunts for redemption through art and love. *Niels Lyhne* occupies a pivotal position along the Existential highway that leads from Kierkegaard to Camus. Rainer Maria Rilke, Jacobsen's grateful disciple, placed the Dane alongside Auguste Rodin as "the two inexhaustible ones, the masters". Thomas Mann also drew from the novel's mood of fervid, even doom-laden quest, in *Tonio Kröger* and *Death in Venice*. As for his search for passion as a secular fount of meaning, he shares both longing and disenchantment with the protagonists of novels from Flaubert's *Madame Bovary* to DH Lawrence's *Sons and Lovers*. As much a victim of the age as his over-burdened hero, Jacobsen died of tuberculosis in 1885, aged 37.

Translation: Although *Niels Lyhne* first reached English in 1919, a much superior version appeared in 1990 from Tiina Nunnally.

See also: Flaubert, *Madame Bovary* (1857); Rilke, *The Notebooks of Malte Laurids Brigge* (1910); Thomas Mann, *The Magic Mountain* (1924); Albert Camus, *The Outsider* (1942)

Selected works by the same author: *Mogens and Other Stories* (1872); *Marie Grubbe* (1876)

23 | THE BROTHERS KARAMAZOV (1880) by Fyodor Dostoyevsky.

Russian

Translated by Richard Pevear and Larissa Volokhonsky (Vintage Classics)

Real or imagined, children play a decisive role in *The Brothers Karamazov*. The novel turns on the unfinished business between parents and offspring, powerful and powerless, both in the family and society at large. As this lurid tale of avarice, desire, rivalry, murder and redemption in a Russian town accelerates towards its climax, Dostoyevsky (as he so often does) shifts the mood and varies the pace. We learn about the childhood exploits of the clever scamp, Kolya Krasotkin. Once, for a dare, he lay down between the railway tracks and, by now paralysed with fear, let the "approaching monster" run right over him. Readers of *The Brothers Karamazov* often feel a little like Kolya. This steaming, clanking express of a book comes laden with such an inexhaustible freight of meaning that figures of the stature of Einstein and Freud ranked it above all other fiction. Many partisan interpretations – religious, political, philosophical, psychological – seem to demand that we lie in its tracks and allow this mighty machine of wisdom to roar across us.

In practice, especially in modern translations that bring us nearer to Dostoyevsky's voice (or rather voices), this monumental, but infinitely varied, novel does not set out to shock and awe. Like his earlier *Crime and Punishment*, the plot pivots on a killing: of the dissolute gentleman, Fyodor Karamazov, a "repulsively sensual" ageing buffoon. His puerile pleasure-seeking reverses the poles of authority between the generations. The bulk of the novel's later "books" (it has twelve, divided among four parts) present the police investigation of the crime, the scrutiny of evidence, the tangled arguments over culpability and, finally, the drawn-out, nail-biting godfather of all courtroom dramas. Did Fyodor's eldest son, "a brute of an officer who drinks cognac and goes whoring", commit a dreadful parricide in the course of robbing his father in order to clear debts? Or does blame lie with the cunning servant Smerdyakov, reputedly Fyodor's bastard by the abused simpleton "Stinking Lizaveta"? Meanwhile, Fyodor's three sons from two wives – feckless, hell-raising Dmitri; rebellious, gifted Ivan; saintly, innocent Alexei – spar and wrangle over matters sacred and profane. Dmitri and Ivan also wrestle with their father over the affections of the local minx Grushenka, for whom Dmitri – in fits and starts – forsakes his high-minded fiancée, Katya.

Add to this domestic imbroglio knockabout scenes of provincial life, from tavern to courthouse, with lashings of lust, greed, envy and backbiting. Eventually we share the bewilderment of a Polish noblemen caught up in mayhem at the inn: "This is Sodom!" Or, perhaps, it's soap opera. Stripped of the insulation of Victorian gentility, the raucous, hectic carnival of Dostyevsky's prose shows its comic mettle. Alcohol in excess fuels showdowns, erotic or financial, between out-of-control adults, while gentler episodes involving children – the moral focus here – have a kinder sense of fun. In charge of the narration, a nosy, garrulous "author" not only tells the story but, like a gossipy neighbour, tries to steer our judgement. Plunge into the brothers' boozy, bitchy world, as "one more clownish and almost incredible scene" follows another, and redemption feels a galaxy away. Rather, these slaves of appetite embody what Ivan calls "the whole offensive comedy of human contradictions".

Yet around this squalid stage of fools Dostoyevsky builds the most awe-inspiring architecture – emotional, spiritual and intellectual. His visions, debates and dialogues sear themselves into the mind and heart, never to fade. Among them stand out Ivan's parable of the Grand Inquisitor who accuses the returned Jesus of having burdened mankind with the unwanted gift of free will and snatched from us the consolations of "miracle, mystery, and authority"; his recurrent speculation that, in the absence of God, divine judgement and the soul's immortality, "everything is permitted"; Alexei's devotion to the "active love" and "deep infinite compassion" preached by his mentor, the holy monk Zosima; and Alexei's final insistence that a single memory of goodness, "especially a memory from childhood", may be enough to serve "some day for our salvation". The supreme dialectician among novelists, Dostoyevsky puts his own faith through the severest tests. None is more harrowing than Ivan's fury at the idea that divinely-ordained free will might justify the torture by abusive parents of a young girl. For Ivan, "The whole world of knowledge is not worth the tears of that little child".

Crucially, these magnificent set-pieces do not drop into the action as ready-made sermons or playlets. They emerge organically from character and conflict. Intensely theatrical, the novel's epic antitheses – belief and unbelief, hope and despair, social revolution and spiritual renewal – strive towards a synthesis that forever eludes its protagonists (though not, perhaps, the kids who lark and scrap in the background). When Ivan posits that "man has, indeed, invented God" or the "mysterious visitor" in Zosima's testimony avows that modern materialism forces each solitary man to seek "seclusion in his own hole", their arguments always arrive framed by the tumultuous drama unfolding around them. As Dmitri stands trial, parricidal longings emerge as the norm in a society cursed by its derelict patriarchs: "Everyone wants his father dead". The prosecutor warns of "some general malaise that has taken root among us". But the prosecutor is a bullying windbag, possibly deluded: always, the novel pushes back against its own theorems. Even the Devil, who appears to delirious Ivan in the shape of a genteel, down-at-heel sponger, has mislaid his infernal swagger and now feels like "an x in an indeterminate equation", a "ghost of life who has lost all ends and beginnings". Dostoyevsky himself gives us a suspenseful end, with the promise of future reversals to come. Among the angels and the demons, and with humankind's "amazing mixture of good and evil" in between, life's performance – both a tragedy and a comedy – will continue.

Translation: Richard Pevear and Larissa Volokhonsky's mission to reclaim the Russian classics through re-translation struck gold in their exhilarating 1990 version: bracing, vibrant, faithful.

See also: Gogol, *Dead Souls* (1842); Turgenev, *Fathers and Sons* (1862); Tolstoy, *War and Peace* (1869); Céline, *Journey to the End of the Night* (1932)

Selected works by the same author: *Notes from Underground* (1864); *Crime and Punishment* (1866); *The Idiot* (1869); *Demons* (1872)

24 | Germinal (1885) by Emile Zola.

French

Translated by Roger Pearson (Penguin Classics)

At its greatest, topical and documentary fiction rises to the height of myth. However dogged the research, however meticulous the gathering of facts and testimonies, chroniclers of social life who choose the novel as their vehicle must transform time-bound detail into time-defying form. The thirteenth in the epic sequence of twenty Rougon-Macquart novels of France under the Second Empire of 1851-1871, *Germinal* first of all outraged Zola's contemporaries with its unsparing realism: about conditions in the pit villages of north-eastern France, where it takes place; about the squalor, misery and danger of the colliers' lives; about the daily violence, physical and sexual, of a benighted place where a teenage girl in the mines can anticipate "the usual thing… raped behind the slag-heap, a baby at sixteen and then a poverty-stricken home if her lover married her".

Zola went down the mines of the Nord department, which he presents as growing monstrously into "a single industrial city", and studied the economics of coal production. This background toil enriches, but does not explain, the overwhelming power of *Germinal.* For one thing, his novels – like Charles Dickens's – seem to illuminate present woes but generally unfold in the past. Reform had mitigated some glaring abuses in pit work by 1885. From the start, Zola also depicts the mining districts as a contemporary inferno, scorched by flame, blackened by soot and pierced by the cries of tormented souls as they sweat amid and underneath "the nocturnal fires of the land of coal and iron". The pits become great predatory animals, "crouching ready to devour the world". When, in the frenzied, hallucinatory final act of *Germinal*, flooding caused by an act of sabotage destroys the mineshaft of Le Voreux, "The evil beast… sated with human flesh, had drawn its last long heavy breath".

In a setting that resembles classical myth or Biblical prophecy as much as the France of its day, human beings battle with a system that strips them of dignity, hope and, frequently, life itself. Etienne Lantier, the flawed hero, arrives to work in the Montsou mines as an outcast wanderer. Followers of earlier Rougon-Macquart novels will know of his accursed parentage and how his character, torn between nobility and savagery, bears out the theories of genetic inheritance and ancestral legacy in Zola's "experimental" novels. However, the science, or pseudo-science, behind the doctrines of Naturalism will scarcely bother readers now, although Zola does haul them into view; for instance, by ascribing Etienne's attack on a rival as "the onrush of his hereditary taint".

Etienne finds a protector in the veteran pitman Maheu. He works alongside Maheu's spirited teenaged daughter Cathérine; their relationship, intimate but largely chaste, will prop up the novel. Zola's underground scenes have all the dread and precision of a nightmare, repeated every shift. His frankness about the mine girls' exploitation – by the coal owners and their male co-workers alike – scandalised critics. Confronted with the child labour, squalid lodgings and starvation wages that lead to "the promiscuity of poverty", polite society preferred to shoot the messenger.

Even the doughty Cathérine, Zola writes, shares that "inherited submissiveness which laid low the girls of her race while still children". For all his insistence on victimhood passed down across the generations, the older women prove bonny, sharp-tongued fighters. After the harrowing, winter-long strike which gives the plot of *Germinal* its backbone, an outburst of rioting sees the village matrons castrate the corpse of a profiteering shopkeeper and, in a famously grizzly scene, parade "this miserable piece of flesh" on a stick "like an odd piece of meat on a butcher's stall".

During the strike, the self-educated Etienne becomes an orator and agitator who, "with the excitement of the new convert", plunges into the squabbling politics of revolution in the age of the First International. Zola dramatises a three-way dispute between moderate reformers such as the innkeeper Rasseneur, socialist disciples of the International, fired by their hunger for justice and "the ecstatic vision of a promised land", and the Russian anarchist Souvarine, who dreams not of redistribution or equality but of "pure destruction". In the event, all this "sectarian wrangling" comes to nothing. Hunger, despair, and a massacre of fourteen men, women and girls by government troops, drive the miners back to work. However, the anarchist apostle has one more card to play. His deed pushes *Germinal* into its apocalyptic, and masterly, finale, when this pioneering social novel morphs into something closer to a heart-pounding disaster-movie.

For all the workers' defeat, Etienne has studied Darwin and glimpses a future stage of evolution with "the strong people devouring the effete bourgeoisie". The novel gives little hint of that, despite its parting glimpse of springtime seed whose germination will "crack the earth asunder". It did show to writers of the next century that exemplary tales of injustice and revolt could mine the subterranean powers of archetype, vision and fable. The bitter struggle to make "your own happiness in this world" may draw on buried treasures of the storytelling past.

Translation: LW Tancock's 1954 version for Penguin Classics has a muscular forthrightness that recalls DH Lawrence. It remains a benchmark, although Roger Pearson's 2004 Penguin rendering deploys modern scholarship and brings Zola closer to our time.

See also: Hugo, *Les Misèrables* (1862); Platonov, *The Foundation Pit* (1930); Laxness, *Independent People* (1934-35); Cela, *The Hive* (1951)

Selected works by the same author: *Thérèse Raquin* (1867); *Nana* (1880); *The Ladies' Paradise* (1883); *The Beast Within* (1890)

25 | HUNGER (1890) by Knut Hamsun.

Norwegian

Translated by Sverre Lyngstad (Canongate)

Near the start of *Hunger*, the penniless and malnourished young writer who recounts his grim existence plans a knockout monograph about "Philosophical cognition" that will "deal a deathblow to Kant's solecisms". Alas, this breakthrough in the history of thought has to wait because "I didn't have a pencil on me anymore". He has pawned his jacket and left the pencil in a pocket. Hamsun's blazing, fervid and hallucinatory novel of despair and delirium on the streets of Kristiania (now Oslo) has become such a revered text that its aura can mask its texture. Absurdity partners its intensity, and a self-lacerating comedy – as close to Beckett or Bernhard as to Kafka – punctuates its moments of fleeting rapture and howling misery. Our hapless narrator, burning with shame and rage in his "living everlasting hell", may be a haggard prototype of the lonely wanderer in the hard, cold cities of modernity. He's also figure of bleak fun, a self-harming blunderer who squanders every chance that comes his way.

Hunger, published in 1890 after the young author had himself suffered rejection and destitution after his return to Norway from the US, does indeed break acres of new ground. Its inner journey through dejection and solitude into "the sheer madness of hunger" takes the fiction of tormented consciousness into uncharted realms of darkness. The nightmare episodes of alienation on the streets of Kristiania match in date, place and mood the spectral nocturnes painted by Edvard Munch. Yet part of Hamsun's originality consists in showing how a life that can feel utterly tragic from within – "defeated, defiled and degraded in my own estimation" – can look, from a distance, clownish and comical. Dialogue, often painfully funny as our hero wheedles, cadges, fibs and boasts his way into the odd loan or subsidy, sets the tone just as much as the bouts of famished introspection that leave him "hollowed out, spiritually and physically". This dark night of the Nordic soul concludes, after all, not with a suicidal demise in a frozen garret but a job offer on a merchant ship and a brisk, not unhappy, farewell to Kristiania, "where the windows shone so brightly in every home".

Critics bracket Hamsun's immersive style, so rapt, swift and inward, as a breakthrough on the road towards the stream-of-consciousness fiction that would dominate the standard histories of 20th-century literature. Yet *Hunger* takes care to mark a distance between narrator and reader. It lets us see this pitiable but also proud – indeed, downright offensive – loner though many other eyes. There are the editors who buy or reject his articles and stories, the policeman who treats him with bluff indulgence, the young woman whose sympathy he arouses and exploits, the landladies who show him kindness as well as contempt.

Emaciated and injured (he picks up wounds he then neglects), his half-starved body disgusts him. His writings – sold, if he's lucky, for a handful of kroner – can prompt bursts of conceit and "a wonderful sense of pleasure", but also spasms of self-hatred. *Hunger* pioneers the post-Romantic "artist novel", with the creative process no longer a divine wind but a draining, Sisyphean labour. The narrator's search for a language of despair helps keep him alive: in the pit of his "brooding darkness", he strives to find "a word so horribly black that it would dirty my mouth when I uttered it". These efforts often misfire. On the Kristiania dockside, he scribbles an overblown Decadent drama of the Middle Ages while the port's bustling industry thrums and clangs around him. The contrast between "the incessant clanking of the railcar couplings" and "that thick, musty air of medievalism" in his misbegotten play traces a symbolic divide between one phase of culture and another.

Although a thoroughly urban novel, *Hunger* draws threads from the pastoral strand in Norwegian literature. Our narrator registers the passing seasons with an almost Japanese precision. Autumn, that "carnival of transience", makes him feel like "a crawling insect doomed to perish". (Two decades later, Kafka would write *The Metamorphosis*.) Just as the starving writer thinks of himself as a frail speck on the hostile surface of the city, so Kristiania itself huddles like a fragile cluster of competitive humanity pitched uneasily between fjord and forest. Both traditional religion, and the high ideals of the philosophers, wilt beneath this amoral struggle for survival. Each ruse our narrator devises to snatch his next meal belongs in a Darwinian domain. Animal cunning – theft, cheating, seduction, coercion – may prevail where his evolved intellect fails. Given the older Hamsun's Nazi sympathies, the vision that seizes his narrator has a special frisson. He wants to write an allegory about "a fire in a bookstore", and grasps the true meaning of this image: "it wasn't books that were burning, it was brains, human brains". Feverish with resentment, as well as sheer need, the lowly but haughty outcast cuts both a sorry and a sinister figure.

Translation: Sverre Lyngstad's scrupulous and powerful 1996 version improves vastly on its English predecessors.

See also: Jespersen, *Niels Lyhne* (1878); Rilke, *The Notebooks of Malte Laurids Brigge* (1910); Beckett, *Trilogy* (1951-53); Salih, *Season of Migration to the North* (1966)

Selected works by the same author: *Mysteries* (1892); *Pan: From Lieutenant Thomas Glahn's Papers* (1894); *Victoria* (1898); *Growth of the Soil* (1917)

26 | The Duel (1891) by Anton Chekhov.

Russian

Translated by Richard Pevear and Larissa Volokhonsky (in *The Complete Short Novels*; Everyman's Library)

No agency or academy ever did, or ever could, define the length at which a short story becomes a novella, then a novel. It seems apt that Anton Chekhov, such a peerless comic dismantler of prescriptive and dogmatic thinking in every genre he touched, should in some of his own greatest works both pose that question and then – with idiosyncratic brilliance – answer it. Although brief (120 pages in the edition recommended here), *The Duel* blends levity and gravity, foreground detail and depth of field, as it presents a series of discoveries and reversals that feels entirely novelistic. Like other concise masterworks of the 1890s and 1900s –

notably, by Joseph Conrad and HG Wells – it chillingly looks forward to an era in which "an ideal race of people" will trample on the generous humanism that Chekhov the doctor-reformer both preached and practised.

In a sleepy, sultry resort on imperial Russia's Black Sea coast, the idle, even parasitic Ivan Andreyich Laevsky has tired of his affair with the married Nadezhda Fyodorovna. She has left her sick husband for this genial wastrel. He's also bored with the dream of the sunny, sensual south, and pines to return from the "Asiatic" Caucasus to the cold, damp cities of the intellectual north where "one could be honest, intelligent, lofty and pure". In reality, Laevsky is none of those things. Still, he cares fitfully for his mistress's feelings, enjoys the company of the good-hearted army doctor Samoilenko – and recognises a natural enemy when the haughty, clever and pitiless zoologist Von Koren arrives to smash this somewhat tatty seaside idyll.

With exquisite footwork, Chekhov sets the stage for a showdown between Laevsky, the ultimate "superfluous man" of the Russian literary tradition, and the brisk, heartless Social Darwinist Von Koren. The latter believes in "the struggle for existence and selection", scorns most people as "puppies and nonentities", and identifies love with "the strong overcoming the weak". His arrogance appals the kindly church deacon who views both Von Koren and his rival as privileged dilettantes, "spoiled since childhood by good surroundings". They should rather – as their author did – do some proper work to alleviate squalor, sickness and ignorance.

Every minor character, and every facet of the sub-tropical landscape and atmosphere, glows with the richest colours, painted in the subtlest strokes. We glimpse the multicultural, largely Muslim, hinterland where poor folk of various sorts do their best to live in harmony. After the crisis has passed, the deacon chats with a Tatar innkeeper in a lovely valley about the difference – if any – between the deities they worship. "Only the rich man sorts out which God is yours, which is mine," the host remarks – surely with his author's blessing. "Eat, please."

Guilty but lazy, Laevsky hopes to free Nadezhda from the "tight mesh of lies" in which he has entangled her, but finds neither the will nor the means. Blunder by blunder, he traps himself in a knot of debt and jealousy, and seeks to break his bind by flinging down a rash challenge to Von Koren. In 1891, of course, duelling for the sake of "honour" feels to everyone concerned like a quaint and silly throwback. But then Chekhov treats Laevsky's self-pitying "crippled by civilisation" shtick, and Von Koren's superman fantasies, as equally outworn postures. At the farcical showdown, Laevsky deliberately fires wildly into the air. Chillingly, his adversary – the Nietzschean, the eugenicist, the man who believes that "What reason achieves, your flabby, worthless hearts destroy" – takes aim at the "superfluous man's" forehead.

By the time he wrote *The Duel*, Chekhov had begun his career in the theatre. In its surprise twists, as in its wonderfully paced and nuanced dialogue, his prose fiction shows its kinship with his dramatic gift. Yet *The Duel* no more concludes in a neatly-tied denouement than do the plays. As his chastened foe sets sail into a new life, Laevsky (who did survive) reflects that "No one knows the real truth". A penumbra of mystery, and possibility, surrounds every being, every action. This is Chekhov's rebuttal in art to the delusional clarity of the Von Koren doctrine, with its claim that the clever and the powerful should enlist the rest of humanity as "cannon fodder, beasts of burden". His fiction ironises, but forgives, both the feckless drifter and the ruthless planner. *The Duel* draws back to observe their petty pride through the deacon's eyes, as he hopes that both might instead "direct their hatred and wrath" to relieve the misery of the poor.

Translation: Partisans of Chekhov's many translators often bicker like his own characters, but Pevear and Volokhonsky's bold approach (2004) to his longer fiction pays rich dividends.

See also: Lermontov, *A Hero of Our Time* (1840); Gogol, *Dead Souls* (1842); Turgenev, *Fathers and Sons* (1862); Roth, *The Radetzsky March* (1932)

Selected works by the same author: *The Shooting Party* (1884); *Ward No. 6* (1892); *The Seagull* (1896); *The Cherry Orchard* (1904)

27 | The Murderess (1903) by Alexandros Papadiamantis.

Greek

Translated by Peter Levi (New York Review Books)

As the 19th-century closed, many "advanced" works of European  literature set out to challenge, to innovate, even to shock, in their portrayal of disturbed minds and diseased societies. A handful of masterworks aside, most of these once-bold provocations now read as quaint period pieces and no more. At the same time, on the backward Greek island of Skiathos, a poor, pious and conservative writer was mining the scant resources of his home and his neighbours for stories that can still alarm, unsettle and horrify. His short novel *The Murderess* implicates readers in a nightmare – both psychic and social – that leaves us feeling, like its accursed heroine, that "grief was joy and death was life and everything was upside down". In general, glib invocations of Athenian tragedy do no favours to Greek authors. In this case, with a work whose restrained artistry complements and intensifies its visceral impact, the comparison seems justified.

Published in 1903, Alexandros Papadiamantis's story takes us a little further back in the harsh history of his Sporadic island: the old people here have memories of the 1820s war for Greek independence. For the sixty year-old grandmother Hadoula, in any case, the grind of duty and toil remains as relentless as it has always been for women in this impoverished patriarchy of seafarers and shepherds. Also known as "Frankojannou", after her husband, she has "never done anything except serve others", a slave to parents, spouse, children, grandchildren. At the same time her "cleverness and thrift" (which includes the odd theft) have given them a better life than many in this "small, provincial spot" where sons – like Hadoula's own three – habitually emigrate or go to sea.

One of her boys, the "neighbourhood scoundrel" Mitro, has gone to the bad; he knifed his sister Amersa, and is now serving time on the mainland for murder. However, the plight of girl children vexes Hadoula above all. All in need of unaffordable dowries, perpetual drains on the near-empty purses of their parents, this tribe of surplus females look to Hadoula like burdens to themselves and their families. She rejoices when the diseases of childhood, incurable in this forsaken backwater, carry them off like "wingbeats of the little angels" who will welcome them to heaven. As she watches unsleeping over her sickly granddaughter, the child of her eldest daughter Delcharo, "memories rise like ghosts" of her life, in all "its futility and its emptiness and its hardness". Why should "the infinite multitude of female children of the poor" endure the same misery?

So she begins to kill them. First, without arousing suspicion, she suffocates the little girl. Then she drowns two young villagers as they play beside an old cistern. "Remorse and worry" plague her but the urge to liberate girls from "this world of sins and tortures" has become a compulsion. Only when, by coincidence, she witnesses (but fails to prevent) an accidental drowning do the authorities, sluggish and negligent, begin to suspect her. She flees across the rocks, woods and shores of an island that Papadiamantis conjures in all its pitiless beauty. The daughter of a "witch", Hadoula can buy silence and assistance with her skills as a herbalist and healer. Even here, though, the bumbling police pursue her while the accusing ghosts of her victims hang in dark dreams "like a necklace". In her madness, in her flight, she stumbles through the secrets and crimes of a place where natural loveliness, like the woodland "twitter of nightingales" in "a sweet May dawn", seems to mock the plight of men and (above all) women without hope or rest. For her, as for them, "Tomorrow held no vision of golden sunrise." She seeks out the hermit monks who have refused in their chastity to bring "other unhappy creatures into the world". Although memory scourges, conscience bites and "Heaven and Hell were within her", secular authority closes in. Her bid to escape runs out "midway between divine and human justice".

Far from any progressive metropolis, in spirit as much as in geography, Papadiamantis cannot offer Hadoula or the village womenfolk any glimpse of redemption through social change. Chained to custom, to biology, to poverty, a slave in every sense, she rebels in a psychotic but logical form. Her murderous revolt defies fate but – here the echoes of classical drama grow louder – brings down its blows. Papadiamantis's narrative has a pulsating force and sensuous clarity that turns *The Murderess* into a fictional force of nature, as unyielding as the island's seas and rocks. Yet he stands squarely with Hadoula and the villagers, a messenger for their struggle and sorrow, never a detached observer of "primitive" or exotic folk ways. She is no anthropological curiosity but a genuine tragic heroine, driven towards savagery by sympathy. For this afflicted woman whose rage at injustice drives her into evil, everything in life "came to her at the wrong time and upside down".

Translation: The eminent classicist Peter Levi's version (1983) has all the pace, force and fire that this inexorable tragedy demands.

See also: Undset, *Kristin Lavransdatter* (1920-22); Camus, *The Outsider* (1942); Rulfo, *Pedro Páramo* (1955); Kadare, *Chronicle in Stone* (1971)

Selected works by the same author: *The Emigrant* (1882); *The Gypsy Girl* (1884)

28 | The Gate (1910) by Natsume Sōseki.

Japanese

Translated by William F Sibley (New York Review Books)

A lowly government clerk, Sosuke doesn't often stir from the modest home he shares with his wife, Oyone, on the suburban fringes of Tokyo. So even a visit to the dentist – a front tooth has begun to wobble, another sign of flying time – counts as an event. In the waiting room, he picks up a magazine brashly entitled "Success". However, "'Success' and Sosuke were poles apart." Justly, readers and critics have heaped praise on Natsume Sōseki for the exquisite refinement of his novels of petty bourgeois Japanese life a century ago, in an era torn between a ritual past and a frantic future, and often peopled by diffident misfits. Along with this filigree sensitivity, however, comes a deadpan irony – even absurdity. It lends his harassed Everyman heroes a comic touch that only deepens their pathos. "People like us don't have the right to expect very much, do they?" Oyone reflects. Sōseki did not enjoy the years he spent in the London suburbs as a state-funded scholar of English literature. But any reader familiar with that milieu may recognise in his fiction elements of bittersweet, lower-middle-class sitcom amid the courtly graces of Japan.

The Gate – Sōseki's favourite among his works – is exceptionally rich in his wistful, melancholic hues. However, it also sparkles with a pin-sharp attentiveness to the changing world that so discomfits the loving but lonely couple at its heart. Sosuke wanders the thronged city centre streets of Tokyo, drinking in the "restless, superficial" energy of modern advertisements, streetcars, luxury shops. Public events happen at the corner of his vision: a politician is assassinated; Field-marshal Kitchener visits Japan from Britain, and he wonders whether he and this fêted warrior belong to "the same human race". His reality is Oyone, his spruce home and perpetual money-worries – above all, how to pay for the college education of his feckless playboy brother, Koroku. Precious few great novels endow with poetry, even heroism, the heavy weather of making do, and getting by, in the bewildering cities of modernity. *The Gate* does. Sosuke's emerging friendship with their bluff, jovial landlord Sakai – his pleasure-loving antithesis – promises a solution to the Koroku problem. Yet deeper, hidden troubles fuel his "nameless dread of things to come".

Step by step, with masterly discretion and control, Sōseki reveals the emotional turmoil veiled by this placid and polite surface. Born to privilege, once a student in Kyoto, Sosuke has wrecked his prospects through his rash liaison with Oyone, formerly married to a friend. Scandal and disgrace more than innate timidity have made him "an outsider at a banquet". The "storm wind" of their transgressive love has blown them into shared solitude as a protective unit, "part of a single organism", condemned to a "lonely peace". Three times, Oyone has fallen pregnant only to lose the baby to miscarriage or stillbirth. Sōseki's account of Oyone's anguish, sharpened by her belief that marriage to Sosuke branded her "a criminal guilty of the most horrendous acts", has, for all its delicacy, a lacerating edge. Sosuke wrestles with their destiny. "For her part, Oyone simply wept." Obscure, childless, patronised, the couple cling to each other, "mere wraiths that barely cast a shadow on the world".

In its final chapters, *The Gate* takes a wonderfully unexpected turn. Indifferent to religion until now, Sosuke seeks to settle his spirit through a ten day retreat at a Zen Buddhist temple. A mediocre writer might make this refuge the venue for some life-changing discovery, a starburst epiphany or "satori". For all his efforts at meditation, however, Sosuke can never quite cross the threshold of enlightenment. Again, his frustration has its wryly comic side. He remains "among those unfortunate souls fated to stand in the gate's shadow, frozen in his tracks". Maybe his "gate" lies closer to home, in ordinary married love with its daily duties and rewards? On a rare visit to the bath house with his landlord, Sosuke hears from Sakai about the bush warbler he has heard trying for the first time to sing as the cold months end: "It really made a mess of things." As do we all. Still, winter has fled and – in a novel that marks the passage of the seasons with unerring grace – spring has returned at last. As a student, before his fall, Sosuke had paid a visit to the "Pavilion of Compassion" in Kyoto. In Sōseki's creed, this is the holiest shrine of all.

Translation: Sentence by flawless sentence, William F Sibley (2012) proves equal to Sōseki's subtlety, tenderness – and humour.

See also: Machado, *Epitaph of a Small Winner* (1880); Svevo, *Zeno's Conscience* (1923); Kafka, *The Trial* (1925); Tanizaki, *The Makioka Sisters* (1946-48)

Selected works by the same author: *I Am a Cat* (1905); *Botchan* (1906); *Sanshirō* (1908); *Kokoro* (1914)

29 | The Notebooks of Malte Laurids Brigge (1910) by Rainer Maria Rilke.

German (Austria-Hungary/France/Switzerland)

Translated by Michel Hulse (Penguin Classics)

As he remembers his father's death, the young man who narrates Rilke's only novel insists that our imagination can never hope to equal a reality that bursts beyond all description with "so many unique details". We think or imagine only in broad, crude strokes, whereas "realities are slow and indescribably detailed". Malte Laurids Brigge is the book's 28-year-old Danish drifter and dreamer. He shares many of the author's youthful travails. Earlier, Malte has sat (as usual), lost in contemplation, in his chilly fifth-floor room in the Paris of the 1900s. Here he lives as a penniless nomad. He frets that we have not only "remained on the surface of life" but smothered it with "unbelievably boring material", so that existence resembles "drawing-room furniture in the summer holidays".

Because it occupies such a significant place in the development of 20th-century European literature, this feverish, tormented – but sometimes droll and satirical – monologue by the Prague-born poet has often been as heavily cloaked in critical theory as that forsaken furniture. True, you can hardly plot a route through the history of Expressionism, Modernism or even Existentialism without passing by Rilke. In Paris, the young poet and critic became the friend, student and champion of painters and sculptors – from Cézanne to Rodin – as the new century dawned. With it came revolutionary ways of transforming that elusive reality into enduring art.

The Notebooks, however, track the lonely, sensitive Malte's efforts not so much to elaborate high ideals as to perceive the world around him, and within him, in all its majesty and misery. His quest for authenticity built a prototype that regiments of young, artistic rebels would borrow and adapt. An old world is dying – the world, in Malte's memory, of the hidebound and stultifying Danish family he has fled. The new one, meanwhile, struggles in anguish towards birth, still concealed behind the hypocritical shams and masks of the past. "We should like to remove our make-up and whatever is false and be real," Malte writes. But our former disguises stick to us, so that "we go about, a laughing-stock and a demi-being, with neither a real existence nor a part to play-act".

Written with all the intense, rhapsodic and mystical beauty of Rilke's verse, *The Notebooks* also contain long passages of remembrance in which Malte evokes his upbringing in Denmark. With its unhappy, stifled womenfolk and self-destructive patriarchs, the family house at Ulsgaard veers close to the secret-haunted decor of an Ibsen play. So do the book's almost-comic interludes at dinners and parties. Rilke revered Ibsen, whom Malte cites as a "timelessly tragic writer". Like Rilke, the playwright had sought to make visible "what you had seen inside". Malte's Ibsen-esque sympathy with the sufferings of women, either starved of love or else loved into slavery, threads through his narrative. As a little boy, we hear, his mother even dressed him as a girl: "Maman's little Sophie".

Lines of gender blur as Malte re-enacts the doomed passions of women who never found men worthy of their love, from the forlorn maidens in medieval tapestries to the poet Sappho herself, that prophet "entirely of the future" who measured "a new yardstick for love and the grief of the heart". "Now that so much is changing," asks Malte, should not men change as well? In a visionary passage, he urges men to start to learn "the labour of love that has always been done for us".

The Notebooks have their period peculiarities: for example, Malte's excursions into the courtly, heraldic tales of the 15th-century, inspired by his childhood reading and close to the medieval fantasias of Marcel Proust's narrator. Even here, we glimpse the mortal, sometimes, morbid combat between a dying era and its successor. Through this lurid period of interregnum dance "the demons of the twilight".

Mostly, however, the contemporary streetlife of Paris presses in on Malte, with its paupers, invalids and wastrels. Its ghastly, vivid actuality oppresses yet exhilarates him. Among the paintings of the time, think Munch rather than Monet. Malte breathes "the existence of the terrible in every particle of the air". Yet this hallucinatory journey of a soul passes through patches of sheer ecstasy. When he sees a half-demolished apartment building – a common sight in great cities, now as then – Malte with his painterly eye traces the outlines of life on the exposed walls, the leftover signs of "the midday meals and the illnesses and the breath exhaled and the smoke of years". Nothing could be more sensuous and concrete than this astonishing passage. Yet the philosopher Martin Heidegger later quoted it as a sort of scripture of modern phenomenology. All the experience stained on those tatty walls – "the acrid tang of urine and the smell of burning soot and the steamy greyness of potatoes and the slick, heavy stink of old lard" – becomes part of Malte's being: "it is at home in me". Outward and inward life, the world and the mind, converge in the rapture of consciousness, and the permanence of art.

Translation: The writer-philosopher William H Gass devoted a book to the challenges of translating Rilke. Michael Hulse's edition (2009) reveals a remarkable translator of German modernism on peak form.

See also: Jespersen, *Niels Lyhne* (1880); Hamsun, *Hunger* (1890); Proust, *In Search of Lost Time* (1913-1927); Bernhard, *Correction* (1975)

Selected works by the same author: *Sonnets to Orpheus* (1922); *Duino Elegies* (1923); *Letters to a Young Poet* (1929)

30 | In Search of Lost Time (1913-1927) by Marcel Proust.

French

Translated by CK Scott Moncrieff and Terence Kilmartin, revised by DJ Enright (Vintage)

In *The Guermantes Way*, the third of the seven volumes that compose *In Search of Lost Time*, the narrator returns to see the great actress Berma perform again. As before, her lofty reputation almost blinds him to the reality on stage, so that "I admired too keenly not to be disappointed by the object of my admiration". How many readers of Proust have felt the dazzle of this work's renown so acutely that it turns into their Berma, a revered idol dutifully applauded thanks to "preconceived ideas" rather than spontaneous enjoyment? It need not be. Read at leisure, without prejudice, and with the sort of openness to the rapture of discovery that the narrator brings to his encounters with people and works of art, these seven books that build into one book can become a never-ending source of joy.

Proust is not just much funnier than his reputation as fiction's champion aesthete and extreme subjectivist allows. He is braver, broader, less snobbish, more political, more topical. Too few routine critical homages salute, for instance, the extraordinary, almost documentary portrait of blacked-out Paris in the First World War in the final volume, *Time Regained*. How typical of Proust, as well, that in this section the narrator should denounce the "falsity of so-called realistic art" just after he has given luminous proof that he commands this, among so many other, modes of expression.

Yes, the great arc of his novel investigates the operation of memory and time through the filter of a single consciousness. Memory is that "mountain landscape rich in minerals" which the ailing narrator hopes to mine before he dies, and so refine into the novel that we're reading. Proust is never obscure; but he is always exact. He never scorns the trivia of everyday social life but he does re-frame and re-imagine them. Always up-to-date on trends such as movies, motoring and aviation, he scorns critics who want the novel to be "a sort of cinematographic progression". For all that, Proust's torrentially eloquent mapping of the mind also delivers a witty and precise cartography not only of French high society a century ago, but of its unrespectable shadow-side of servants, courtesans, actors, tailors, gay men and women, and so on. Not quite all human life is here. All human feeling is. If Proust's account of the private mysteries of "involuntary memory" waymark the narrator's development, so too does the public passion unleashed by the Dreyfus Affair that "divided France from top to bottom" and sets his liberals and reactionaries at loggerheads.

Between the wide horizon of French social and cultural life, and the sumptuous inner chamber of memory-driven consciousness, *In Search of Lost Time* also dwells in an inter-subjective space of love and desire. Most of its movement takes place here. That love may assume the form of the narrator's childhood longing for his absent mother in his bedroom at Combray, with the to-and-fro of power in their relationship (a master motif of the novel) that leads him from pure desolation into a "puberty of sorrow, a manumission of tears". It may crystallise into the pursuit through memory of a lost past, which threads through all seven volumes. This quest finds its focus in visionary moments of absolute recall, prompted by triggers such as the famous madeleine dunked in a tisane when "Combray sprang into being, town and gardens alike, from my cup of tea".

Attachments to mother and cherished grandmother aside, the narrator learns love by observing the urbane, marginal, Jewish Charles Swann – first in Proust's pantheon of alluring outsiders – in his affair and marriage with Odette de Crécy. In later volumes, the narrator will replicate, and deepen, Swann's agonies and ecstasies in his own, equally tangled liaison with the elusive Albertine. That affair and its jealousies will prompt passages that contain the most forensically brilliant explorations of the hidden byways of desire ever committed to print. The narrator explains how "We fall in love for a smile, a look, a shoulder" but then, "in the long hours of hope or sorrow, we fabricate a person, we compose a character". Love, carnal and spiritual alike, also drives the courageous account of the homosexual condition within a censorious and persecuting society that binds the novel's central volumes. From the absurd, heroic Baron de Charlus, both a comic buffoon and a sort of gay martyr, to the same-sex attachments of Albertine herself with her "little band" of girls at the seaside resort of Balbec, Proust gives multiple voices and faces – as no novelist had before – to this "race upon which a curse is laid and must live in falsehood and perjury… their honour precarious, their liberty provisional". Proust likens Oscar Wilde to Captain Dreyfus. They are twin poles of attraction in a novel that honours the otherness of the scorned and the slighted in conventional society, even as – with incomparable finesse – it shows that time and memory make us strangers to ourselves.

The narrator's growth coalesces in his slow-blooming love of art; above all, the kind of art that furnishes us with "the sole means to discover lost time". From the connoisseurship of Charles Swann to the snobbish aestheticism of the Verdurins' salon; from the fiction and essays of Bergotte to the music of Vinteuil, the acting of Berma and the paintings of Elstir (modelled in part on Whistler and Monet): engagements with artists and their critics frame almost every major episode. The narrator's endlessly baffled yearning to distil memory and insight into the material form of a novel tethers the entire span of the seven volumes. Through his admiration for creators such as the composer Vinteuil, whose violin sonata with its tantalising "little phrase" becomes a mysterious theme-tune for the book, the narrator comes to understand each authentic artist as "the native of an unknown country" – a place revealed in their works alone. Proust builds, and charts, just such a domain. Although the "mighty dimension of time" deepens his perspective beyond the surface flatness of "realistic" fiction, the narrator insists that "real life, life at last laid bare and illuminated… is literature". The art of time, the time of art, can redeem experience from the erosion of the years. The toll of those years lays both a comic, and a tragic, burden on the old friends the narrator meets as his story concludes at the aristocratic Guermantes' party in Paris. "Everybody in the room appeared to have put on a disguise" of grey hair or wrinkled skin. Time has done its worst. Only art can arrest its corrosive flow. "Through art alone are we able to emerge from ourselves, to know what another person sees of a universe which is not the same as our own."

No one thinks of Proust, the hyper-sensitive dandy who scrutinises every masquerade and manoeuvre of boudoir, salon or studio, as a Utopian novelist. Yet the narrator's imagined paradise of an art within and beyond time glows with all the magic of a liberated state. Proust need not paralyse or disappoint us, as the diva Berma does her over-eager fan. Instead, we may come to share the writer Bergotte's dying rapture over "a little patch of yellow wall" in Vermeer's cityscape of Delft. The "obligations" of genuine, transformative art – such as this painting – have "no sanction in our present life". Rather, they "seem to belong to a different world, a world based on kindness, scrupulousness, self-sacrifice", which, perhaps, "we leave in order to be born". Reading Proust hints at what art and thought might be like on that alien planet of grace and truth.

Translation: Urbane, companionable, CK Scott Moncrieff's original translations from the 1920s form the still-secure foundations on which the revisions by Terence Kilmartin (1981) and DJ Enright (1992) have built.

See also: Cao, *Dream of the Red Chamber* (1792); Colette, *Chéri/ The Last of Chéri* (1920–1926); Musil, *The Man Without Qualities* (1930–1943); Pamuk, *The Black Book* (1990)

Selected works by the same author: *Pleasures and Days* (1896); *Jean Santeuil* (1952); *Against Sainte-Beuve* (1954)

31 | Reeds in the Wind (1913) by Grazia Deledda.

Italian

Translated by Martha King (Italica Press)

For the country folk of eastern Sardinia, early in the 20th-century,

elves, monsters, sprites and other supernatural beings throng the rivers, woods and mountains just as they always have. At the river's edge, the "panas" – ghosts of women who died in childbirth – beat the clothes of unseen children with "a dead man's shin bone". Efix, the servant burdened with guilty secrets, whose journey towards redemption drives *Reeds in the Wind*, hears them at the novel's start and again as his own death nears, when he senses "the light flutter of innocent souls transformed into leaves, into flowers". In this insular peasant society, even those who survive into adulthood will endure malaria, hunger, flood, drought and semi-feudal servitude. Emigration, to the "Continent" of mainland Italy or across the oceans, may attract. But the little town near Efix's rented patch of poor land is not so remote that it fails to pay attention to reports from disenchanted returnees. They warn that, although America may look like "a lamb ready for shearing", "Go near it and it eats you like a dog."

Born in 1871 into this ancient patriarchy, where the Middle Ages felt as close as the wandering ghosts of the "Barons" who once held court in now-ruined castles, Grazia Deledda defied her lack of formal education to become both a prolific and a sophisticated witness to its way of life. She never patronises this "Third World" Europe that bred her, but never prettifies it. Her novels (with *Reeds in the Wind* her personal favourite) do much more than record with a painter's eye and a dramatist's ear the scenery, customs, myths and howling injustices of a region where beauty frames backwardness, women have few rights but endless duties, and the "melancholy" poor live "waiting for leftovers from the tables of the rich". Working within the framework of Italian "verismo", she greatly enriched the range of this school's anti-romantic naturalism. She incorporates into her prose not only a lyrical, even mystical, sensitivity to the spirit-crowded landscapes of her birthplace, but a forensic scrutiny of the social and mental underpinnings of this culture. We meet Efix as he weaves a mat, "seven reeds across a willow twig", from the beds around his hut. Symbolically, those flexible grasses will return when he says that "We are reeds, and fate is the wind." Donna Ester, one of three noble but impoverished Pintor sisters whom Efix serves a tenant farmer and faithful retainer, asks, "But why this fate?" Deledda's people often forge their own chains of deference, loyalty and humility. She lays that process of self-abasement painfully, grippingly, bare. Meanwhile, she measures the barriers that, like the hulking mountains, block off every possible escape.

Lia, the sister of Efix's "padrones" Ester, Ruth and Noemi, did flee the long-dead Barons' domains. With the connivance of Efix, she ran away to the mainland and married there. During her flight Efix – by accident, or as planned revenge? – killed the Pintor sisters' father, Don Zame. That is the sin he feels bound to expiate through a lifetime of devotion. Deledda shrewdly balances the social weight of gender and of class. Although a "worm" of a tenant-servant, Efix also controls the family. When Lia's feckless son Giacinto visits them, he brings a breeze of freedom that stirs up hidden shames and desires. The Pintors' "shadow of dishonour" falls again. Over her fast-flowing swerves of plot – most involving the sisters' indebtedness to the witch-like money-lender, Kallina – Deledda dramatises the grip of hierarchy and superstition in a place where "the past still ruled". Bible stories and local folklore, even Kallina's resemblance to a figure out of Greek myth, "a Nemesis with her club", soak the present with fable.

Yet the boldest women here have tasted liberty. Lia's scandalous flight, and Giacinto's city-bred frivolity, shock and tempt the sisters. The youngest, Noemi falls for golden boy Giacinto but is courted by their kinsman Don Predu, whose wealth may rescue them from disgrace. Church festivals, which double as carriers of pagan lore, give these poverty- and fever-stricken people brief respite. But "the fiesta soon passes". In ritual processions, Deledda notices pale young women who "hid their passion like embers under ashes". Here, "All eyes are full of life and death." Laden with remorse, Efix pursues his "terrible voyage towards divine punishment" by joining beggars on the road. Deledda never sentimentalises: among the tramps, he finds tricksters and bullies, "all the emotions of more fortunate men". Efix will return to die with the Pintors, while Noemi reluctantly agrees to wed Predu. Escape routes close. The past reaffirms its mastery. In the graveyard, white bones have broken through the earth and "lay like margaritas on the green weeds". Only Efix himself moves, from life to death, on his "journey towards eternity".

Translation: Martha King (1998) captures Deledda's human and natural landscape in all its bold colours: radiant and serene in one scene, rugged and violent the next.

See also: Papadiamantis, *The Murderess* (1903); Tagore, *Home and the World* (1916); Pavese, *The Moon and the Bonfires* (1950); Rulfo, *Pedro Páramo* (1955)

Selected works by the same author: *Elias Portolu* (1900); *After the Divorce* (1902); *The Mother* (1920); *Cosima* (1937)

32 | PETERSBURG (1916; revised 1922) by Andrei Bely (Boris Nikolaevich Bugaev).

Russian

Translated by John Elsworth (Pushkin Press)

Huddled on their shores and islands, a "mongrel breed" between sea and sky, the citizens of Andrei Bely's Saint Petersburg seem "not quite people, not quite shadows". As a tale of political unrest and conspiracy by a Symbolist poet of genius, Bely's dazzling, hurtling novel of Russia's imperial capital during the first revolution of 1905 is a gloriously hybrid creature in itself. Bely crafts a ticking-bomb thriller in which a high official's son, Nikolai Apollonovich Ableukhov, has agreed to murder his own father on behalf of an anarchist cell. Then he repents and seeks to disable the primed device. At the same time Nikolai tangles, almost in Tolstoyan style, with a married woman and her outraged husband. Meanwhile, the conspirators plot, feud and self-destruct at a feverish moment in Russian and European history when, as a harlequin sings at a masked ball, "behaviour terroristic is the time's characteristic".

Ringed by its smoking, strike-prone factories, *Petersburg* itself breathes and stretches through these frantic October days. This city-monster devours its inhabitants between the "greenish blue" waters of the Neva and its lurid crimson dusks and dawns. Its populace becomes a single, multi-stranded being, a "crawling, howling myriapod" that lives and dies on this narrow "point" in space and time. Humanity is dwarfed and yet cradled by "the entire spherical surface of the planet" and the infinities of space: "We feel the seething of Saturn's masses in the spine". With extraordinary fluidity, Bely knits into the pulsing action a series of philosophical, even mystical, reflections on order and chaos, east and west, and the limits of human intellect as the planned city's "network of parallel prospects expanded into the abysses of the universe". In a homage to Alexander Pushkin, the statue of the Bronze Horseman – Peter the Great – comes to life to haunt the dreams of these "shadows" in the city he decreed.

A great urban panorama bearing wagonloads of speculation, *Petersburg* can sound in summary like a heavyweight edifice to match the grandiose palaces among which its characters scurry. In fact, Bely whips the plot along with caustic wit, lightning-bolts of poetic insight and a cumulative mood of menace and suspense. Fractured, comic, rhythmic and imbued with sardonic humour, his street-level dialogue – especially among the shabby revolutionaries in pubs and garrets – has an elliptical informality far distant from the salon elegance of the Ableukhovs' circle. Even in high society, however, Bely writes with a brilliance and brevity that aligns him with the Symbolists and modernists of his generation. Compare the masked ball at the Tsukatovs, a "labyrinth of mirrors" in which identity dissolves into a maze of feints and disguises, with the set-piece parties of *War and Peace.* You feel the depth of change in Russia, and in prose.

A "poet's novel" in the best sense, *Petersburg* condenses its ideas into chains and clusters of images and motifs: the geometry and mathematics, for example, that make Senator Ableukhov a rational embodiment of "proportionality and symmetry", while the isolated Nikolai becomes "a human numeral one… an emaciated little stick, running his course through time". Yet their relationship, as the son grasps what it will mean to murder his own father, acquires enormous poignancy – on top of the inbuilt tension of the bomb ticking away in a sardine-tin. Nikolai feels a surge of love "for the old despot who was condemned to be blown to bits".

After 1917, Bely – the pseudonym of Boris Bugaev – reached a wary accommodation with the Bolshevik regime. Nonetheless, he depicts his revolutionaries, like his rulers, as the playthings or instruments of time, space and chance. The indifferent universe mocks their "world of shadows" while even the individual personality can never achieve solidity and permanence. Nikolai remembers that his father would hold his infant child up to mirror and say: "Just look, son: there are strangers there".

Bely wrote as the First World War raged. He looked back to the time when Russia's defeat by Japan had spread a cultural crisis of confidence. His conspirators often talk of the rising East and the declining West; of the twilight of the "period of humanism". They pretend that "a period of healthy barbarism was at hand". Yet these windy geopolitical abstractions convince no more than the complacent geometry of Senator Ableukhov's doomed order. The planets swing in their orbits as the bomb-clock ticks. Love and fear, error and happenstance, propel the tiny human "grains of caviar" that subsist on the "open sandwich" of the teeming city.

The image, typically with Bely, startles and disconcerts. If we must live as trivial fragments of nothingness, far better to be caviar than sand. Vladimir Nabokov, that great gourmet of literature, placed *Petersburg* near Joyce's *Ulysses* – and above Proust – in the first rank of his pantheon of 20th-century fiction. After the deluge, before the explosion, it makes every crimson moment glow.

Translation: After long neglect, Robert Maguire and John Malmstad's pioneering 1978 translation brought Bely's masterwork to English life; John Elsworth's complete version (2009), more readily available, follows dashingly in their wake.

See also: Gogol, *Dead Souls* (1842); Döblin, *Berlin Alexanderplatz* (1929); Cela, *The Hive* (1951); Pamuk, *The Black Book* (1990)

Selected works by the same author: *The Silver Dove* (1910); *Kotik Letaev* (1922)

33 | HOME AND THE WORLD (1916) by Rabindranath Tagore.

Bengali

Translated by Sreejata Guha (Penguin Classics India)

A conservative young wife in the rural Bengal of the 1900s, Bimala falls for a flashy bully of a politician. This shameless, seductive "ocean of maleness" embodies everything her husband – a high-minded aristocrat – detests. In her turmoil, she asks, "Why does God make us such mixed beings?" In *Home and the World*, Rabindranath Tagore splits his story of division and contention – in the heart, the household, the community – between three such "mixed beings". The Bengali poet, polymath, educator and cultural leader has cast such a vast shadow over South Asia – his lyrics are sung in the national anthems of both India and Bangladesh – that the temptation arises to reduce his work merely to its values or ideas. But Tagore was a questing artist-thinker, above all. In 1913, he had become Asia's first Nobel laureate for his poetry. His novels stage conflicts within and between their protagonists so intractable that the fiction can scarcely contain them.

Three voices share the narration of *Home and the World.* Bimala herself is a born-again traditionalist who, despite her modern education, seeks to recreate old-fashioned modesty and chastity as a sort of "poetic craft". A landowner of ancient lineage, her fastidious husband Nikhilesh fears that, for all his liberal ideals and do-gooding paternalism, the "temple" of his soul "lies vacant". Sandip, his thrusting rival, finds him "almost lifeless". The disruptive element, Sandip is a rabble-rousing, "post-truth" nationalist agitator against the British Raj. He tramples on integrity, believes in "Victory for illusion!", but still sucks Bimala into his vortex of passion and power.

In turn, these narrators report and reflect, with the same incident seen from three angles. Readers who come to this novel seeking the timeless wisdom of some cartoon sage may be shocked – and thrilled – by its restless modernity. Sexual liberation, feminist awakening, anti-colonial militancy, religious doubt, underclass revolt: the "world" that Bimala's dream of domestic grace tries to keep at a distance not only hammers at the gates of "home", it breaks through into its "inner chambers", and the most intimate recesses of the self. Tagore wrote as the First World War shook Europe and parts of Asia; as demands for gender and racial equality grew; as avant-garde art and cutting-edge science eroded secular and spiritual authority. This big world rushes into the idyllic landscape that brings joy to Nikhilesh (and Tagore). Framed by this "destructive dance of reality", reversals and paradoxes shake each human corner of the novel's romantic – and political, and philosophical – triangle.

Nikhilesh yearns to release his wife from the status of "a mere doll, confined to a small space" (her progress matches that of Ibsen's heroines). But how can a man decree a woman's freedom? Besides, he has never let go of his attraction to his widowed sister-in-law, Mejorani. Bimala's project to re-establish traditional order and beauty is itself a modern exercise in retro-fitted nostalgia. She discards it when Sandip's super-modern pragmatism enlists her as a "Queen Bee" icon of national renewal – a goddess-like pin-up for the anti-Raj movement. Even Sandip himself, drawn as a Nietzschean demagogue with a bloated ego who believes that "I want" is "the core chant of creation", has his patches of self-doubt, even self-hatred. They tussle with themselves as with their lovers and rivals.

Meanwhile, colonial-era commerce and globalised manufacturing drive the "swadeshi" movement to buy Indian goods and boycott foreign imports. Through the impoverished peddler Panchu, we understand that this great campaign can harm the poorest of the poor – especially when local zamindars (landowners) compel them to join. Ever the tortured liberal, Nikhilesh insists that "My India doesn't belong to gentlemen alone." For Sandip, the "swadeshi" unrest is a wave that may carry him to power, with lies, fraud and violence – a "layer of pure filth" – the silt that underlies every "noble deed". For him, might is right. Liberated India must emulate the deceit and coercion practised by all empires: "Those who rule need not fear lies." When he suborns his lover Bimala into a theft from Nikhilesh's treasury and the social protests take a menacing sectarian turn, pitting Hindu against Muslim tenant farmers, all the conditions for a tragic denouement fall into place.

Tagore the poet threads his story with images of fire that warms but also burns. Near its close, Nikhilesh reflects that "We are not flames, we are embers, dying ones". These domestic feuds and passions appear as frail imitations of the epic desires that convulse gods and heroes in Hindu mythology. Tagore depicts Sandip's idolatrous cult of the nation-state, shorn of what the populist "seller of spells" calls "the toxin of religiosity", as absurd and blasphemous. His human embers dance and glow between one dimension and another, unable to thrive in any. Tagore's novel, too, hovers among different planes. Colloquial dialogues, and the trio's self-revealing soliloquies, bind all its warring elements: erotic fervour, mythic allusion, political debate and poetic rapture. Illusions rise and swirl like the monsoon waters of a Bengal July. "Truth" forever slips from human grasp. Neither "home" nor "world" alone can put a stop to the endless "quest for one's identity".

Translation: Sreejata Guha (2005) has a vernacular vibrancy, a music of clashing voices, but she also restores key passages omitted in the 1919 translation by Tagore's nephew, Surendranath.

See also: Flaubert, *Madame Bovary* (1857); Turgenev, *Fathers and Sons* (1862); Lampedusa, *The Leopard* (1958); Husain, *Basti* (1979)

Selected works by the same author: *Gitanjali: Song Offerings* (1910); *Gora* (1910); *The Post Office* (1912); *Farewell My Friend* (1929)

34 | Kristin Lavransdatter (The Wreath; The Wife; The Cross) (1920-1922) by Sigrid Undset.

Norwegian

Translated by Tiina Nunnally (Penguin Classics)

Kneeling in the church at Trondheim, by now respectably married and a mother, Kristin Lavransdatter remembers the time when she felt "her passion temper her will until it was sharp and hard like a knife, ready to cut through all bonds – those of Christianity, kinship and honour". Kristin's illicit passion for the impulsive libertine Erlend Nikulausson has already shaken her loving family on their estate in Gudbrandsdal, and wrecked her betrothal to the stalwart neighbour Simon Darre. It will never quieten, or fade, through three decades of stormy marriage, through her raising of seven sons and her tireless administration of farms and families, through Erlend's madcap meddling in political conspiracy, and through Kristin's own journey towards a more settled, secure faith.

Desire, with its unfathomable origins, its helter-skelter progress and its catastrophic outcomes, governs almost every step in this three volume family saga set among the Norwegian farming gentry of the early 14th-century. Simon never stops loving the woman who spurned him; his unquenchable yearning marks the third point of a grand amorous triangle. He reflects that "whatever is inscribed" on a young heart "is carved deeper than all the runes that are later etched". Vast in scope but tightly-knit, never loose or shapeless, Sigrid Undset's modern-minded period epic measures the lifelong repercussions of early love, and hate. Its force and finesse may bring to mind the near-contemporary work of Proust. While she prepares to end her life as a lay sister in a convent, Kristin decides that "Life on this earth was irredeemably tainted by strife". Wherever "physical love" flings people together, "sorrows of the heart and broken expectations were bound to occur as surely as the frost appears in the autumn". Amid these lonely, glorious valleys and slopes, where the relatively new Christian creed does battle with the stubbornly enduring cult of pagan gods, sexual love proves the fiercest divinity of all.

To spend years on a medieval blockbuster in the age of Proust or Joyce sounds like an act of reactionary defiance to match any of the sacrificial vocations Kristin admires among the Trondheim nuns. In fact, Undset's irresistible, immersive trilogy stages a revolution of its own. As a young author in the Norway of the 1900s, she had begun with a conventionally "shocking" modern novel of adultery. That theme, with children born out of wedlock who both break the peace between houses and help to heal blood-stained rifts, does resonate through *Kristin Lavransdatter*. Undset's growing fascination with the histories and sagas of the traditional Norse world never overrode the insight, and the frankness, of her 20th-century voice. She wears her enormous learning about the age and its customs, from food and clothes to feuds and sex, with astonishing ease and grace.

Her trilogy lets us experience the struggle – psychological as much as social – between the ecstasy, and guilt, of Christian faith and the domain of the "trolls and goblins and elves" who still live "under every rock". Blood feuds and honour killings co-exist, uneasily, with written laws and moral consciences. Nothing about *Kristin Lavransdatter* feels anachronistic. Nothing feels archaic either – even when Kristin herself backslides from the priests' creed into pagan ritual during a terrifying "troll night". Undset pays the distant past the rare compliment of assuming that its people had inner lives as complex as our own. In her vast cast, every woman, down to the poorest serving girl, has a depth and weight to match every man's. Each landscape, each season, blazes on the page. This alien world feels completely real; completely ours. Unlike her Victorian forebears, Undset sinks into the farmsteads and townships, pastures and mountains, of the medieval north not as an escape but an emancipation.

Proud, sensual, honourable, courageous, hard-working (not a single page goes by without some tough physical labour), Kristin flourishes in this 14th-century novel more mightily than she could have done in some story of the recent past. With few exceptions – George Eliot and Germaine de Staël among them – the women novelists of the 19th-century had no choice but to define their heroines as creatures made and broken by love. Yet the passion that drives Kristin, tugs her away from her clan and thrusts her into a relationship that spreads scandal across three decades, never imprisons or devours her. Supremely self-aware, with a "fever-like inner vision", she repeatedly condemns but then absolves herself. The "sin" of her disobedient surrender to Erlend, which others view as a curse on her land and her kin, never prevents her from thriving as a wife, a matriarch, a manager; a woman of substance, clout and consequence. Undset dramatises not only the lurching carousel of her marriage to Erlend but her love for her seven boys, each finely characterised, with a supremely sensitive inwardness. No early 20th-century heroine – scarcely any of the 19th – matches Kristin's fulfilled abundance. As she reflects at her journey's end, after one more extraordinary deed while the Black Death scourges Norway, "there was not a single day that she would have given back to God without lament or a single sorrow she would have relinquished without regret". The reader will echo that gratitude.

Translation: In 2000, Tiina Nunnally's magnificent version revitalised Undset's epic in English: each page glows and sparkles like the landscapes she so wonderfully evokes.

See also: Staël, *Corinne* (1807); Tolstoy, *War and Peace* (1869); Proust, *In Search of Lost Time* (1913-1927); Laxness, *Independent People* (1934-35)

Selected works by the same author: *Gunnar's Daughter* (1909); *Jenny* (1911); *The Master of Hestviken* (1927)

35 | Chéri/The Last of Chéri (1920;1926) by Colette (Sidonie-Gabrielle Colette).

French

Translated by Roger Senhouse (Vintage)

Of all the liberated heroines who begin to fill the pages of fiction in the early 20th-century, few can match the mingled aura of seduction and subversion that lingers, like one of her fragrances, around Colette's Léa de Lonval. A "richly kept courtesan", now aged forty-nine, she has for five years loved the "graceful demon" Chéri. He is really Fred Peloux, the pampered son of another high-maintenance mistress, whom Léa has known since his infancy and taken as a lover when he was nineteen. In other hands (in male hands?), the story of this affair between one ageing Parisian demi-mondaine and the child of another, amid a milieu of expensively disguised paid-for sex where love means "money, infidelity, betrayals, and cowardly resignation", would sink fast into squalor, horror and tragedy.

That is not Léa's, or Colette's, way. True, the twin *Chéri* novels – one set, with flashbacks, just before the First World War, the other just after – do end in one lover's despair. But that agony belongs to Chéri himself, who (almost blasphemously, given the period) brackets his passion for a woman twenty-four years his senior with the Great War itself as joint sources of his incurable alienation: "Léa, the War… the two together have driven me outside the times I live in". As for Léa herself, 19th-century writers would have shunted her into the madhouse, the terminal ward, the cemetery. Here, she fights through into the post-war era as a brisk, brusque and "altogether virile" battle-hardened survivor. She tells the shocked Chéri at their final meeting that "I love my present. I'm not ashamed of what I had, and I'm not sad because I have it no longer." Can we believe her?

Distraught by her cheerful indifference, Chéri considers this sexless, "'merry friar' joviality" of "a healthy old woman" to be merely an act. Although no longer draped in "negligées like the gossamer clouds of dawn", Léa still tantalises, still mystifies, even under a thatch of "thick grey vigorous hair, cut short like his mother's". Her shape-shifting powers lift her fate far beyond the space of self-abasing victimhood so often measured out for older women drawn to younger men. Yes, Léa loves, she regrets, she mourns, she suffers searing loneliness after three decades devoted to the charms of "radiant youths and fragile adolescents". Still, she does so as the conscious agent and fashioner of her own destiny: a brazen heretic, not a pitiable freak. In the devastating scene that closes *Chéri*, she resists "the most terrible joy of her life" when her lover returns to her. She sends him back to his unloved, unloving wife, Edmée.

Colette's scandalous choice of theme, even her bracingly free-spirited approach to it, would count for little without the quicksilver subtlety of her art. She tempers the gorgeous sensuality of her prose with a muscular economy. Each item that depicts elegance and luxury in Parisian high society a century ago – from langoustines and strawberries to rose gardens, silk gowns and antique furniture – comes with a price tag discreetly attached. In the bickering intimacy between Léa, Chéri's mother Charlotte and Edmée's mother Marie-Laure, she counts the cost these women have paid for selling not just bodies but a slice of their souls to their plutocratic patrons. For all its sumptuous grace, her style hides a razor's edge. Much more than fancy décor, the spangled accessories of the top-drawer courtesan also serve as richly freighted symbols. We first glimpse Chéri trying on Léa's pearl necklace: a sign of the implicit femininity that his role brings. Those pearls will recur at crucial junctures in the plot, tokens of the chain of beauty and desire that binds the couple.

In *The Last of Chéri*, the Great War has fallen like an axe between one state of mind – one state of society – and another. In swift, bold strokes, Colette shows that privileged women have left the boudoir – Edmée becomes a dynamic hospital administrator – but that pre-war discontents and disparities still sabotage marriages and affairs.

Spendthrift Americans guzzle champagne in night-clubs, Charlotte goes in for "company promotion" and Edmée revels in her prestige as a "non-commissioned angel". The settled love of equals eludes them all. Movingly, Chéri (or Fred) replaces Léa as the forsaken slave of passion. He flees his frozen marriage to take refuge in the poky apartment of an opium-addicted former prostitute. Colette touches on his wartime ordeals, and hints at the trauma of the returned warrior plagued by "nostalgia, listlessness, disillusion, neurasthenia". When Léa glibly diagnoses his troubles, we feel for him, not her; the balance of our sympathy shifts. As the forlorn Chéri creates a shrine to lost love from photographs of the radiant young Léa, the past engulfs the present in a Proust-like reverie. Only in images, in imagination, can he bridge the chasm between them. For Colette, who understands so much and judges so little, an age-defying desire unites her "adolescents and time-worn courtesans, who are akin in their credulity and passion for romance".

Translation: Roger Senhouse's English voicing of Colette (1951) serves not only her lyricism and finesse, but her emotional rigour and insight.

See also, La Fayette, *The Princesse de Clèves* (1678); Proust, *In Search of Lost Time* (1913-1927); Undset, *Kristin Lavransdatter* (1920-1922); Duras, *The Lover* (1984)

Selected works by the same author: *Claudine at School* (1900); *The Vagabond* (1910); *Ripening Seed* (1923); *La Chatte* (1933)

36 | Zeno's Conscience (1923) by Italo Svevo (Aron Ettore Schmitz).

Italian

Translated by William Weaver (Penguin Modern Classics)

In his wild youth, Saint Augustine prayed for the Lord to make him pure – but not just yet. Defiantly secular, Italo Svevo's sensual, self-centred but kind-hearted and open-minded hero vows to give up smoking. But he forever delays his last cigarette. That final puff, he thinks, will gain its intense flavour from "the feeling of victory over oneself and the hope of an imminent future of health and strength". The Triestino businessman Zeno Cosini will – like his nicotine-addicted creator – never forsake his smokes. "Victory over oneself", and its unruly desires and drives, would mean no less than death.

Droll and farcical, lyrical and philosophical, Zeno's first-person account of his youth, marriage, affairs and business dealings revels in all the contradictions of the teller. Published in 1923, Svevo's third novel appeared after his former English teacher in Trieste – James Joyce – had encouraged this part-time author and manager of the family paint business to resume his literary vocation. Indifference had greeted his first two books. As the premise for his narrative, Svevo has Zeno consult a psychoanalyst: an early bow for the Freudian shrink in European fiction. The therapist recommends that he record his memoirs as part of the treatment. Zeno, however, seeks not so much to lay the past to rest as to recover, understand, even celebrate, its scandals and errors. Almost like Proust, he seeks to rescue and cherish memory as blessed "Days go by, suitable for framing", rather than confront and bury his mistakes. Besides, Zeno's misadventures in love and at work thread his recollections on a string of rueful comedy that binds the entire book.

Self-deceiving but self-revealing, Svevo's bourgeois Don Quixote manages to sabotage or complicate every dream that he chases. His marriage begins in confusion, as he loves one daughter of the merchant Malfenti – Ada – but weds another: Augusta. Typically, in this life of paradox, the couple prove perfectly suited to each other.

Still, as a man of his class and time, he embarks on an affair with the singer Carla – but mainly to feel the relief that comes when he returns home to his beloved spouse. "Where could there be any remorse in me, when, with so much joy and so much affection, I was speeding to my legitimate wife?" When he aims to transgress, Zeno ends up on the path of virtue. Conversely, his overt generosity in bailing out his indebted business partner – and brother-in-law – Guido has tragic, unforeseen consequences. "We were neither good nor bad," he decides; rather, "Goodness was the light that, in flashes and for moments, illuminated the dark human spirit".

Hypocrite, hypochondriac, middle-class and middle-of-the-road, Zeno becomes the prototype of the everyman hero – or anti-hero – who will stumble through the comic fiction of the 20th-century. His pioneering stream-of-consciousness can sometimes resemble a confessional stand-up comedy routine. Kindness and sensitivity, an absence of malice and fury, will redeem this flawed bungler for readers, if not for purists. Early critics of Svevo scorned his vulgar Triestine prose, and Zeno himself laments that his "horrid dialect" falls far short of Dante's noble Tuscan tongue. Democracy in fiction requires "low" speech as much as base emotions, even though Svevo also lends Zeno passages of radiant memory which glow with all "the solidity, the colour, the insolence of living things".

Protected by his status in the golden twilight of the Habsburg Empire (Trieste did not join Italy until 1920), Zeno can bounce between reversals and embarrassments under the benign star of comedy rather than tragedy. However, Svevo – the pen name of Ettore Schmitz, a comfortably secular Jew whose family had flourished in Trieste – told his story from across the gulf of hindsight carved by the First World War. Zeno's account closes with the outbreak of hostilities; in the countryside outside Trieste, Austrian troops create a "new and impassable frontier". It will slam the door on the era of easy-going tolerance that has shaped Zeno's outlook on his world. In the final paragraphs, this businessman who shares his creator's professional interest in technology even imagines – decades before atomic weapons – an "incomparable explosive" that will end all human life.

Behind the merrily unfolding scenes of farce and intrigue, Zeno hints at a pessimism worthy of Schopenhauer, a favourite author of Svevo's. "Life does resemble sickness a bit," but, unlike other diseases, "life is always fatal". Between the twin lures of sloth and frenzy, flight and fight, Zeno seeks a "golden mean" of health. Perhaps he merely yearns for it. For health – or cure, in the psychoanalyst's terms – would mean stepping off the carousel of desire and disillusion that gives his life, and this book, its enduring charm. There's still time for one more cigarette.

Translations: Beryl de Zoete first translated *The Confessions of Zeno* in 1930. William Weaver (2001) not only corrects the title but gives Zeno a new, enchanting lease of life.

See also: Cervantes, *Don Quixote* (1605-1615); Proust, *In Search of Lost Time* (1913-1927); Hašek *The Good Soldier Švejk* (1923); Musil, *The Man Without Qualities* (1930-1943)

Selected works by the same author: *A Life* (1892); *As a Man Grows Older* (1898)

37 | The Good Soldier Švejk (1923) by Jaroslav Hašek.

Czech

Translated by Cecil Parrott (Penguin Classics)

If the cruelty and futility of war runs like a scarlet thread through the

history of fiction then so does its sheer idiocy. Before *The Good Soldier Švejk*, however, few authors had grasped that it takes an "obvious imbecile" – or, at least, a shrewd survivor who acts like one – to unmask collective madness clad in frock-coats and uniforms. With Švejk, the "malingerer of weak intellect" who somehow spots, and dodges, the fatal truths that elude generals and politicians, Jaroslav Hašek drew the prototype of every later hero of the awkward squad who must save his skin in armies, and countries, ruled by delusional blockheads. Joseph Heller, as he acknowledged, could never have composed *Catch-22* without the Czech satirist's inglorious soldier as a model. The "vicious circles" of military bureaucracy that Švejk learns to escape spin down the conflicts of the century until they entangle Heller's Yossarian in Italy.

For Hašek, the brass-hatted folly he encountered in the Austro-Hungarian army's 91st Infantry Regiment was but a special case of the officious insanity that ruled the Habsburg empire in its twilight years. As an anarchic Czech humorist (a true Bohemian), Švejk's creator had fallen foul of the imperial-and-royal authorities in Prague long before the outbreak of the Great War in August 1914. At this moment, his peerless comedy opens as news of the Archduke Franz Ferdinand's assassination in Sarajevo reaches Švejk, courtesy of his charlady. Later, in The Flagon pub (licensed premises being the natural habitat of both anti-hero and author), Švejk's seditious mockery lands him in trouble with the political police. This is the first in a chain of arrests, detentions and interrogations in which the good soldier's not-so-dumb insolence lets him outwit his "superiors" and fight – or shirk – another day.

Episodic, discursive, fuelled by backchat, gags and anecdotes, Švejk's misadventures could, in clumsier hands, outstay their welcome. Yet, as he bounces his alter ago around the jail cells, detention barracks, guardrooms and taverns of the doomed empire, Hašek's flair for absurdist dialogue, his hawk eye for official fraud and obfuscation, keep the flame of satire – and slapstick fun – alight. Like every long distance comedian, Hašek knows that running gags can help bind a picaresque meander between one fine mess and another. So Švejk's expertise in the stolen-dog trade – a line of business not unknown to Hašek – crops up time and again.

Aptly enough, Švejk specialises in passing off mongrel mutts as pedigree hounds. Likewise, in the ramshackle, multi-ethnic Habsburg domains, confident effrontery allows mongrel chancers to act as officer class thoroughbreds. Recruited again into the army, Švejk has most in common with the self-aware – as opposed to the self-deluding – impostors. He serves as assistant to the Catholic chaplain Katz; Jewish in origin and atheist by inclination, happy to act the part of "a little tin god" in a system that demands that its troops submit to divine blessing "before proceeding to die in battle". Later, Švejk becomes batman to the equally cynical Lieutenant Lukáš. Nothing can keep him down for long: certainly not arrest as a suspected Russian spy, when a sergeant decides that his seemingly dumb detainee is "as artful as a cartload of monkeys".

Across all of these behind-the-lines escapades, Hašek never misses the chance for satirical target practice. He indulges, but then often upends, the ethnic stereotypes of Habsburg popular culture – from snooty Austrians to lecherous Magyars, wily Jews and (of course) cunning Czechs. He parodies the bombast and balderdash of official jargon: in military communiqués, propaganda journalism, deceitful regimental histories, government edicts. We even hear about a book by a jingoistic German professor, already dead in August 1914: "How to Die for the Kaiser! A manual of self-instruction."

That's not a work Švejk will be opening. His various scrapes and charges – sedition, insubordination, espionage, desertion – cleverly keep him far from the front line. Finally, even *his* luck runs out. Švejk finds himself passing by train through a battlefield in the Carpathians: a panorama of corpses, crosses, shell craters, burnt-out villages, "so that the whole battalion was able to feast its eyes on the joys of war". Ever practical, Švejk looks forward to the farmers' fine post-war harvest: "They've got a whole regiment rotting away on their fields". Still, within Hašek's comic orbit, the good soldier faces a future not as "bone-meal" but as a POW: mistaken for a Russian, and captured by his own side. Švejk at one point mentions a Czech writer he once knew, one "Ladislav Hájek". This "cheerful gentleman" used to read out his yarns in the pub: "They were very sad stories and they made everybody laugh." Because, not in spite of, the immeasurable sadness of a continent's collapse into industrialised slaughter, those stories still make everybody laugh.

Translation: The unabridged 1973 translation by the diplomat-scholar Sir Cecil Parrott is authoritative; however, Paul Selver's first English version from 1930 lends a beguiling, music-hall mischief to its period patter.

See also: Musil, *The Man Without Qualities* (1930-1943); Andrić, *The Bridge On The Drina* (1945); Hrabal, *I Served the King of England* (1971); Kundera, *The Book of Laughter and Forgetting* (1978)

Selected works by the same author: *The Red Commissar* (1981)

38 | The Magic Mountain (1924) by Thomas Mann.

German

Translated by John E Woods (Everyman's Library)

At the Berghof sanatorium, high above the Swiss resort of Davos, space collapses – like the tubercular lungs of the clinic's patients – into the "little world of illness". Time, on the contrary, expands. It stretches into leisurely cycles of summer and winter, remission and relapse, in a succession of "semi-elastic turning points" broken only by the final departure of some once-hopeful performer in this stuttering dance of death. Young Hans Castorp, "neither a genius or an idiot" but an apprentice shipyard engineer from the prosaic "flatlands" of Hamburg, plans to stay on the mountain for three restorative weeks. But the "guest" will become a "comrade": an enlisted member of this "tubercular crew", gathered from all over Europe and beyond. The patients obsessively pore over their symptoms, their X-rays and their prognoses with one another, with the bluff medical director Dr Behrens, or with his psychoanalytically-inclined sidekick Dr Krokowski, for whom "illness was merely transformed love". Seven years later, unhealed but undefeated, Hans will depart for the trenches of the Western Front to play his part in "the worldwide festival of death".

To Thomas Mann, writing in the early 1920s, Hans's Alpine interlude appears "on the far side of a rift" hollowed out by the Great War. The passage of nine decades has, on some scales, deepened our distance from the bourgeois Europe of the 1900s. In large measure, though, this monumental yet intimate novel, which probes so cunningly into the gaps between clock time, body time, story time and the time of history and evolution, feels as bracingly fresh as the thin, dry air of the Berghof. On the "narrow stage" of its sanatorium, many kinds of drama overlap. An erotic comedy, a lyrical tragedy, a dialectical symposium, a *Bildungsroman*, a phantasmagoric tableau that animates the hidden forces of biology, history and philosophy: Mann's Alpine expedition mines treasures in abundance. Confiding and ironic, its narrative voice saves the reader from altitude sickness. For all its renown as a semi-allegorical portrait of European civilisation on the brink of a self-willed downfall, *The Magic Mountain* avoids portentousness. For sure, the shadow of the coming war adds a lens of hindsight. Mostly, Hans, his gravely ill cousin Joachim, and their fellow travellers on this slow ship of death, live in the ever-flexible moment. Mann enlivens their highland limbo with scenes of lust and learning, farce and mystery; of tipsy parties, furious debates and moments of numinous ecstasy in "this winter valley under a deep blanket of snow".

Apart from the stalwart cadet Joachim, whose friendship grounds the thoughtful but impressionable Hans, the young engineer forges three key bonds. He falls in love and lust with the enigmatic Clavdia Chauchat, that "Kirghiz-eyed, softly slinking woman" married to a Russian imperial bureaucrat. Their minds and, briefly, their bodies connect. The idea of Clavdia, as much as her flesh-and-blood reality, knots love and death into a single entity for Hans. Dr Behrens affirms this kinship in his speculations on life itself as nothing more than "the oxidation of cell protein". For Behrens, "Life is dying". When Hans and Clavdia kiss, the narrator insists that love means "the touchingly lustful embrace of what is destined to decay". In the human body, as in the communities it forms, youth heralds age. Ripeness brings rot. A disease such as consumption is merely "life's lascivious form".

In his tumult of sense and intellect, Hans wrestles with the rival theories of two "hyper-articulate mentors". They tug "at both sides of his soul". Long-term sufferers who now lodge down in the village, the Italian author and activist Settembrini, and the Jesuit-trained teacher Naphta, spar and joust for the allegiance of the malleable young engineer. Settembrini, an apostle of "the powers of reason and enlightenment that will liberate the human race", voices the secular, progressive liberalism of the 19th-century. His dialectical antithesis, the Jewish-born Catholic convert Naphta scorns with his "caustic" tongue the godless "gospel of reason and work". This cynical "revolutionary of reaction" defends the authority of the Church; the sanctity of hierarchy; the virtue of war; the "necessity of terror". To Naphta, "unbiased science is myth". Human beings crave "discipline and sacrifice". Settembrini, for his part, detests illness and yearns to abolish suffering; to him, "Metaphysics is evil". In our new age of fundamentalism, and irrationalism, the duo's exchanges feel thrillingly up-to-date. Yet Mann, always the ironist, seeds this dualistic spectacle with ambiguity. Settembrini becomes a dogmatic champion of doubt; a knee-jerk sceptic. Naphta, for whom "the principal of freedom has outlived its usefulness", reviles nationalism and treats capitalist wealth as "fuel for the fires of hell". He relishes the prospect of working-class revolution to overthrow bourgeois hypocrisy. The Jesuit morphs into the Bolshevik.

These duellists, twin principles of a decaying European order, need each other. Their ends diverge, but their means, of rational argument and knowledge, coincide. After an absence, Clavdia returns with the inarticulate but mesmerising Dutch coffee planter, Mynheer Peeperkorn. Like "the elderly priest of some alien cult", Peeperkorn casts a strange spell over the Berghof. This "masterful zero", devoid of talent or intellect, "has us all in his pocket". Naphta and Settembrini spot a deadly foe in this dunce-like divinity: the avatar of a modern cult of mindless instinct and charisma. Soon, the melancholy merriment of the Berghof melts like the snows in spring. A "love of quarrels" poisons its chilly air. "Outbursts of rage" climax in a ridiculous duel between Hans's mentors. We hear, on the mountain, the early rumbles of a "historic thunderclap". Soon, Europe's "accumulated stupor and petulance" will erupt in the "deafening detonation" of total war. History will devour young Hans, "life's faithful problem child". Down in the flatlands, his plight, and his problems, remain ours.

Translation: In its wit, its pace, its rhythm, its lively attunement to Mann's erudition and irony, John E Woods's version (1995) re-opened the Berghof's doors to a new generation.

See also: Voltaire, *Candide* (1759); Musil, *The Man Without Qualities* (1930–1943); Roth, *The Radetzsky March* (1932); Mahfouz, *The Cairo Trilogy* (1956-57)

Selected works by the same author: *Buddenbrooks: The Decline of a Family* (1901); *Death in Venice* (1912); *Lotte in Weimar* (1939); *Doctor Faustus* (1947)

39 | The Trial (1914-15; published 1925) by Franz Kafka.

German (Austria-Hungary; Czechoslovakia)

Translated by Mike Mitchell (Oxford World's Classics)

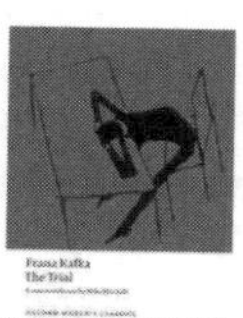

The "great legal organism" that slowly swallows Josef K. after his arrest on an unknown charge turns out to have offices and officials everywhere. It grinds away in tenement slums, painters' studios, boarding-houses, "in almost every attic"; even in the bank where K. works as an up-and-coming accountant. Yet these ubiquitous premises are always mean, dirty, dilapidated. In one of the dingy, airless rooms where low-level lawyers toil, an unrepaired hole in the floor means that "if one of them did get stuck, his foot would hang down in the lower attic, right in the middle of the corridor where their clients waited".

Kafka admired Dickens. The grotesque shabbiness of the surroundings in which K.'s ordeal veers between farce, absurdity and sheer dread recalls the choking world of *Bleak House* quite as much as the legalistic serpent-coils that strangle him. Readers who come fresh to *The Trial*, awed by its reputation as the ultimate modern parable of guilt and innocence, persecution and victimhood, are sometimes surprised to find themselves plunged into a sinister circus. Here, knockabout black comedy, lewd jests, bawdy stunts, near-slapstick mishaps and the day-to-day anxieties of office routine occupy as much space as anguished metaphysical debates. Even if K.'s entrapment in an opaque and unfathomable legal process drags him to "the very limit of what was endurable for human beings", many of his misadventures arrive in the guise of slumland vaudeville. This bizarre cabaret plays out in seedy, soot-smeared corners and corridors; not in some dystopian dreamland but a city much like Prague during the Habsburg Empire's final years.

K.'s initial arrest in Frau Grubach's boarding house takes place to the sound of "brief laughter in the neighbouring room". At his first hearing, in a grotty tenement block before a guffawing audience, his avowal that he isn't a decorator but "a senior accountant with a large bank" results in a gale of mirth. People "shook as if they had a violent fit of coughing". When K.'s case reaches its inevitable finale, in an encounter with a "double-edged butcher's knife" in a moonlit quarry, he complains – ever the self-important yuppie – that "They send old, second-rate actors for me". The theatre-loving Kafka's flair for comic pratfalls, backchat and misprision, brings hilarity to the edge of panic – and vice versa.

Josef K., newcomers to Kafka will also swiftly learn, is no weedy, craven drudge but an entitled careerist. Often a bully and a snob, he neglects his aged mother, buys sexual services from a barmaid called Elsa, preys on vulnerable women and, after his arrest, assaults his fellow-lodger Fräulein Bürstner with unwanted kisses "like a thirsty animal". Although he "had rights, the country was at peace, and the laws had not been suspended", his subjection to this parallel shadow justice system seems to come about because the implacable machine "is attracted by guilt". In some readings, K. has even called his entire ordeal into existence himself. He seeks out the court and its bureaucrats as much as they seek him, hopes that a self-justifying "account of his life" will exonerate him, and even in his dying moments frets that "he could not do all the authorities' work for them".

Does K. try and convict himself? What's undeniable is that Kafka, who lets his vain accountant carry on working as the invisible deliberations churn away, presents the relationship between everyday reality and quasi-judicial nightmare as a porous, breathing membrane. Behind every door, around every corner, horror and mystery wait. Stray gossip about the trial suddenly breaks into K.'s conversations with clients. His first evidence of the savagery concealed behind the court's obscurities comes when the "thrasher" beats the guards who first arrested him in a dusty storeroom at the bank itself. Crucially, they are chastised because K. has complained about their heavy-handed tactics. He has caused their punishment. The guard called Franz lets out "one unchanging, uninterrupted scream".

During a financial consultation with a factory-owner, K. hears of the painter Titorelli, who "knows lots of judges". Titorelli will explain to K. about the impossibility of "genuine acquittal", and the faint hope of either "apparent acquittal" – where the trial may resume at any point – or an endless "protraction of the proceedings". At no point does Kafka detach the religious or philosophical dimensions of K.'s quest for an unattainable law and truth from the humdrum minutiae of his existence. No novel is less abstract, more precise, than *The Trial*.

Later, in the cathedral, K. comes across a prison chaplain and hears the great parable of the countryman who waits for lifetime at the gate of the Law. But he has rushed there in order to meet a valuable Italian client who wanted a tour of the city's art treasures. Primed for a dull morning of business diplomacy, K. drops suddenly into the realm of mystery and revelation. He learns of "a radiance which streams, inextinguishable, from the entrance to the Law", and of the sorrow of a supplicant who never asked to enter even though, as the door-keeper tells him, "this entrance was intended for you alone". Even here, at the novel's metaphysical climax, we slip into a fussy, tit-for-tat dialogue between K. and the priest over what it all means. K. feels that "the simple story had become misshapen". Interpreters have since re-moulded Kafka's tale into every plausible or preposterous shape. Its concrete immediacy, its dark humour, its hallucinatory clarity, both invite and withstand each raid on its secrets. As for a final judgement, that remains like the highest court of all, in Titorelli's words, "quite out of the reach of you, of me, of us all".

Translation: Willa and Edwin Muir's pioneering Kafka translations of the 1930s still rightly win admirers; Mike Mitchell's 2009 version – which draws on the complete manuscripts – has verve, pace and precision.

See also: Dostoyevsky, *The Brothers Karamazov* (1880); Hašek, *The Good Soldier Švejk* (1923); Buzzati, *The Tartar Steppe* (1940); Camus, *The Outsider* (1942)

Selected works by the same author: *The Metamorphosis* (1915); *In the Penal Colony* (1919); *The Castle* (1926); *Amerika (The Man Who Disappeared)* (1927)

40 | Berlin Alexanderplatz (1929) by Alfred Döblin.

German

Translated by Michael Hoffman (Penguin Classics)

Although Alfred Döblin's narrator tells us that "The world is made of sugar and shit", we taste precious little sweetness in the year of strife and misfortune recounted in *Berlin Alexanderplatz*. Yet this picaresque journey through the lower depths of life in the German capital just before the final crisis of the Weimar Republic hums with an exhilaration, even an excitement, that marks it as one of the first – and greatest – tales of big-city frenzy in the mass-media age. Assuredly, Döblin, a restless and prolific doctor-writer who moved from style to style, had learned much from Joyce's *Ulysses* in his scenes of urban montage. Newspaper headlines, pop song lyrics, advertising slogans, municipal notices and a dozen other idioms of the modern metropolis collide. But, compared to Leopold Bloom's largely genial saunter through Dublin in June 1904, the progress of the ex-convict Franz Biberkopf from mischance to disaster unfolds under a lurid neon glow rather than gentle Irish gaslight.

Once a furniture mover, Franz leaves Tegel jail. He has served four years for manslaughter after beating his lover Ida to death in a fight. Throughout the book, the violence that dispossessed men inflict on the even more powerless women who become their victims recurs in a sorry refrain. As the seasons of the year 1928 pass in hectic, raucous Berlin, Franz tries to stay on the straight and narrow. Yet, time and again, fate – or a force something like it – "crashes into our man". Döblin writes not only as a literary Modernist enthralled by the sensory overload of the electrified metropolis in the first media age; he becomes a forensic sociologist who registers each barrier – whether built of bureaucratic edicts or class prejudice – that blocks the path of a former prisoner who has "sworn to all the world and to himself that he would remain decent". Dead-end, short-term jobs (the most enduring of them, ominously enough, as a vendor of extreme right-wing newspapers) push him back towards the criminal underworld. In a bar, a broken down one-time teacher warns against the "cult of destiny. I'm not believer in fate. I live in Berlin, not ancient Greece". But even free-willed 20th-century Berliners, it turns out, need money and status to ward off the blows of fate in this world made "of iron" that "rolls up to you like a steamroller".

At first hesitantly, Franz falls in with the Pums gang of burglars and swindlers. As his haphazard criminal career as fixer, fence and pimp veers towards mortal danger, a trio of girlfriends – Lina, Cilly, Mitzi – offer poignant proof that underclass women have even fewer defences against the "hammer blows" of destiny than men.

Around Franz's reluctant rogue's progress, the city sparkles, seethes and shouts. From department-store sales pitches to cinema posters, official statistics to press propaganda, every clashing jargon and idiom of the mass-society metropolis crowds Döblin's narrative. The corny moralistic summaries that precede each "book" of Franz's story recall street ballads. Döblin's *Alexanderplatz* lies very close to the milieu of Brecht and Weill's *Threepenny Opera*. From time to time, fragments of Biblical and Classical sources – the sufferings of Job, the family bloodbath of the Oresteia, Abraham's willingness to sacrifice his son Isaac – lend an ancient, epic resonance to these modern tales of woe. Meanwhile, the interludes of reportage that bring the seamy side of city life to light have a symbolic as well as documentary function. The Berlin central slaughterhouse evoked in a terrifying passage of bravura prose comes to stand for the bloody sacrifice of all defenceless creatures: "For it happens alike with man and beast."

Franz encounters a kind of butchery when he has an arm amputated in the wake of a botched crime. Pathetically, and with no other option, he persists in low-level criminality. Franz has vowed to "lead a decent life" and comes to care, even as a pimp, for the prostitute Mitzi. But in this city, at this time, he cannot keep his oath. Despite flashes of tenderness, even serenity, Death "beats his drum roll" and begins to sing his slow song of annihilation. Reinhold, Franz's sadistic partner in crime, kills Mitzi, and Franz takes the rap. Consigned to an asylum after a kind of catatonic breakdown, he seems doomed – until the fate in which sophisticated Berlin refuses to believe, begins to twist again. Döblin confesses that he has taken his readers "down a dark alley". Yet his original audience in Germany in 1929 could not have known how much darker that street would become. Far-right thugs, like left-wing militants, wander in and out of Franz's working-class settings of pub, cafe, street market and doss house. Still, the absence of historical hindsight gives *Berlin Alexanderplatz* a buzz and tingle of immediacy that no retrospective portrayal of Weimar Germany from the far side of Hitler's Reich has ever matched. "There are no grounds for despair," affirms the storyteller as Franz's journey approaches its "rough, awful, bitter conclusion". All ironies aside, he – and his readers – could not have known that there were.

Translation: Connoisseurs of Berlin slang have not always approved the 1931 translation by Eugene Jolas, although it still has a feverish, demotic dynamism. The virtuosity of Michael Hofmann's exhilarating new version (2018) brings us closer to the Weimar whirlpool.

See also: Zola, *Germinal* (1885); Bely, *Petersburg* (1916-1922); Cela, *The Hive* (1951); Mahfouz, *Cairo Trilogy* (1956-1957)

Selected works by the same author; *The Three Leaps of Wang Fun* (1915); *Wallenstein* (1920); *November 1918: A German Revolution* (1950); *Tales of a Long Night* (1956)

41 | The Seven Madmen (1929) by Roberto Arlt.

Spanish (Argentina)

Translated by Nick Caistor (Serpent's Tail)

In *The Seven Madmen*, we meet a criminal mastermind – the Astrologer – whose world-conquering schemes align him to the megalomaniacs familiar from fiction and film in Roberto Arlt's day, as in ours. The Astrologer, though, has some startlingly prescient ideas. He argues that in the chaotic cities of the 20th-century (in Arlt's case, Buenos Aires), the disenchanted masses need not merely a strong dictatorial hand but a consoling diet of fake news and alternative facts. "The person who can find the lie the masses need," muses the Astrologer, "will be King of this World."

In this hectic, visionary novel, with its demoralised hero adrift in the heartless metropolis, Arlt did not explicitly set out to design a speculative dystopia along the lines of HG Wells, Aldous Huxley or George Orwell. Along the way, though, this unsettled Argentinian journalist and small-time inventor devises for his arch-villain some notions that have a strikingly prophetic ring to them. A marginal figure in the literary life of Argentina, Arlt died young (in 1942) and only slowly gathered a posthumous reputation as a reckless maverick and wild pioneer. His Astrologer hankers after a ruling elite of "the elect" who will "administer the herd's pleasures and miracles". To him, the regime run by his "secret society" might equally be Bolshevik or Fascist, though he does admire the Ku Klux Klan. He speaks, though, not so much like an ideological propagandist from Arlt's own time as a social media tycoon in ours. He and his gang will profit even-handedly from every yearning felt by the lonely crowd. "Just like in a pharmacy," he foresees, "we'll have a wide variety of perfect lies, each one labelled for a different disease of the mind or soul."

Crazily inventive, eccentric and extravagant, *The Seven Madmen* still reads like a bolt from the blue. The novel veers in tone and voice between pulp fiction and philosophical dialogue, tough urban noir and existential angst. Remo Erdosain, its browbeaten hero, is a small-time drifter and would-be inventor (like his creator) in the brash Buenos Aires of the late 1920s. Unhappily married to Elsa, Erdosain embezzles six hundred pesos and seven cents in the course of his debt-collecting job. Seeking to escape jail, he falls into the snares set by the Astrologer and his fellow hoodlums. He consents to take part in a kidnap and extortion plot, which should end in the murder of its victim: his wife's cousin Barsut, whom he hates with "an insipid, cowardly rancour". Yet around this tabloid intrigue, set against the bleak streets of a down-at-heel city pock-marked by filthy cafes and sleazy brothels, Arlt conveys a surreally intense sense of a mind and a world at the end of its tether. Amid "the monstrous turmoil of cement and iron cities", Erdosain becomes the modern Everyman devoid of faith and hope, in search of salvation – even when peddled by crooked charlatans. If he owes a debt to the frantic dreamers of Dostoyevsky, Erdosain looks ahead to the alienated heroes of post-war European fiction. Confined to "the anguish zone" of his miserable life, he feels a "constant pressure of dread". His identity frays until he feels that "I'm not at the centre of my being." His gratuitous offence will, he thinks, make him real to himself and to society: "it is only thanks to crime that I can affirm my existence". Proto-existentialist gloom aside, he's also a hapless booby whose bumbling entanglement with major-league gangsters has its comic side. Neither does Arlt overlook the sheer pathos of his and his friends' plight. The former prostitute Hipolita, originally a humiliated maidservant, decides that selling your body means "having your mind and your will free".

The Astrologer and his sidekicks accept that the modern society that crushes the Erdosains and the Hipolitas "is based on the exploitation of men, women and children". They have learned from the violence of Lenin and Mussolini (what matters is that "both came out on top") but now plan a smarter system of control. It will rule by force when it must, but fantasy when it can. Erdosain agrees that, "We have to usher in the realm of falsehood, of magnificent lies." Beyond his hard-boiled thriller plot and his scrutiny of the rootless urban soul, Arlt jumps forward to an era of elite manipulation in which smooth plutocrats, not rough tyrants, will govern. "Ford is a God," declares the Astrologer. Metropolitan fret and stress have denatured humanity but left it stranded, nostalgic for vanished meaning – just as the decorative copper roses that Erdosain hopes to patent recall the organic life they mimic. The "aristocracy of cynics" he hopes to join will pacify today's "maelstrom of outcasts" with an artificial paradise. Erdosain, it turns out, will himself become the dupe of a big lie. But the future conjured by the Astrologer does feel suspiciously like ours.

Translation: Nick Caistor (1998) copes zestfully, and creatively, with the novel's wild swings of tone, register and voice.

See also: Dostoyevsky, *The Brothers Karamazov* (1880); Döblin, *Berlin Alexanderplatz* (1929); Camus, *The Outsider* (1942); Murakami, *Hard-boiled Wonderland and the End of the World* (1985)

Selected works by the same author: *Mad Toy* (1926); *The Flamethrowers* (1931)

42 | The Man Without Qualities (1930-33; 1943) by Robert Musil.

German (Austria/Germany/Switzerland)

Translated by Sophie Wilkins and Burton Pike
(Picador Classics)

Writing in the 1920s and 1930s, Robert Musil often points out the chasm that separates this time from the setting of *The Man Without Qualities*: Vienna in 1913. Women's fashions, for example, then consisted of tantalising layers and drapes, a "cleverly curtained theatre of the erotic", not the functional, sexless tunics of today. The Great War and the revolutions it triggered play no overt part in Musil's gigantic yet tightly-focused portrait of the Austro-Hungarian empire on the eve of its demise – 1100 pages published in his lifetime, five hundred more of posthumous additions. Yet the novel's tentacular architecture spreads out from this offstage, unforeseen catastrophe. Its plot can be read as a miniature or microcosmic drama of civilised Europe's serenely oblivious stumble into disaster.

Musil's central consciousness, Ulrich, is a super-bright but directionless mathematician whose smug lawyer father belongs to the empire's "intellectual aristocracy". Ulrich drifts into the amorphous job of "secretary" to the so-called Parallel Campaign. Steered by Count Leinsdorf, this is the pretentious but inchoate preparatory work for a "Year of Austria", that "true home of the human spirit", in 1918. A grandiose public-relations stunt, the Campaign aims to celebrate seven decades of Emperor Franz Josef's reign as Imperial-and-Royal ("K-und-K") sovereign of the constitutionally mixed-up entity which Musil dubs "Kakania" – "Crapland". By the by, it seeks to outgun a rival German jubilee to mark thirty years of Kaiser Wilhelm's rule. Designed as a jamboree for the "Emperor of Peace", the Campaign, as protean and confused as the empire it promotes, winds from one twisted impasse to another. The mighty forces of "cannons and business deals" – the former embodied in the gruff but conniving General Stumm, the latter in the charismatic, unfathomable financier Paul Arnheim – threaten to push this innocuous festival of multi-ethnic statehood into a pretext for military and capitalist aggression. Musil need not spell out what 1918 – the date of the empire's death – was really like. From the level of the single sentence to that of the novel, the ironies of history, culture and psychology scramble motives and sabotage desires. They transform both the Campaign and the lives of its prime movers into a tragi-comic havoc of unintended consequences.

The Man Without Qualities can often feel urgently contemporary. With the Parallel Campaign, it dissects innovative techniques of spin, hype and ideological "branding" through media manipulation. The ethnic nationalism that gnaws away at Austro-Hungarian identity, that nebulous creature "with no concept of itself", in our day still does its divisive work as "a substitute for religion". Arnheim, the genius entrepreneur and "regal man of business", fuses cash and culture to mesmeric, and topical, effect. This "brilliant outsider" merges "soul and economics". His glamour anticipates an epoch when the "Business King" will "take over the leadership of the masses". We inhabit that time. In prose of microscopic subtlety and rigour, leavened by sophisticated comedy, Musil – an engineer by training – applies the tools of both philosophy and science to modern psychological and social life. For Ulrich, changing times have brought about "the dissolution of the anthropocentric point of view". They have knocked traditional humanism from its pedestal, and shaped a type of restless mind that has forsaken "all the great ideals and laws". It now "regards nothing as fixed, no personality, no order of things", because "our knowledge may change from day to day". Ulrich himself acts as both barometer and avatar of this relativistic age, "without qualities" because his gifts and aims cannot coalesce into a solid selfhood. In a mind like his, in a city like Vienna, "countless views, opinions, systems of ideas" converge, yet "the central nodal point tying them all together is missing".

In this age of "pseudo-reality", with its "gaseous fluidity", other doubt-befogged moons circle around Ulrich's planet. Diotima, his cousin and the wife of a foreign ministry official, becomes the high-minded hostess of the Campaign's luminaries, and advocate of "Global Austria" as prototype of the multi-cultural state. Ulrich's married mistress Bonadea pursues pleasure above all, but in this shape-shifting city her sensuality might represent thwarted ambition, "a desire for distinction". His friends Clarisse and Walter, spouses at war, fall for various brands of the "superstitious claptrap" – mystical, irrational, Nietzschean – that outright charlatans or self-anointed saviours sell in the salons of Vienna. The cunning servants Rachel and Soliman – one a Jewish peasant, the other an African boy kept as a protegé-pet by Arnheim – take their own comic-opera revenge on the lords and masters. In the novel's third part, Ulrich's intense, quasi-incestuous bond with his sister Agathe dominates. Ulrich has tended to treat women as "prey" to be "struck down by "the amorous male spear". Gifted, introspective, anguished, Agathe proves more than an equal partner in her brother's spiritual quest to master the "inner hovering life". They pursue an "essayistic" way of being, in which morality means not obedience to some empty husk of faith but "living the infinite fullness of possibilities". The close-knit siblings dream of a "quintessential love", a platonic union of "two identical yet different forms". Agathe, though, is plagued by a "fundamental sense of being superfluous". She feels the nihilistic tug of suicide, and spurns bourgeois happiness with "the total contempt of the born rebel".

We also meet Moosbrugger: one of the most darkly inspired creations in all fiction. Moosbrugger is a sex murderer, the callous butcher of a street-walker, yet an amiable, charming fellow with a face "blessed… by every sign of goodness". Is he mad, or bad? Where on the scale of evil, or freedom, do his vile deeds belong? Ulrich's pedantic father, whose death reunites Ulrich with Agathe, has studied "diminished responsibility". That concept seeps out from Moosbrugger's cell in the Dante-like "abyss" of the asylum to infect all Vienna. The cheerful, impenitent Moosbrugger's crimes haunt almost every character. Does this "pathological comedian" merely embody "repressed instincts common to all"? Could he, more than suave Arnheim, represent the essence of this "messianic age"? If "the rules of the moral life" have decayed into "metaphors that have been boiled to death", Moosbrugger and his ilk, rather than the intellectual cavalier Ulrich, may aspire to fill the vacuum that results. "Crimes are in the air," argues Ulrich. They "seek the path of least resistance, which leads them to certain individuals". Musil never finished work on *The Man Without Qualities*. By the time of his death, exiled in Switzerland from Nazi-occupied Austria, Moosbrugger no longer sat behind bars, studied by psychiatrists, "the wild, captive threat of a dreaded act". His spirit ruled Europe.

Translation: Supple, energetic, readable, Sophie Wilkins and Burton Pike's complete translation (1995) shows a formidable command of Musil's enormous linguistic, and intellectual, resources.

See also: Dostoyevsky, *The Brothers Karamazov* (1880); Rilke, *The Notebooks of Malte Laurids Brigge* (1910); Mann, *The Magic Mountain* (1924); Roth, *The Radetzky March* (1932)

Selected works by the same author: *The Confusions of Young Törless* (1906); *Three Women* (1924)

43 | THE FOUNDATION PIT (1930; published 1973) by Andrey Platonov.

Russian

Translated by Robert Chandler, Elizabeth Chandler and Olga Meerson

Many excellent novels look back in sorrow, anger or nostalgia to the upheavals and calamities of history. Much rarer are those that, in the heat of the moment and without any luxury of hindsight, not only inhabit the essence of a time of transformation but intuit its final outcomes. Completed in 1930, but unpublished in Russia until 1987, *The Foundation Pit* miraculously found a way to channel both the present and the future of the Soviet experience into a livid, bitter, touching and bleakly comic fable. Neither does Platonov's achievement stop at the borders of the Soviet Union, whose eventual failure can be detected in the literal, and metaphorical, foundations of this book. His characters internalise the dream – and the tragedy – of the breakneck modernisation and urbanisation that would soon spread across the globe. "Don't people get to feel smaller as their buildings get bigger?" wonders the labourer Voshchev. He has lost his former job because his vice of "thoughtfulness" slowed down "the general tempo of labour" in the brisk Soviet age. With the Cold War fading from memory, Platonov's parable endures as an elegy for the victims of "progress" that can resonate from China to Peru.

In a poor province ravaged by forced collectivisation and ensuing famine, Voshchev and his co-workers toil to dig the foundations for a huge municipal complex. It will serve as "a common home for the proletariat" and replace the demolished old town, with its private plots. In a nearby village, the "liquidation" of the kulaks – so-called rich peasants, although their wealth existed solely in the lies of Soviet propaganda – has left a landscape of nightmare, a killing ground of starvation, execution and despair. Although unmistakeable, the allegorical overtones of this unbuilt Utopia, this tomb of human hope, never feel forced. The black farce and compassionate inwardness of Platonov's prose mean that his microcosm of a revolution betrayed avoids any sense of the schematic sermon. Through the lives of his people, rather than authorial steering, he disproves the doctrine spouted to Voshchev by a party line trade unionist: "Happiness will come from materialism… not from meaning".

Platonov wrote from inside the Soviet furnace of coercive change. He shows that, for so many in Russia, that "meaning" had until this point found a home in revolutionary idealism. An engineer with deep philosophical knowledge, he had himself been a Bolshevik true believer. Even Stalin praised him before persecuting him and his family. Several of his main figures – the engineer Prushevsky, the high-minded navvy Kozlov, even the crippled court jester Zhachev, his tongue liberated by the marginal role of "miserable freak" – want to believe they are building a better world. Even after he has witnessed ghastly evidence of mass death around the new collective farm, Voshchev collects the stray effects of the "terminally liquidated" kulaks – a tin ring, a rough sandal, a "homespun trouser leg" – as relics of "lost people" who "had lived without truth and had perished before the final victory". Step by heart-breaking step, Platonov reveals that truth as a sham and that victory as a nightmare. As Voshchev mourns over the corpse of the little girl Nastya – a factory owner's granddaughter, and an almost Dickensian doomed angel – he reflects that "he no longer knew how Communism could ever come to exist if it didn't appear first of all in a child's feelings". *The Foundation Pit* would lose its authority, and dilute its anguish, if it did not stir the embers of that child-like longing for a promised land. Prushevsky himself aches to have faith in the future in spite of the "dark wall in front of his groping mind". He both seeks and flees the idea of happiness, which seems conceivable as "just something the trees rustled about, or that a band serenaded in the Trade Union Park".

Elements of absurdist satire defy the lingering idealism of Prushevsky and his comrades. As the peasants expire, their "collectivised" horses trot off to feed in a "compact formation" at their leader's behest. Animals too may be class enemies, since "in the hands of a rampant kulak even a goat could be a lever of Capitalism". The ousted village priest has got a secular "jazzy haircut" and is on probation to join the Atheist Club. Propaganda blaring from loudspeakers alienates language from real meaning. Public speech itself, like the people whom it saves or slaughters, has lost its soul. The nameless "activist" who enforces state decrees spouts deadly slogans, as do the directives that instruct him. The comrades at the farm have "gone dashing off into the leftist quagmire of rightist opportunism". Prophetically, Platonov sketches the mental scenery not only of Orwell's *Animal Farm* but of his *Nineteen Eighty-Four*. As words fray and souls shrink, the workers who yearned to erect Utopia dig their own graves, "seeking eternal salvation in the abyss of the foundation pit".

Translation: The Chandlers and Meerson (2009) revise Robert Chandler and Geoffrey Smith's pioneering version, and do full justice to the pathos, satire and thwarted idealism that converge in Platonov's vision.

See also: Gogol, *Dead Souls* (1842-55); Zola, *Germinal* (1885); Bulgakov, *The Master and Margarita* (1940); Han, *A Dictionary of Maqiao* (1996)

Selected works by the same author: *Chevengur* (1928); *Soul* (1935); *Happy Moscow* (1936); *The Return* (1946)

44 | Journey to the End of the Night (1932) by Louis-Ferdinand Céline (Louis-Ferdinand Destouches).

French

Translated by Ralph Manheim (Alma Classics)

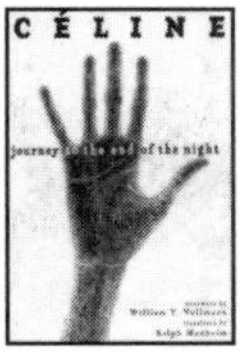

Ferdinand Bardamu, the shell-shocked and self-loathing narrator of this tragi-comic nightmare of a novel, finds a musician girlfriend called Musyne amid the chaotic Paris of the First World War. If she considers this tormented veteran of the trenches "repulsive", well, "Maybe I'm an artist in that line. After all, why wouldn't there be an art of ugliness as well as beauty?" Hardly any other work of its century pushes that "art of ugliness" to such soul-scorching extremes as *Journey to the End of the Night*. Every later writer who reports from that burning edge of reason where mind and culture crumple into horror and absurdity – from Heller to Grass, Welsh to Houellebecq – stands in its dire shadow. Some of Louis-Ferdinand Céline's lesser disciples merely played with the nihilism and misanthropy that Bardamu often – not invariably – voices in his corrosive contempt for humankind as "nothing but packages of tepid, half rotted viscera". But for Céline, as for the anti-hero who shares many of his author's youthful misadventures, the damage, and the disequilibrium, went deep.

The *Journey*, along its sulphurous way, defends the poor against the rich, black Africans against their colonialist predators, and rages against the blind cruelty that in modern life drives pity "to the bottom of our bowels along with our shit". In the years following this incandescent debut, however, Céline would notoriously slip into deranged anti-Semitism. He collaborated with the Nazi occupiers of France, endured jail and exile, and passed his last years as a national disgrace. That unhappy obsessive did not write the *Journey*. On the other hand, the obscenely disordered world that it conjures did made such breakdowns, personal or collective, far more likely to occur. Céline could finish his voyage, which he recounts through Bardamu in a slangy, scabrous monologue that thrilled his countless literary heirs. He could not heal the wounds it left behind.

Like the author, Bardamu is a medical student who has volunteered for war service. Although the grisly surrealism of his ordeal only occupies the novel's first quarter, the trauma of battle repeats for the rest of its length. Again like Bardamu, Céline went on to practise medicine in a shabby suburb of Paris. A physician's clear-eyed alertness to symptoms, organic or psychiatric, helps him to keep a foothold in the age of reason and science. At the front, Bardamu sees an officer's head blown off, with blood in the open neck "bubbling and gouging like jam in a kettle". Later, he attends the aftermath of a botched abortion that reminds him of "the colonel's decapitated neck". The *Journey* may figure as the scandalous scripture of 20th-century malcontents and nihilists. Do not discount its value as a hideously exact fictional record of post-traumatic stress and the long-term toll it takes.

After the war, "phobically allergic to heroism" and the whole patriotic racket, Bardamu flees the "putrid carnival" of Paris for colonised West Africa. In the malarial hell-hole of Fort-Gono (as in gonorrhoea), European brutality vastly exacerbates the dangers of seething and diseased nature. The "flabby, heartless sons of bitches" sent from France prey on their native victims. "The poetry of the tropics turned my stomach," confesses Bardamu, but as always Céline mitigates the bile with scurrilous, unforgiving wit. Next stop America, and a ribald but occasionally rhapsodic view of the Roaring Twenties from the illusion-free perspective of a steerage-class migrant. Typically, Bardamu first encounters New York in a subterranean lavatory, a "faecal grotto". In Detroit, where he toils on the Ford assembly line, the workers "became machines". The dehumanising regime of the modern factory (which Céline had studied) recalls the deadly din of the Western Front. For once, our itinerant cynic hitches up in Detroit with a sympathetic partner, Molly. But his sporadic lapses into ranting misogyny represent one florid symptom of a generalised male pathology. From time to time, flaring bursts of lyricism hint at a forgotten realm of peace and loveliness, as when the city night fades and "On pavements sticky with the small rain of dawn the pavements glistened blue". Then the sun rises again on a stricken century, with its "vast maelstrom of apocalyptic ambitions".

Back in down-at-heel Paris, Dr Bardamu tempers (as did Céline) his ennui with a commitment to his ragged patients in an era when "Glory, in our time, smiles only on the rich". The mental and medical crises of his old comrade Leon Robinson, even more acute than the narrator's, hasten the story towards its gory finale. A local "crime of passion" distantly echoes the Great War that has poisoned these minds and their entire world. For all its vernacular verve and swagger, its beggar's banquet of satire and profanity, the *Journey* leads into dark places indeed – as when Bardamu witnesses a couple of slum tenants mete out a "terrible thrashing" to their cowed daughter. "I believed I gained strength listening to such things," he comments, "the strength to go further". Yet compassion must survive, even if relegated to the bowels of a society blighted by its mechanised inhumanity. "Beyond the plaints we hear," other voices cry out to us; voices that "we haven't yet heard or understood". From its depths of cynicism and despair, Céline's *Journey* can still attend to them.

Translation: With exuberant vulgarity, Ralph Manheim (1988) lets Céline in English sing – and curse – at the top of his rasping voice.

See also: Hašek, *The Good Soldier Švejk* (1923); Döblin, *Berlin Alexanderplatz* (1929); Sartre, *Nausea* (1938); Grass, *The Tin Drum* (1959)

Selected works by the same author: *Death on Credit* (1936); *Guignol's Band* (1944); *North* (1960); *London Bridge* (1964)

45 | The Radetzsky March (1932) by Joseph Roth.

German (Austria-Hungary /Germany/ France)

Translated by Michael Hofmann (Granta)

A few years before the First World War, the elderly Emperor Franz

Joseph of Austria-Hungary insists on paying a visit to his eastern frontiers to watch the autumn military manoeuvres. During the draining round of official ceremonies, a Jewish elder bestows on the "Imperial and Royal" monarch a ritual blessing: "Thou shalt not witness the end of the world!" Strictly speaking, that prophecy proved correct. Franz Joseph died in 1916, two years before his empire's collapse. But the elder's words forge another link in the chain of ironic foreboding that snakes through Roth's elegiac, but exuberant, novel. *The Radetzsky March* plots the fortunes of the Trotta family, once Slovenian peasants, across three generations. Through their destinies, Roth traces the decline and fall of the Habsburg dynasty and – by extension – of the traditional European civilisation it upheld.

Writing in the early 1930s, as a nomadic cultural orphan raised in a Jewish community on that Habsburg eastern fringe, Joseph Roth had every reason to lament the "boundless catastrophe" that had swept away the stuffy, hierarchical – yet tolerant and graceful – order of his youth. The drums of doom, as ubiquitous here as the jingling tune of Johann Strauss Sr's "Radetzsky March", sound a muffled thump through every chapter. Above every twist in the Trottas' path beat "the dark, rushing wings of death". Through pointless shootings in duels, the suicide of ruined officers, the peaceful, and indistinguishable, departures of a venerable servant or a venerable emperor, or simply the inexorable age that creeps up on women with "cruel and silent tread", every figure will face "an assignation with Death". In the final act, after so many premonitions and foreshadowings, the "red veil of war" descends to finish off this world for good.

For all its autumnal wistfulness, nostalgia even, *The Radetzsky March* is not a gloomy or mournful work. Exactly the opposite: the imminent dissolution of the society that bred him impels Roth to chronicle its dying days with unconquerable brio, panache, wit and even mirth. From the bandstands of Moravia to the barracks of Galicia by way of palaces or cafés in Vienna, the Trottas' empire glows in every shade of a resplendent twilight. Although tomorrow will bring storm and calamity, the sheer sensuous immediacy of Roth's prose almost convinces us that the skies over the whiskered emperor's multi-cultural domains "were never anything other than blue".

At the Battle of Solferino in 1859, the first Lieutenant Trotta snatches his family's place in the sun. By a fluke, he saves the young Franz Joseph's life. Newly ennobled, Baron Trotta and his clan rise in the world, although the proud Lieutenant feels outrage when a patriotic schoolbook wilfully misrepresents his exploits. He learns, as will his descendants, that "it was guile that ruled the world". So Joseph Trotta has already been expelled from "the paradise of simple faith" as his family saga starts. Disillusioned, he steers this son Franz away from the army and into the less prestigious civil service, and a middling bureaucratic post in sleepy Moravia.

Franz's son Carl Joseph, who takes the lion's share of plot, does join the cavalry. But, as a mere mediocre lieutenant, he drifts into a becalmed career of garrison time-wasting, desultory affairs, gambling debts and unfulfilled ambitions on the empire's edge. Meanwhile, Franz Joseph himself – whose own kindly but confused musings punctuate the story – strives like his subjects to avert the reckoning to come with routine, pomp or domesticity. At a grand parade in Vienna, a sultry lovers' tryst at a cheap hotel, or a hunting-lodge buffet piled high with caviar, ham, "heavy slabs of carp and slender slippery pike", we might conclude that "the world was not doomed". For the most part, the Trottas act rather than reflect. Although it recaptures a period of fretful rumination, the novel hurries from one cinematically vivid scene to another at a brisk canter. Curiously, even comically, the crusty old ruler of the "dual monarchy" has a more deeply imagined inner life than the Trottas themselves. Around him, fitfully and messily, change happens: nationalism becomes "the new religion", and on the frontier young Trotta reluctantly orders troops to fire on unarmed strikers. The officers' code of honour now appears "the final residue of… childish tales". Cast down by debt and doubt, Carl Joseph feels an accursed creature, on whom "an evil power has cast an evil eye".

As the Great War's tempest begins to rage in August 1914, after a spectacular, symbolic lightning storm, Carl Joseph walks through the garrison town and spots the Friday night candles alight in Jewish homes. "Death itself," he thinks, "had lit the candles", on this "Sabbath of blood". After the bewitching pageant of colour and comedy, and all his high-spirited, luminously painted escapades, Roth darkens the mood from bittersweet elegy into outright dread. He would die, exiled and broken, just before an even greater calamity struck his Europe. For all the doom remembered or foreseen, the prose, and the people, of this valedictory parade still march by in a defiant blaze of joy.

Translation: Crisp, forceful, rhythmic and beautifully phrased, Michael Hofmann's version (2002) rightly helped to restore Roth's fortunes in the English-speaking world.

See also: Hašek, *The Good Soldier Švejk* (1923); Musil, *The Man*

Without Qualities (1930-43); Andrić, *The Bridge on the Drina* (1945); Lampedusa, *The Leopard* (1958)

Selected works by the same author: *Hotel Savoy* (1924); *Job* (1930); *The Emperor's Tomb* (1938); *The Legend of the Holy Drinker* (1939)

46 | Independent People (1934-35) by Halldór Laxness.

Icelandic

Translated by JA Thompson (Vintage)

Although he is an artful oral poet in the medieval Norse tradition, the sheep farmer Gudbjartur Jonsson can be a man of few and terse words when asked by outsiders to justify his ways. When a townie visitor praises the "lovely valley" in remote rural Iceland, where Bjartur labours to make a bare living against the land, the weather, the gentry and the grasping merchants, he flings back this simple credo: "I fear neither ghosts nor men. I own good sheep." But the "ghost" who supposedly curses his property will take her revenge. Men's greed and selfishness will shatter his faith in the supreme dignity of the independent farmer as "a king in his own kingdom". He will even lose his beloved sheep, martyrs to "worms", always prone to sicken and to stray. At his nadir, in this novel where ewes, lambs, horses, cows and dogs often have personalities to rival its human figures, the bruised Bjartur muses that, whatever happens, "a man always has the memories of his dogs".

Class tensions, economic shifts, political upheavals, a world war and its aftermath: all these factors will hammer Bjartur's dream of peasant self-sufficiency, and the well-being of his family, into the frozen ground. His story covers two decades from the turn of the 20th-century – almost an immemorial dream-time of legends and phantoms – to the 1920s. Bjartur breaks away from service to the Bailiff of Myri's snobbish clan. He borrows heavily to purchase his own, stony and sodden, grazing land. There, two unhappy wives, Rósa and Finna, will languish and die, as will several newborns.

Two sons, Gvendur and Nonni, struggle into adulthood, as does Asta Sóllilja ("dearest sun-lily"). She is Rósa's daughter not by Bjartur but by Ingólfur: the slick, ambitious son of the Bailiff's genteel wife.

Asta's tormented relationship with her adoptive "father" anchors the entire book. As stubborn and mutinous as Bjartur himself ("We are also a sovereign state," she says when she has her own baby), Asta is a wonderful creation. This ungainly, visionary girl with "a different soul" yearns to know, to love, to live joyfully, but suffers the curse of her upbringing with Bjartur in silence, hardship and guilt: "She had lived with him in troll's hands, thinking that she was a troll herself". Stricken by her almost-incestuous bond with Bjartur, betrayed by the tutor who promises "tidings to uplift the soul" through books but then turns into a sexual predator, she sinks from a childhood of happy solitude into the self-devouring loneliness and doubt of one who "stood alone, outside the whole world".

In bald outline, *Independent People* may sound like a relentless rural tragedy to match the bleakest works of Thomas Hardy. Laxness, however, makes of Bjartur's curmudgeonly but heroic resistance to modernity, and Asta's thwarted longings for love and freedom, so much more than a backcountry catastrophe. Pastoral idyll, social satire, economic critique, poetic myth, above all the scorchingly intimate drama of a family broken more by fate than by choice – these elements build into an epic of majestic authority and range. From uncanny tales of the witch Gunnvör, who has laid "a curse on this fold", to Bjartur's almost occult skill in rhyming and alliterative verse, the traditional past shadows the encroaching present, with its monopolist merchants, its agricultural cooperatives, its debts, banks, mortgages and lying politicians. (Ingólfur will eventually become Prime Minister). Elves, trolls and the Norse deities feel more at home here than new-fangled Christianity. Laxness transforms this harsh spot that the patronising tutor calls a "tiny world behind the mountains" into the gale-lashed arena for a universal combat, between people and – even more – within people. He can evoke the cycle of the seasons with a spellbinding lyric grace, comically impersonate the backbiting gossip of Bjartur's neighbours over endless cups of coffee, or enter the consciousness of little Nonni as – in a bravura section – he slips out of "sleep-language" into "the laws of day".

Decades before authors such as Gabriel García Márquez restored the world's forgotten backwaters to the front rank of fiction, Laxness had staked his own, magnificent claim. Bjartur inherits one thousand years of solitude in a place where nature and man combine to crush the "lone worker's" ideal of the freehold, self-sustaining farmstead. Like his nation's, Bjartur's personal cult of self-sufficiency ("Keep your mind free and your path your own") becomes a fetish, an idol, a self-harming ritual. Bjartur's poetry, we hear, was "technically so complex that it could never attain any noteworthy content; and thus it was with his life itself". But if his knotted character helps darken his destiny, so too do much wider forces. As Icelandic solitude dissolves in the aftershocks of war, in booms, busts, and strikes, the inequities that shipwreck "independent people" stand revealed as symptoms of a worldwide pandemic. After the bank has seized the farmhouse he so proudly built, the indebted Bjartur meets a socialist militant for whom "the only thief… is capitalism". For this timeless epic written in the spirit of the sagas also belongs to the strife-ridden 1930s. Whether seen through ancient or modern eyes (and Laxness has both), Bjartur's doomed pursuit of self-reliance becomes "the story of a man who sowed his enemy's field all his life, day and night".

Translation: In his only translation, J A Thompson (1945) achieved a masterpiece of his own, with its springing north-country rhythms, its rainbow spectrum of epic, poetic and colloquial speech.

See also: Deledda, *Reeds in the Wind* (1913); Undset, *Kristin Lavransdatter* (1920-1922); Lampedusa, *The Leopard* (1958); García Márquez, *One Hundred Years of Solitude* (1967)

Selected works by the same author: *World Light* (1940); *Iceland's Bell* (1943); *The Fish Can Sing* (1957); *Under the Glacier* (1968)

47 | Journey by Moonlight (1937) by Antal Szerb.

Hungarian

Translated by Len Rix (Pushkin Press)

Among Etruscan monuments, in a Rome museum, the scatty but brooding hero of *Journey by Moonlight* learns the motto that governed the worldview of that long-extinct people. "Enjoy the wine today, tomorrow there'll be none." Szerb's picaresque novel – comic, high-spirited but tinctured with a deep melancholia – both champions and mocks that urge to "seize the day" in wild bids for freedom. An extra, and unavoidable, patina of poignancy now covers a story much concerned with the fatal charms of nostalgia, that European ailment for which "there is no cure". Loved and admired in his native Hungary, its author – an anti-fascist Catholic of Jewish descent – was battered to death in a concentration camp in 1945.

Journey by Moonlight concocts a savoury goulash blend of screwball comedy, *Bildungsroman* parody and almost-Freudian inquiry into the collective drives and demons of 1930s Europe. Its dancing irony, bittersweet wit and nimble storytelling recall those other survivors of the wreck of the Habsburg Empire: Joseph Roth and Stefan Zweig. Yet an undercurrent of anxiety about the spiritual malaise of European culture in such "apocalyptic times" pushes the jesting Szerb into the gloomier company of Thomas Mann or Robert Musil. Mihaly, our protagonist, feels from time to time that "the door of the dead was open", and that the jaws of annihilation gape not just for him but for his age.

Already in his mid-thirties, feckless Mihaly – the cosseted son of a wealthy Budapest businessman – has belatedly resolved to grow up properly by marrying Erzsi. He has, after all, already broken up her own first marriage to the steady Zoltan. Throughout, he feels like "a failure in his adult, or quasi-adult life". Respectable matrimony cannot alter that. In Venice, almost as soon as his honeymoon with the equally privileged Erzsi has begun, he realises his mistake. In memory, he sinks back into his obsessive youthful friendship with the glamorous and doomed Tamas and Eva: a brother and sister from a home in which life "was non-stop theatre, a perpetual commedia dell'arte". In their company, reality fades as a beguiling world of fantasy beckons. Mihaly feels the delirious sensation of "standing on the brink of a terrifying vortex". He can often sound like a ditzy Danubian prototype for the post-war existentialist hero.

The ill-matched couple's springtime journey through the historic cities of Italy becomes a farce that hovers on the edge of breakdown. Raised as "the model of a good girl", Erzsi frets about her nuptial bonds as soon as they are tied. Mihaly's morbid fancies return to Tamas, with his cult of the "supreme ecstasy" of suicide. By the time they reach Perugia, the pair go their separate ways. As in some Freudian dream, set-designed in 1930s Hollywood, figures from Mihaly's past turn up by accident in Italy – the louche adventurer Janos; Ervin the Jewish intellectual who has converted to become a saintly Franciscan friar; Eva herself. After a crisis in Foligno, talks with a half-English doctor inclined to mysticism remind Mihaly of his own brushes with unseen powers during a dank November in London. Erzsi flees to Paris to seek her own kind of low-budget liberty.

Mihaly's lurching progress down the leg of Italy sometimes glows with the colours of "a happy fairy-tale" – as when a naïve but sweet-natured American called Millicent bails him out with dollars. In Rome, however, shadows from the world of the dead loom ever larger in his mind. Rudi Waldheim, the erudite chum who explains the Etruscans to him, believes that, since the triumph of European Christianity, "the raw, ancestral pagan death-desire has gone into exile". Now it only surfaces in superstitious fads such as witchcraft and Satanism. He might have mentioned fascism, but Rudi's speculations remain his – not Szerb's. The muse of comedy still reigns on this stage of chance, farce and folly. In Rome, Mihaly pays a visit to the grave of John Keats, who – rather like the Etruscans – sensed that "only the present matters, and moments of beauty are eternal".

In a twin-track denouement, Szerb saves both Mihaly and Erzsi from themselves. Erzsi's bourgeois soul recoils in time from her fantasy of being bought and sold by rich men, "like some Eastern whore in the Bible or the Thousand and One Nights". Zoltan, the husband she abandoned, even wants her back. In Trastevere, Mihaly rebounds from dark dreams of the Etruscan "death-demons" to find "a normal, friendly Italian summer morning" outside his window. When his father arrives from Budapest to collect his errant son "like a truanting schoolboy", every nightmare seems to have evaporated in the sunlight of reason. The "entire middle-class establishment" that Mihaly fled is back in the saddle. Within two years of the publication of this delightful, hypnotic romp, the "death-demons" would begin their savagely thorough elimination of the culture, and the author, that created it.

Translation: Witty, speedy and graceful, Len Rix's 2001 version reflects both the sunlight and the shadows of Szerb's style.

See also: Mann, *The Magic Mountain* (1924); Roth, *The Radetzsky March* (1932); Musil, *The Man Without Qualities* (1930-1943); Bassani, *The Garden of the Finzi-Continis* (1962)

Selected works by the same author: *The Pendragon Legend* (1934); *Oliver VII* (1942); *The Queen's Necklace* (1943)

48 | The Gift (1938;1952) by Vladimir Nabokov.

Russian (Russia/Germany/United States)

Translated by Michael Scammell, Dmitri Nabokov and the author

Exiled in 1920s Berlin among White Russian émigrés, the hero of *The Gift* dismisses the idea of a return to his homeland as "idiotic sentimentality". "Our nostalgia," he insists, "is not historical – only human". Beyond the accidental displacements forced by war and politics, every person must, whether home or away, live in exile from "the hothouse paradise of the past", and especially from childhood. For the impecunious writer Fyodor Godunov-Cherdyntsev, whose scientist-explorer father has disappeared in the chaotic wake of the Russian Revolution, this dispossession takes various forms. Ill at ease in Weimar-era Germany, scornful of the fantasies and prejudices harboured by his fellow émigrés and, above all, by the squabbling exiled literati, he ekes out a bare living as a language tutor, "a poor young Russian selling the surplus from a gentleman's upbringing".

Fyodor's first volume of poems has sold fifty-one copies. The editor of a Russian-language paper tolerates his scribblings. He moves from one shabby, gossip-ridden boarding-house to another. Solitary, shy, fastidious, "living always uphill", Fyodor is an exotic fish out of water whose plight touchingly – and wittily – captures the lonely pride of migrants in many places. As if mimicking his own divisions, the storytelling flips and hovers between Fyodor's own voice and a third person narration. Eidetic memories of his father the intrepid lepidopterist (Nabokov's own scientific specialism), and of a childhood magic "unknown in other families", torment but also console him. Torn between countries, between ambitions, he also migrates between languages. He instructs vulgar executives in the rudiments of other tongues while in his own he might make anything, "a midge, a mammoth, a thousand different clouds".

Written in the late 1930s, just as history's next earthquake forced him out of Berlin and towards his American exile, *The Gift* is Vladimir Nabokov's spectacular farewell – not only to an epoch and a city but to the Russian language as his creative medium. He never again published a novel in his mother tongue. His close involvement with the English edition, its prose as freighted, nuanced and radiant as any book that he first wrote in that language, spreads another layer of richness, and of ambiguity, across the novel. This is a portrait of the artist as a not-quite-so-young man, with many circumstantial details that correspond to the record of Nabokov's Berlin years. But it also affirms, through Fyodor's craft and thought, that the house of fiction must stand or fall by itself: an autonomous domain rather than an annex of memoir or politics.

First through lyric poetry, then critical biography, Fyodor is searching for the authentic expression of a gift that he feels "like a burden inside himself". For material, he plunders that golden but vanished childhood with an idealised father, the frets, shocks and humiliations of a downwardly-mobile refugee routine, but also the heritage of the Russian language and its masters. Fitfully, *The Gift* shows Fyodor's ardent courtship of the Russian-Jewish émigrée Zina. The author, not entirely teasingly, stated that "Its heroine is not Zina, but Russian Literature". Certainly, the giant shadows of Pushkin and Gogol fall across his style, while a concise book-within-a-book purports to be Fyodor's spirited but sceptical account of the 19th-century realist and reformer, Nikolai Chernyshevsky. His militant novel *What Is To Be Done?* inspired Lenin and the Bolsheviks.

Fyodor's portrait of the artist as activist – the complete antithesis of Nabokov – salutes Chernyshevsky's noble idealism and his long self-sacrifice. It also evokes the bravely endured Siberian exile that links the otherwise chalk-and-cheese pairing of critic and subject. Nabokov, though, enlists this chapter as a platform for his own principles. He presses his case against realist or "materialist" literature because it neglects the unique, particular truths of the life it pretends to reflect. For Fyodor/Nabokov, the literal-minded Chernyshevsky "saw everything in the nominative" whereas "any genuinely new trend is a knight's move, a change of shadows, a shift that displaces the mirror". With the scrupulous exactitude of the lepidopterist as his model, Fyodor will aim to net the darting, shimmering butterflies of existence. Meanwhile, the windbags and the propagandists crank out the sort of "realism" that betrays reality.

True to his hero's word, Nabokov will later invite the reader to "go into the forest together". In passages of almost mystical illumination, he pins down Fyodor's experience of lake-swimming in Grünewald on a torrid summer's day. Supreme verbal artistry, the writer's answer to "those magic masks of mimicry" on a butterfly's wing, rescues memory from oblivion: this is art not for art's, but for real life's sake. Typically, in a novel laden with as much comedy as sadness, this enchanted epiphany collapses into farce. Fyodor has his clothes stolen and makes his naked way back to his digs. Always, through episodes of rapture or slapstick, the suspended animation of exile – this "void, a gap in life" – is incubating his talent. When fate at last conspires to unite Fyodor and Zina, he glimpses "the plot of a remarkable novel": the one that we are reading. Across frontiers of time, of culture, of language, the gift will be delivered intact.

Translation: Refining his son Dmitri and Michael Scammell's text, Nabokov in 1963 fashioned a second masterpiece from his original.

See also: Gogol, *Dead Souls* (1842); Rilke, *The Notebooks of Malte Laurids Brigge* (1910); Bely, *Petersburg* (1916-1922); Döblin, *Berlin Alexanderplatz* (1929);

Selected works by the same author: *Laughter in the Dark* (1933); *Lolita* (1955); *Pnin* (1957); *Pale Fire* (1962)

49 | Nausea (1938) by Jean-Paul Sartre.

French

Translated by Robert Baldick (Penguin Modern Classics)

Antoine Roquentin, the young traveller and historian marooned in a gloomy French port city called "Bouville" that much resembles Le Havre, often snipes at made-up stories and their readers. To Roquentin, in the first-person "diaries" that make up *Nausea*, the phoney dimension of fiction belongs with the bourgeois bad faith of the establishment "Bastards", whose pompous portraits hang in the municipal museum. It smacks too of those smug "professionals in experience" – doctors, priests, magistrates, soldiers – who package their life-stories into "anecdotes wrapped in silver paper"; and of the oppressive 19th-century culture of the public library, where at random he scans a page or two of Balzac's *Eugénie Grandet.* When, horror of horrors, Roquentin actually begins to share the contentment of the town's Sunday strollers, drinkers and cinema-goers, he says: "I am as happy as the hero of a novel". In other words, an antiquated fake. Yet at the end of Jean-Paul Sartre's first novel, which both foreshadows his later work in philosophy and fiction and maps out its own self-sufficient domain, our misanthropic scoffer fondly idealises the writer and singer of an old pop song he loves. He sees this pair as "a little like the heroes of novels", who have "cleansed themselves of the sin of existing". By now, Roquentin himself longs for nothing more than the gift to write a novel himself. "Beautiful and hard as steel", this work of art will let him "recall my life without repugnance".

The later status of *Nausea* as the first, brilliant lightning-flash of existentialist thinking has proved a mixed blessing for the novel itself. Yes, Roquentin in his dismal harbour town does pass through a crisis of selfhood, and of consciousness. Scenes of hallucinatory fervour lead him into the "blinding revelation" of the absurd, gratuitous nature of his, and the world's, existence. They expose the terrifying reality of a freedom that feels "rather like death". He loses, and finds, himself: "I know that the world exists. That's all. But I don't care… Everything is gratuitous, that park, this town and myself".

The morose drifter struggles with the mind-bending "nausea" that signals his dissociation from the objects and people around him. His visionary spell of agony and ecstasy beside a chestnut tree illuminates this absurd, contingent world in all its "frightening, obscene nakedness". Roquentin's puddle-strewn road to freedom, through the recognition of his own "superfluous" existence, became a hallowed pilgrim's progress that beat a path for post-war literature and thought.

Still, for all its philosophical scaffolding, *Nausea* is more than a strikingly original "novel of ideas". Having plunged Roquentin into his vortex of naked existence, far from "the world of explanations and reasons", it then breaks with the opiate lure of pure speculation. At first, our surly researcher is engaged on the biography of an Enlightenment-era diplomat, Monsieur de Rollebon. Roquentin also remembers his slightly improbable globe-trotting over the past six years – his travels from Morocco to Cambodia, London to Berlin. These "real adventures" come to resemble vain fictions. Now, "my past is nothing more than a huge hole". Besides, "all I have ever wanted was to be free". That freedom, though, lies at the bottom of a fearful abyss. Wandering alone in this city of "tragic solitudes", he recalls his lost English lover, Anny, who later visits him. She is an actor who "changes faces". Her stage confrontations with the "black hole" of dissolving identity mirrors Roquentin's own plight. *Nausea* takes care to embody all these disorienting trains of thought in the person of an often risible narrator – an absurd guy, in every sense. His tortured anguish at vulgar mortals and their cosy homes (at the edge of Bouville, the rural "Vegetation Belt with its ghastly green paws" begins) is very funny. Despite his disdain for fictional protagonists, he lives on a secure private income, just like some Romantic swashbuckler. Moreover, he edges towards a recovered belief in the sort of story that will re-cast a simple human life – like that of the black woman vocalist in New York who sings "Some of these days" – as "something precious and almost legendary".

Roquentin might sneer at the feeble, outdated "humanism" pathetically espoused by a self-taught clerk ("the Autodidact") he often meets in the library. Whether socialist, liberal or Catholic, that fatuous faith in progress erects a "wall of complacency" like that of the frock-coated worthies – exploiters, hypocrites and reactionaries all – who hang in the gallery. But it becomes hard to read Roquentin's passage through visions of grotesque absurdity towards a place "on the other side of existence", where art consoles, music inspires and stories make sense, as anything other than a tentative rapprochement with that despised "humanism". True, the novel reaches us in the 18th-century guise of a set of posthumous journals. We presume that Roquentin – that "poor fellow who had got into the wrong world" – has lost the inner fight to square the circle of his contradictions. For Sartre, on the contrary, that tension between the bracing liberty of emptiness revealed by sheer thought – "my place is nowhere; I am unwanted" – and the countervailing attraction of stories, commitments and "adventures", would prove a lifelong stimulus. Armed with his 1200 francs a month, Roquentin quits Bouville for Paris with his cherished plan to compose a novel that will rise "above existence". Those Bastards on the museum wall could be forgiven for having the last laugh.

Translation: Robert Baldick (1963) proves valiantly equal both to Roquentin's slangy, profane confessions, and his rhapsodic episodes of philosophical dread and bliss.

See also: Rilke, *The Notebooks of Malte Laurids Brige* (1910); Céline, *Voyage to the End of the Night* (1932); Camus, *The Outsider* (1942); Beckett, *Trilogy* (1951–53)

Selected works by the same author: *The Wall* (1939); *Being and Nothingness* (1943); *No Exit* (1944); *The Roads to Freedom* (1945)

50 | The Invention of Morel (1940) by Adolfo Bioy Casares.

Spanish (Argentina)

Translated by Ruth L C Simms (New York Review Books)

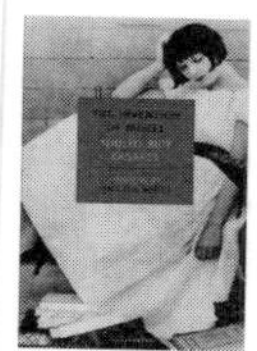

Ever since Mary Shelley dreamed of Dr Frankenstein and his unhappy creature, masterpieces of fantasy in one age have tended, in the next, to evolve into documentary reportage. This is a familiar, and gratifying, way of looking at the fantastic or speculative stories that still excite and disturb readers. We bless them because they prophesied this discovery, that technology, or some other scientific or cultural revolution. They delivered a bulletin from the future back to their baffled or benighted age.

In the 21st century, we can certainly read *The Invention of Morel* through this lens. On his Pacific island, our paranoid narrator – seemingly, a fugitive from justice in Venezuela – slowly grasps the nature of the "invention" that the sinister Morel has devised in this disease-ridden, snake-infested tropical laboratory, with its twin suns and unearthly tides. If he has not yet managed to "create human life", Morel has gone far beyond radio, television, cinema and photography – the cutting-edge communications technology of 1940 – to generate human simulacra or replicants. These living, moving holograms, the fellow islanders whose essence Morel captures, "shall live in this photograph forever". As they endlessly repeat the actions of a single week, the virtual reality figures may lack coherent memory. Still, "no one could distinguish them from living persons". Morel sees "no valid reason" to deny consciousness to the beings "created by my machinery". In this short, memorably weird, novel, Bioy Casares looks backwards to HG Wells (and sinister Dr Moreau, on his island), and forwards to the technological phantoms and dystopian landscapes of Philip K Dick and JG Ballard. With breathtaking prescience, he foreshadows the principles, and the philosophy, of virtual reality, artificial intelligence, and "post-human" selfhood in the digital age.

Mediocre writers, though, can sometimes take a successful gamble on posterity. As Morel outlines his "mechanical and artificial system for the reproduction of life", *The Invention of Morel* does much more than submit a prophetic report on VR, AI and the hi-tech alphabet soup of post-modernity. This island dystopia, with its echoes of Stevenson and Defoe, becomes, like its forerunners, the sultry setting for a philosophical inquiry into the frontiers of consciousness and identity. Perhaps these holograms, or replicants, or facsimiles, merely show us the true nature of human existence. Beings like us, who "cannot understand anything outside of time and space", might inhabit a state "not appreciably different from the survival to be obtained by this machine". Distraught, the runaway narrator wonders whether he has stumbled across "an abandoned insane asylum" – or whether he has lost his mind. As his spectral companions look and walk straight past him, he asks whether he – or they – have died. Who is haunting whom? Could he have entered their "purgatory or heaven", or have they descended "from another planet"? Otherwise, "I think I must be in hell". Faustine, with whom the narrator falls in love but can never talk, resembles some movie idol desired and worshipped through a screen – and was apparently inspired by the silent era diva Louise Brooks. Eventually, the narrator grasps that he can only join the "private paradise" of this second life by forfeiting the first. If "the images have souls", then "the transmitters lose theirs", once cloned by the machines that Morel tends in his hotel-museum on the island.

Both a disciple of his fellow-Argentinian Jorge Luis Borges, and a deep influence on the older writer, Bioy Casares writes with all the playful irony and lucidity that allowed both maverick authors to retool and renovate the fiction of adventure and fantasy. Via the strange phenomenon of Morel's island, this "magical occurrence" or "negation of reality", Bioy Casares helped re-engineer a rusty genre. His story speeds into realms of the imagination unvisited by the modernist fiction of his day.

Borges used his introduction to the novel's first edition as a manifesto for his model of the plot-driven, ideas-laden adventure, more metaphysical than psychological. This kind of fiction aims not to mimic reality but to delight and perplex the reader with "an odyssey of marvels", an "artificial object, no part of which lacks justification". It seems fitting that the anti-realism machine devised by Dr Borges performed its first great feat with this account of a megalomaniac inventor, who seeks to copy nature so perfectly that he has to kill his raw material. Meanwhile, the shadows from Morel's island flit across the internet, which Bioy Casares just about lived to see. Cyberspace preserves our virtual selves "in a vision that no one can ever destroy".

Translation: Ruth L C Simms's 1964 text has just that dry neutrality, poised between pedantry and nightmare, that suits this report from technological limbo.

See also: Voltaire, *Candide* (1759); Kafka, *The Trial* (1925); Lem, *Solaris* (1961); Murakami, *Hard-Boiled Wonderland and the End of the World* (1985)

Selected works by the same author: *A Plan for Escape* (1945); *The Dream of Heroes* (1954); *Diary of the War of the Pig* (1969)

51 | The Tartar Steppe (1940) by Dino Buzzati.

Italian

Translated by Stuart Hood (Canongate)

On "a dead stretch of frontier", where "nothing had ever happened", a young lieutenant joins the army unit that staffs Fort Bastiani. It guards against the potential threat of raid or invasion from a "legendary kingdom" across the bare steppes in the Northern Territories. Although the camp doctor tells him that "everybody comes here by mistake", Giovanni Drogo at the outset treats this first posting as a preparation for a great and glorious battle. It will ensue, so he imagines, when the Northerners cross the plains to wage war among the mountain peaks, cliffs and crests where the lonely fort stands. This story seems to unfold in the storm-swept outpost of some 19th-century European power. Drogo has quit a bourgeois city of cafés, balls, railways and promenades, although only horses ever serve the Fort. Its soldiers' names suggest mixed origins – the commanding officer is Colonel Filimore – while the invisible Tartars of the Northern Kingdom hint at a medieval, perhaps oriental, tradition.

In any case, nothing continues to happen. As the seasons dramatically change around these crags, valleys and summits, years stretch into decades. A "mysterious torpor" seizes and immobilises Drogo. He returns to the city on leave, only to ride back to the Fort and its rigid, meaningless routines as if magnetised by some occult power. Periodic false alarms respond to every suspicion of strategic preparations – road-building, frontier-surveying – out on the desolate steppe, which had "mystery but no meaning". Then, as usual, normal inactivity resumes. Apparently irreparable, the cistern outside Drogo's quarters drips, year in, year out. His youth fades, and with it the hopeful sense of standing "on the threshold of the wonders awaiting us".

Yet "the winds of time are blowing", a little fiercer every season. Drogo plods through middle-age still with some "deep-rooted presentiment of great events". Are those moving specks on the horizon, revealed only by telescopes that the high command then bans, signs that the enemy plans at long last to invade? Drogo concludes that "the Northern steppe will always remain deserted", but he keeps at his absurd post. More than three decades pass; his health fails. He must journey down the valley to die at an isolated inn, "a much harder battle than the one he once hoped for". Has he squandered his life entirely in vain? At this point, with the ineluctable logic of dream or myth, we learn that new black lines sighted on the steppe apparently presage a genuine attack from the North. Drogo must die forgotten after "thirty years of torture merely waiting for the enemy". Fresh recruits will reap "the rewards of glory".

An unclassifiable marvel, Buzzati's third novel was written in 1938 as he worked, himself a slave to repetitive drudgery, as a night editor on a Milan newspaper. Aside from its affinities with the universe of Kafka, *The Tartar Steppe* invites all manner of interpretation through the gates of its own "enchanted castle". Somehow, it resists them all. Its mystery derives from its clarity. Buzzati writes with an easy, graceful and compelling lucidity. He delineates each feature of the Fort, the "iron rules" of its rituals and the inhuman grandeur of the surrounding mountains – whose actual counterparts in Italy the author loved to explore – with sober realism. Scenes of barracks comedy, as the bored troops spar and plot, deepen the verisimilitude. As patrols scour the mountains, Buzzati endows this landscape, sublime and sinister, with an almost cinematic colour. We could not be further from the overloaded symbolism of some arm-twisting allegory. Yes, existential, religious or political readings shimmer over the summits of this novel, composed on the eve of total war. For Drogo himself, the Fort's monotony becomes the dreary abode of life itself. Entered in joy, occupied in hope, at length it declines into "a kind of illness", a state in which all expectation withers as we grasp that "a gate has been bolted behind us, barring our way back".

A pilgrim's progress, an experiment in speculative fantasy, a philosophical parable, a topical prophecy: *The Tartar Steppe* wraps many genres within its enigmatic mists and snows. In the end it eludes definition, just as, to the watching sentries, those flickering specks of light across the steppe never quite coalesce into a firm military shape. The novel's own densely-etched reality exerts such a mesmeric hold on the reader that, like Drogo, we cease to speculate. We too overcome "the vague feeling of punishment and exile" that nags him early in his lifetime sentence. He has chosen this forsaken bastion of solitude and inanition – unless he never had a choice. Those presumed Tartar hordes, meanwhile, exist only as a "remote legend". Until the day that they arrive.

Translation: Clear-voiced and fine-grained, Stuart Hood's 1952 rendering captures all of Buzzati's hypnotic allure.

See also: Mann, *The Magic Mountain* (1924); Kafka, *The Trial* (1925); Bioy Casares, *The Invention of Morel* (1940); Lem, *Solaris* (1961)

Selected works by the same author: *The Bears' Famous Invasion of Sicily* (1945); *Larger than Life* (1960); *A Love Affair* (1963)

52 | THE MASTER AND MARGARITA (1928-40; published in full 1973) by Mikhail Bulgakov.

Russian

Translated by Hugh Aplin (Alma Classics)

Tormented by insomnia, the unquiet spirit of Pontius Pilate, Procurator of Judea, fears that the cowardice he showed when he surrendered the virtuous Jesus of Nazareth for execution ranks as "the gravest sin". Literary cowardice was one sin that the author of *The Master and Margarita* conspicuously lacked. Inset into this novel, the story of Pilate's encounter with the vagrant philosopher Yeshua (Jesus) punctuates a wild fictional ride through the Moscow of the 1930s. Mikhail Bulgakov's multi-dimensional fantasia crosses so many lines and breaks so many taboos that it still astonishes with its boundary-busting, free-form modernity. The year before his death, Bulgakov (who had spent much of his creative life in disgrace with Soviet authorities) horrified friends by telling them that he intended to approach a State publisher with this most incendiary of works. Well, "Manuscripts don't burn," as the Devil tells the Master (a downtrodden novelist, and the ostensible author of the Pontius Pilate story) in this book's most celebrated line. But in Stalin's Moscow their makers ran risks of both professional and physical annihilation. Those risks rose steeply during the decade that the multi-talented Bulgakov – doctor, fiction-writer, dramatist, biographer – revised this stupendously inventive work. In the event, he would die in 1940 not in the gulag but of inherited kidney disease. His magical, satirical bombshell would wait a quarter-century even for partial publication. The sense of living, and writing, on the edge of a precipice stokes the novel's mood of febrile exaltation; a careering excitement like that of Margarita as she gallops with the Devil on flying horses through "the black shawl of night".

Satan, or rather Professor Woland, has arrived in Soviet Russia in the guise of an itinerant magician. An urbane "visiting consultant from abroad", he is trailed by an entourage that includes the sassy, jive-talking giant tomcat Behemoth and the fanged evil angel Azazello. Initially, Satan/Woland overturns the craven existence of the poetic hack Ivan Bezdomny ("homeless") and contrives to have the literary apparatchik Berlioz decapitated by a Moscow tram. (The composer Berlioz wrote a *Damnation of Faust*, and Bulgakov spritzes his double plot with allusions to the legend, especially in Goethe's version.) As Woland brings "all sorts of absurd commotions" to the political intriguers and social arrivistes of Moscow, the Pontius Pilate strand challenges Soviet atheism – and one-party dictatorship – with its tale of a free-thinking vagabond destroyed by secular authority. State literati rebuke the Master for writing "an apologia for Jesus Christ". They set the critics on him, and send him to the asylum – an unavoidable destination in this madhouse of a city. Margarita, meanwhile, has fled her defunct marriage to seek love and fulfilment with the Master. That mission, it turns out, requires the tainted assistance of the demonic, charismatic Woland, with his eye "like the entrance to a bottomless well of all kinds of darkness and shadows".

Woland pulls off his greatest conjuror's coup in the Variety Theatre. He showers the greedy public – hardly an advertisement for socialist asceticism – with free money, posh perfume and fancy frocks. The novel, too, unrolls in a series of spectacular turns, orchestrated by a backstage wizard (Bulgakov had experienced spells of both triumph and disaster at the Moscow Art Theatre). This all-star cabaret takes in metaphysical dialogue, social and literary satire, against-the-odds romance and a head-spinning vein of witches' Sabbath fantasy. It feels, simultaneously, archaic and hyper-modern in its style. To secure Woland's favour, Margarita agrees to host the Devil's Spring Ball: both a decadent phantasmagoria, down to the "simian jazz band" and "polar bears playing accordions", and an upgrade into grotesque delirium of an actual party Bulgakov attended at the US Embassy. Here, outsized cats and naked witches may slip at will through the porous membrane that separates reality and fantasy. Bulgakov lets rips as Woland and his crew unleash mayhem among the climbers, sneaks and grovellers of Soviet Moscow. Some of his most striking images, however, take a subtler course. A foxtrotting sparrow, sinister like many creatures here, pecks "as if with a beak of steel" at the photograph of "an entire university graduation class". This happens as Stalin, the "Man of Steel", begins to eradicate entire generations of Moscow's most talented citizens with no Satanic help.

Woland's supernatural aid may, in some dimension, reunite Margarita with her hapless, idealistic author-swain. In a gnostic twist to the Pilate debate, he challenges the one-dimensional goodness of Yeshua and his clan: "Do you want to strip the whole earth bare?" Shadows and contrast, light and shade, alone give depth and meaning to the human scene. Even in dreary Moscow, which proves a bit of a let-down. "I like Rome better," confesses the shape-shifting sidekick Azazello. Once the infernal gang quit the city, the authorities tidy up history and re-write this outbreak of "blatant devilry" and "clear-cut criminality". A band of "criminal hypnotists" has simply deluded the people. Cats, in particular, suffer cruel reprisals, and learn – as did humans – "what error and slander are". But even the tamed Ivan, later a respectable professor, cannot control the "spring full moon". The sheer devilry of art, of love, of imagination, will ride again in anarchic triumph over Moscow, over all our lives.

Translation: Several English versions now compete; Hugh Aplin's (2007) impressively combines verve, pace and colloquial wit with a scholarly scrutiny of this fiercely contested manuscript.

See also: Gogol, *Dead Souls* (1842); Dostoyevsky, *The Brothers Karamazov* (1880); Bely, *Petersburg* (1916-22); Cabrera Infante, *Three Trapped Tigers* (1965)

Selected works by same author: *Heart of a Dog* (1925); *The White Guard* (1925); *A Country Doctor's Notebook* (1927); *Black Snow* (1967)

53 | The Outsider (1942) by Albert Camus.

French (Algeria/France)

Translated by Sandra Smith (Penguin Modern Classics)

It's not quite the case that Meursault has no regrets when this mediocre clerk shoots five bullets into an unnamed Arab on a beach outside Algiers. After the first shot, he realises that in this god-free temple of sun and sea, he has "destroyed the natural balance of the day". Then he fires four more times, those sharp raps on "the fatal door of destiny". That salvo will help convince judges and jurors that he is a monster of "cold indifference" with an "abyss" where his soul should be. Thus he deserves the guillotine. Yet the clinching evidence of Meursault's depravity derives not from this pitiless execution of an anonymous member of a colonised people in the French Algeria of the 1940s. It lies in his impassive reaction to his mother's death in an old people's home. For the prosecutor at his trial, "the first crime", of his refusal to show overt emotion at his mother's funeral, "paved the way for the second". Meursault must lose his head because of its tearless eyes.

Its prose as dry and fierce as the relentless sun that beats down upon Algiers, Albert Camus's short first-person narrative offers the reader a face almost as blank and inscrutable as Meursault's own. The French title, *L'Etranger*, carries the meanings of outsider, stranger and foreigner: a triple layer of alienation that resists all single track interpretation. Although publication coincided with the Algerian-born author's first major philosophical essay, *The Myth of Sisyphus*, attempts to fold *The Outsider* into Camus's mature thought tend to hit the rocks. In the condemned cell, Meursault does refer to "this absurd life I have lived". Mostly, he remains too frail, too directionless a vehicle to carry Camus's fully-formed reflections on the duties of integrity and solidarity that come with a clear-eyed recognition of the absurd contingency of human life and (as Meursault's monologue puts it) "the tender indifference of the world". This nondescript nobody who likes little more than swimming, sunshine and sex with his girlfriend Marie only begins to grow into an embryonic Camusian hero at the last gasp of the book. He confesses that he killed "the

Arab" (the namelessness of his victim tells its own, troubling story) "because of the sun". That sun, as it greets the morning walker with "a slap across the face" or erupts in an "explosion" at high noon, is the closest that Meursault comes to an idea of divinity. This burning godhead will both bless and curse: "The dazzling sky was unbearable." Camus would later flesh out his "Mediterranean" ethics and aesthetics of life in harmony with nature. Meursault himself is more empty-headed beach rat than eco-friendly metaphysician.

Like the lawyers who trace their own designs on this blank human canvas in court, or the prison chaplain who chips in vain at Meursault's belief that "there is nothing after death", critics inscribe Camus's narrator with the features of their creeds. They may reframe as a sociopathic condition his coldness during the sun-strafed funeral of "Mama", although he recognises that his dead parent has recovered a sort of freedom. So "No-one – no-one – had the right to cry over her". As for the murder itself, it arises from a squalid confluence of racial and sexual violence. The "Arabs" are following Meursault's neighbour, the pimp Raymond, because with Meursault's connivance he has brutalised his mistress. She is an Algerian woman rather than a white French settler. Critics have frequently argued that Camus becomes complicit in the dehumanising cruelties of the colonial regime, which finds in Meursault such a willing drone. The writer Kamel Daoud has recently turned *The Outsider* on its head to retell its story, from the Algerians' perspective, in *The Meursault Investigation*. But we do see that this casual killer lacks empathy or conscience much as he lacks God, or even love. His scale of values hardly extends beyond the touch of Marie's tanned, strong body, "the scent of summer", or "a certain type of sky at night". We must fill Meursault's abyss. He cannot – at least until the closing pages – fill it for himself.

In its harsh, flat, noonday beauty, *The Outsider* challenges the reader to restore all the shades of meaning bleached out of consciousness by Meursault's neutralised progress through a moral landscape "emptied of hope". Camus was the opposite of a nihilist, but *The Outsider* suggests that the reader – not the author – must begin the work of reconstruction on this stony ground. The examining magistrate takes Meursault's apathetic atheism as a personal insult: "'Do you want my life to have no meaning?' he shouted. In my opinion, that was none of my business and I told him so." It is, pre-eminently, ours. Meursault, the "Antichrist" to his aghast scrutineers, can still shock and unsettle us, whether as impenitent unbeliever, as neglectful son, as heedless racist, abusive misogynist, or simply as the man who shrugs off the guilt that society loads on him. He finds his death sentence "ridiculously out of proportion" to the evidence of his crime. Camus spent the rest of his career seeking to restore proportion, and perspective, to a world that had lost its frame and its depth. To do that, however, you must stare hard into Meursault's "blinding sun" of nothingness.

Translation: Although Stuart Gilbert's 1946 version retains its authority, Sandra Smith (2012) updates Meursault's voice without discarding its uncanny strangeness.

See also: Dostoyevsky, *The Brothers Karamazov* (1880); Hamsun, *Hunger* (1890); Arlt, *The Seven Madmen* (1929); Sartre, *Nausea* (1938)

Selected works by the same author: *The Myth of Sisyphus* (1942); *The Plague* (1947); *The Rebel* (1951); *The Fall* (1956)

54 | Suite Française (1942; published 2004) by Irène Némirovsky.

French

Translated by Sandra Smith (Vintage)

History makes literature and also breaks it. In the case of Irène Némirovsky, the Nazi genocide both ended her life and, after her murder in Auschwitz, ensured that her projected five-part epic of the fall of France remained incomplete, and invisible. Rediscovered by her daughter, the two completed movements of *Suite Française* survive as the magnificent prelude to an unfinished, tragic symphony. War and invasion smashed her grand design just as it wrecks the lives and hopes of her characters. Even in its truncated

form, this interrupted epic has a beauty, grace and energy denied to almost all the polished monuments of Second World War fiction.

Born in Kiev to a Jewish banking family, Irène Némirovsky became a serial French bestseller during the 1930s. Little in these books' social and satirical intrigues foreshadows the impact of *Suite Française,* which she began after her flight from Paris in the wake of the German occupation. Grand in conception but intimate in execution, the book paints a funeral portrait of France in defeat, "as it loses its honour and its life". In a working note, Némirovsky reminded herself that an epic theme does not requires a solemn tone: "the historical... facts must be only lightly touched upon, while daily life, emotional life and especially the comedy it provides must be described in detail". From the atmosphere of her high-society novels, she did carry over a gift for the comedy of manners, and a gimlet eye for snobbery and pretension. These attributes lend *Suite Française* a surprisingly urbane perspective on national catastrophe.

The two completed volumes, "Storm in June" and "Dolce", have distinct moods and forms. "Storm" intercuts between groups of characters in an exciting, and often bitterly comic, social collage, as Parisians rich and poor, noble and venal, flee the city and seek refuge in the countryside. For grand clans such as the Péricands, "the compassion of centuries of civilisation fell... like useless ornaments". In this bustling, sensuous fresco, future collaborators plot survival strategies under the new order. Amid all the cowardice and compromise the humble, decent Michauds bewail their "bad luck to be born in century full of storms". As she wrote in the heat, even the thrill, of the moment, her satirist's lens pans from one little drama of bad faith or betrayal to another. Némirovsky seems almost to concur with a contemporary sense of the French collapse as some kind of punishment for "decadence". As society rots, however, spring blooms. Like Zola or Turgenev, Némirovsky draws on natural beauty to counterpoint the passion and panic of erring humankind.

In "Dolce", less cinematic and more lyrical, the tone sweetens, but the feelings deepen. In occupied Bussy, the still-polite and even apprehensive German conquerors get to know the women of the town. Their presence stirs a range of feelings – from loathing to lust – that Némirovsky captures with unsparing honesty. Defeat exposes the toxic hatreds between classes, families and generations that have festered in this "affluent but primitive" backwater of France. Offstage, the Resistance begins to stir. Her notes reveal that it would have come to the fore in the (unwritten) next volume.

In the wealthy Angellier household, the unhappy young wife Lucy – her husband a prisoner-of-war – befriends and even begins to love a billeted German officer, a charming and gentlemanly pianist. She thinks of their liaison as "like stroking a wild animal". As "Dolce" concludes, news of the invasion of the Soviet Union arrives to coincide with an elegant but doom-laden garden party at the local château. Such scenes have a sweeping, panoramic, almost Tolstoy-like sense of perspective. Yet Némirovsky composed them in haste, a victim-to-be in the eye of the terrible storm.

Her irony, her romanticism, even her sometimes erratic moral compass, give *Suite Française* a freshness and immediacy to match its delight in the surfaces of life. The deathly ideology that consumed her denied Némirovsky the wisdom of hindsight or the analytic grasp of French defeat developed, for instance, by Sartre in his *Roads to Freedom* trilogy. Instead, she captures moments of crisis in all their shock, their absurdity – even their tenderness and humour. As the courtly officer plays Scarlatti for her, Lucille thinks, "This is for ever". That yearning for permanence is drenched in bitter irony for the author as much as the character.

The emergency that gave Némirovsky her great theme also robbed her of the chance to fulfil its possibilities. Add to this curtailed destiny the disappearance of the manuscript for more than fifty years, and *Suite Française* commands a peculiar status. Here is a novel of huge historical upheavals written without the privilege of contemplative distance, but instead wrenched from circumstances in a desperate bid to pluck order out of chaos. Sentimental critics like to pretend that great art can vanquish evil and, by the skin of its teeth, the notebook containing Némirovsky's crowning achievement did survive to be discovered. But the racial tyranny that killed her also left the book a splendid ruin. We will never know how many other masterworks it stifled prior to their first breath.

Translation: Sandra Smith's 2006 version captures the lyric grace and rhythmic flow of Némirovsky's prose, and her flair for acid satire.

See also: Tolstoy, *War and Peace* (1869); Grass, *The Tin Drum* (1959); Grossman, *Life and Fate* (1959); Bassani, *The Garden of the Finzi-Continis* (1962)

Selected works by the same author: *David Golder* (1929); *The Wine of Solitude* (1935); *Jezebel* (1936); *All Our Worldly Goods* (1947)

55 | Near to the Wild Heart (1943) by Clarice Lispector.

Portuguese (Brazil)

Translated by Alison Entrekin (Penguin Modern Classics)

What can a novelist in their very early twenties know about life? The example of Mary Shelley, nineteen when she published *Frankenstein*, suggests an answer: almost anything, and above all those hidden or forbidden truths that frightened or blinkered maturity might deny. Clarice Lispector, born in Ukraine but brought as an infant to Brazil, also began her literary progress as a youthful prodigy. In *Near to the Wild Heart,* however, her monster lies within. In part a tumbling, rushing, rhapsodic stream of consciousness, in part a more straightforward story of a gifted, solitary girl who marries rashly and repents at leisure, it illuminates a young woman's growth in lightning flashes of scorching beauty and intensity. Joana, who seems "so restless, so thin and precocious" to the worried father who will soon die, feels from childhood like a "perfect animal". She is a wild creature set apart from society both by her burning passions and (even more) her cool intelligence.

"Solitude mingled with my essence," she will later tell her husband, Otavio. As a girl, she thinks of herself as "a viper all on my own". If so, she envenoms her own mind rather than strikes others. At the same time, she exults in her difference, her strangeness, as a "free and solitary creature" with access to moments of vision and revelation that no one else can know or share. "She was in herself, her own end."

Near to the Wild Heart owes its title to James Joyce's *A Portrait of the Artist as a Young Man*. The torrential introspection of Joana's story confirms that side of her literary lineage. In childhood, during adolescence, as a thrilled lover and then a thwarted wife, every epiphany flows through a super-heated imagination that transforms experience, "bubbling like a sheet of hot lava". Joana's home element, though, is not fire but water. She loves the sea; marine metaphors wash across the book, the inner landscape for a heroine who pulses to "the tidal wave of blood". Through "the dark cavities of her body, waves come surging, light, fresh and ancient". This liquid language gives expression to a sense of selfhood forever seeping or flooding over the boundaries of assigned roles. As a daughter, a pupil, a lover, a spouse, the cascading realities of her body, and her mind, wash away the defences family and society build around her. Others, such as the aunt she lives with as an orphan, find something demonic in this breaching of boundaries. In childhood, Joana fears that "I'm heading for evil". In one of the novel's many starbursts of synaesthetic imagery, she imagines evil's taste: "chewing crimson, devouring sweetened fire".

Alongside this drama of heightened consciousness, a more conventional narrative unfolds. Joana marries the law student and would-be philosopher, Otavio. He returns to his former girlfriend Lidia, now pregnant with their child. She confronts Lidia, viewing herself as a scrawny de-sexed outcast next to the "tranquil, primary matter" of Lidia's stolid, ample femininity. Joana seeks solace with a mysterious stranger, dives into despair but then surfaces to seek – via a sea voyage – a new life that will allow her true self to flourish: "I shall rise as strong and comely as young colt."

Lispector interrupts Joana's flow of sensations to show the separate perspectives of Otavio and Lidia, even of the teacher who becomes a surrogate father to her. With Joana herself, we move seamlessly between first- and third-person narration. She always lives in a solid social milieu, a member of a privileged professional caste, even as she feels herself "leaning away from the earth and out into space". In its verbal creativity and psychological urgency, *Near to the Wild Heart* stands an ocean apart from the brand of South American fiction that revels in flamboyant local lore and colour. Still, Lispector's few concessions to her Brazilian setting do stand out: the teacher's mischievous black servant, for example, or passing references to the carnival season.

At root, Joana's journey to the interior takes place in the undiscovered lands of girlhood and womanhood. "What I desire," Joana muses, "still has no name." In its quest for a flowing, flooding language of female selfhood, *Near to the Wild Heart* would inspire later generations of feminists: in Europe as much as the Americas, theorists and novelists alike. Later books would extend Lispector's reach but, arguably, never shine brighter than this astonishing debut. Its heroine becomes not just a sea or river but a forest: the human equivalent of her continent's vast hinterland, still awaiting discovery and acknowledgement. "Raindrops and stars," Lispector writes, "opened the gates of this green and sombre forest, of this forest smelling of an abyss where water flows." In that moist abyss she finds both terrors and treasures.

Translation: Both Alison Entrekin (2012) and Giovanni Pontiero (1990) catch the lyrical excitement of Joana's inner voyage, and her fierce intellectual clarity.

See also: Rilke, *The Notebooks of Malte Laurids Brigge* (1910); Sartre, *Nausea* (1938); Wolf, *The Quest for Christa T* (1968); Duras, *The Lover* (1984)

Selected works by the same author: *Family Ties* (1960); *The Apple in the Dark (1961); The Passion According to G.H.* (1964); *The Hour of the Star* (1977)

56 | The Bridge on the Drina (1945) by Ivo Andrić.

Serbo-Croatian (Yugoslavia)

Translated by Lovett F Edwards (Harvill Press)

Landmark novels need not have a single hero. Neither does a village, a city or even a house have to anchor a far-reaching plot. *The Bridge on the Drina*, which spans four centuries and the rise and fall of two vast empires, takes as its focus the actual monument that gives the book its title. It is a "great clean-cut stone bridge with eleven wide sweeping arches" across the river that runs through the Bosnian town of Višegrad, east of Sarajevo. For centuries it has served as a "link between East and West", a meeting place of faiths and communities that both marked frontiers and crossed them. The bridge and its town host Andrić's teeming, rushing assembly of the yarns, legends and myths thrown up by almost half a millennium of change and conflict on this spot.

History happens willy-nilly to the people around the bridge – Christian Serbs, Muslim Bosniaks (whom Andrić, following local usage, calls "Turks"), Jews, Gypsies, Czechs, Austrians and more – even though, he insists, they alter little. Easy-going and in general tolerant, they may gossip, brawl and feud, sometimes lethally. But the pursuit of happiness drives them, through "an immoderate love of women, an inclination to alcohol, song, lounging and idle dreaming beside their native river". Over that stream, the Ottoman-built bridge stands as a proof of permanence and a guarantor of continuity, so solid and ageless that it "resembled eternity".

Writing under house-arrest in German-occupied Belgrade during the early 1940s, Andrić anticipates – and arguably, with this revered novel, helped to forge – the post-war ideal of Yugoslavia as an integrated ethnic patchwork in which unity sheltered diversity. Although it closes as the First World War breaks out, his novel in effect became the fictional bible of Yugoslavia until the nation's breakdown after 1990 into civil war. As the story ends, and the catastrophe of summer 1914 draws a final line under the mingled traditions of bridge and town, the narrator admits that "there had always been concealed enmities and jealousies and religious intolerance" here, not to mention "coarseness and cruelty". Mostly, however, "courage and fellowship and a feeling for measure and order" flowed through the minds and lives of local folk.

For all his emphasis on mutual respect and co-existence, Andrić designs his 350-year-long fresco of tales as a chronicle of clashes, tensions and even horrors – both in private and public life. The bridge itself exists thanks to the forced abduction of Christian children in an annual levy from the borderlands of the Ottoman empire. One of them, a historical figure, rises at the Sultan's court in Istanbul to become the Grand Vizier Mehmed Paša Sokolović, patron of the bridge (built in the 1560s) that still bears his name. As Ottoman engineers edify this grand instrument of control and contact, morbid folk tales cling to it. Saboteurs try to damage it. The impalement of one would-be wrecker, Radisav, provides both a tour de force of gory prose and a heavily symbolic episode, as despotic power splits ordinary humankind apart.

Andrić is sometimes accused of hostility to the Muslim past of his native Bosnia, and a corresponding prejudice in favour of his own, Serbian, heritage. In fact, he takes care to differentiate the characters of different faiths who live, trade, love, quarrel and die around the bridge from the two imperial systems, Ottoman and Habsburg, that demand their loyalty. Drama succeeds drama – a reluctant bride's suicide, a ruined gambler's tipsy dance along the parapet, great floods and the heroic solidarity they inspire – whichever distant capital claims sovereignty over the bridge. In the 1870s, with the Ottoman lands "consumed by a slow fever", Serbian revolt leads not to independence but Habsburg takeover and the eventual arrival of bureaucratic Austro-Hungarian rule from Vienna. The peremptory, intimate atmosphere of Ottoman power yields to an "impersonal and indirect" government of regulations and statistics.

The modern world intrudes. A railway line bypasses the town and leaves the Grand Vizier's stone gift to his homeland "abandoned like a stranded ship or a deserted shrine". Patriotic students squabble and plot. Some hail the coming triumph of "modern nationalism" over "religious diversities". Then, after the assassination of Archduke Franz Ferdinand in Sarajevo and the descent into European war, "the wild beast which lives in man" but which "barriers of law and custom" restrain "was now set free". No longer invulnerable, the bridge is blown part by artillery bombardment. The independent-minded Muslim shopkeeper Alihodja watches the calamity and curses an "impure infidel faith": not the Christianity or Judaism of his neighbours, but ravening modernity itself, which "might make of all God's world an empty field for its senseless building and criminal destruction". The dread of modern sectarian hatred which clouds the final scenes of Andrić's novel proved all too prophetic. During the bloody fragmentation of his beloved Yugoslavia in 1992, Bosnian Serb paramilitaries massacred Muslim neighbours on and beside the bridge.

Translation: Lovett F Edwards's 1959 translation may grate when it follows the terminology of Andrić's time, but its rich period colours and moods suit the novel's tone.

See also: Musil, *The Man Without Qualities* (1930-1943); Roth, *The Radetzky March* (1932); García Márquez, *One Hundred Years of Solitude* (1967); Husain, *Basti* (1979)

Selected works by the same author: *Bosnian Chronicle* (1945); *The Woman from Sarajevo* (1954); *The Damned Yard* (1954)

57 | Only Yesterday (1945) by SY Agnon (Shmuel-Yoysef Tshatshkes).

Hebrew (Austria-Hungary/Palestine/Israel)

Translated by Barbara Harshav (Princeton University Press)

Isaac Kumer, the naïve and drifting hero of *Only Yesterday*, runs across various kinds of storytellers, writers, preachers and teachers during his adventures in the Holy Land – which, in the early 20th-century of this novel's setting, was a neglected and disputed province of the Ottoman Empire. Outside the port of Jaffa, an idealistic secular Zionist named Gorishkin works as a labourer on the housing project that will grow into the city of Tel Aviv: "By day he transports sand and at night he writes memoirs." Like

Gorishkin, every one of the Jewish immigrants or long-settled residents Isaac meets has a story, a sermon, a fable or a manifesto at hand. Our impressionable protagonist must navigate not only the hardships of the poor migrant's lot – after a failed stint as a farm labourer, he works as a jobbing house and sign painter – but find his way across the shifting sand of rival testimonies and doctrines. Even on the packed train that takes him from his remote Galician birthplace to Trieste (where he boards a ship for Palestine), Isaac is assailed by a never-ending "Quarrel" over Zionism, secularism, faith, doubt and identity. That "Quarrel" will endure throughout this picaresque, tumultuous and wonderfully eccentric novel.

Published in Hebrew in 1945, but rooted in SY Agnon's experience as an incomer to Ottoman Palestine during the so-called "Second Aliyah" of immigration in the decade before 1914, *Only Yesterday* will bewilder any reader who expects to find a realistic epic about the building of a Jewish homeland. Rather, Agnon makes Isaac the slightly dim-witted centrepiece of a mind-bending tapestry of scripture, folklore, history, politics and myth. The result is as curious, colourful and enchanting as the paintings of his near-exact contemporary, Marc Chagall. From café to synagogue, from seaside to desert, Agnon's Palestine seethes with competing stories, competing languages. Well-meaning, weak-willed Isaac, the "man of imagination", bounces in a daze between Jaffa and Jerusalem, "Labour Zionism" and sectarian Orthodoxy, socialism and fundamentalism – not to mention the flesh and the spirit. Agnon's storytelling has the rhythmical pulse and drive of a Bible episode, or a rabbinical parable. Behind the revived Hebrew that his own work helped to shape, the Yiddish of his youth gossips, jokes and sings. Deadpan comedy and barbed one-liners abound. (About scurrilous newspapers: "Good news they don't announce, and bad news flies by itself".) The narrator buttonholes us, digresses, interrupts. A vibrant oral tradition speaks on in his prose.

Then there's Balak: one of the most memorable animals in all fiction. Balak is a Jerusalem street-dog whom in a skittish moment Isaac paints with the Hebrew words, "Crazy Dog". Thereafter, his ordeals, shown from Balak's perplexed point of view, break into Isaac's story. The hound becomes a scapegoat. "What is my crime?" Balak yelps. "Bereft of a critical spirit" he may be, but this afflicted canine Job trots free of the prejudices that divide his human tormentors. Balak "saw the world as one whole". He becomes a celebrity; the press and the squabbling migrant communities divide over his significance: "Iraqis say don't rejoice, Yemenites say rejoice." Agnon's many-layered shaggy-dog excursion will end in disaster, but not before Balak acquires the bark of a prophet who howls to the stars over Jerusalem that "there was no just judge".

Agnon also strews fragments of what will become the founding myths of Israel across his plot. Around Jaffa, "the citrus groves gladden the eye"; the house-building scheme has rescued the future Tel Aviv from "desolation", so now it is "humming like a settled land". Arab workers, fellow-proletarians, figure as folkloric "enemies", but Isaac witnesses the ploys of divide-and-rule bosses. He sees that the Arabs come "not for war but for work". Legend and spin, hope and hype, skew every tale. Isaac's "ascent" into the Holy Land begins amid Austro-Hungarian propaganda for a bountiful empire, "blessed with everything". In Palestine he is bombarded with the homilies of mystical rabbis, the speeches of trade union militants, the pipe dreams of café-table scribblers. Agnon teases each Utopian dream with the sting of his sly ironies. Wisdom eludes even poor Balak: "I, who possess the truth, don't know what it is."

Agnon's life-long immersion in the Torah, the Talmud and a groaning storehouse of Jewish lore enriches every page. This inherited faith, though, resists practical incarnation. Under the Levantine sun, it crumbles into ritualism, fanaticism or kitsch. Isaac has entered "the house of doubt". When his pilgrim's progress leads him from his artistic girlfriend Sonya in Jaffa ("a great actress she didn't become") to the ultra-Orthodox rabbi's daughter Shifra in Jerusalem, their marriage appears not as a sanctified homecoming but as one more wrong turning for a not-so-holy fool. Agnon no more endorses the backstreet superstition of Jerusalem than the progressive windbaggery of Jaffa. When the rabbi denounces a generation "which has not created a new life but has gone away from the old", his jeremiads hardly amount to an author's signature.

If Agnon opts to throw his ironic weight behind any perspective except Balak's, it's that of the truth-seeking artist. Working as a "smearer" of house walls, Isaac befriends the painter Bloykof and learns about the "lives of grief and suffering" that artists lead. Much later, the owl Lilith tells Balak about a hyena immortalised by stuffing at the hands of the taxidermist Arzef, "the artist who made me live for ever". In this generous compendium of fugitive visions and thwarted dreams, the preserved likeness of an unlovely creature is as near as these seekers and wanderers may come to a glimpse of eternity in the promised land.

Translation: Admirably often, Barbara Harshav (2000) hits the right, mingled note for Agnon's unique alloy of folksiness and sophistication.

See also: Hašek, *The Good Soldier Švejk* (1923); Singer, *The Slave* (1962); Salih, *Season of Migration to the North* (1966); Grossman, *See Under: LOVE* (1986)

Selected works by the same author: *The Bridal Canopy* (1931); *A Simple Story (1935); A Guest for the Night* (1939); *Shira* (1971)

58 | The Makioka Sisters (1946-48) by Jun'ichirō Tanizaki.

Japanese

Translated by Edward G Seidensticker (Vintage)

When Yukiko Makioka and her sisters scent another ageing suitor in the wings, the usual alarm bells ring. "Wealthy bachelors past forty generally had something wrong with them." Once spoilt for matrimonial choice, Yukiko has passed thirty. A place on the spinsterhood shelf beckons. Beautician Mrs Itani, the local matchmaker, must look harder for the right sort of groom. In the fast-developing Japan of the late 1930s, the illustrious name of Makioka no longer lifts the social weight that once it could. Has the family entered an irreversible cycle of decline? Besides, neighbours suspect that this merchant clan of Osaka "made too much of family and prestige".

All the same,"stubborn" Yukiko will again go through the matchmaking motions – the "miai" – with another gauche, or widowed, gent who carries with him a respectable lineage and income. Meanwhile, elder sisters Tsuruko and Sachiko, mistresses of the "senior" and "junior" branches of the house, struggle with their husbands to hold the family together – and to prevent wild child Taeko from running off the rails. "The skeleton in the family closet", the "heretic" Taeko falls into entanglements with unsuitable men. She pursues her dream of an independent career as an artistic doll-maker or – worse – a fashion designer. "If dress-making was vulgar, let it be vulgar."

Western devotees of novelists such as Jane Austen or Vikram Seth (whose *A Suitable Boy* owes a heavy debt to Tanizaki's masterpiece) will marvel at *The Makioka Sisters*. As a beautifully engineered domestic saga, as a gentle, affectionate panorama of a vanishing world, or as a deeply sympathetic group-portrait of women limited in their deeds but not their minds, it rivals any counterpart in any other culture. Shrewd, precise, quietly ironic, Tanizaki's storytelling is capable of exquisite delicacy and robust frankness too. After another neo-feudal nuptial dance between Yukiko and some portly swain, we learn that Taeko has fallen pregnant. Her lover is a bartender. Harsh, punishing modernity – gruelling jobs, commuter trains, suburban lodgings, hospital visits – scribbles over the fine brushstrokes of the "marriage plot". "Maidenly" Yukiko, "never at home in the modern world", finds it forever barging into her "hard core" of selfhood – most often, in the shape of some bank manager or pharmaceutical executive with a widening girth, a fondly-recalled first wife, and a willingness to overlook the "blemish" of her dark spot over one eye.

For all the trappings of modern life – not least the elaborate doctoring, with its armoury of tests and X-rays for disorders that may lie in the spirit more than the flesh – the Makioka women still bend or beat against the bars of a gilded cage. Tsuruko and Sachiko continue to wield a matriarchal authority. Yukiko suffers from an inward civil war between her "docility" and that "hard core" of self-sufficiency. Taeko, the "scapegrace sister" and artistic tearaway, has already caused a scandal with the feckless wastrel Okubata – still her official fiancé. Meanwhile, the lower-class, free-spirited photographer Itakura shows her another path to fulfilment. Tanizaki writes wonderfully about making art. When Sachiko looks at Itakura's shots of Taeko dancing, the author captures the essence of his own gift. Each glance, each gesture, has an "astonishing clearness", while the photographer's skill blesses "inconsequential things". Every page of this long, but gravity-defying, novel does the same.

Itakura has learned his craft in America. Osaka snobs treat his breezy manners as the "peculiar coarseness" of a returned emigrant. Throughout, the formal gentility of the Osaka-Kyoto region wrestles with the Western influences that arrived with industrial growth. The Makiokas have foreign friends and neighbours. The strains of Chopin or Schubert drift through gatherings. Among émigré Russians, we learn that "All Japanese read Tolstoy and Dostoyevsky". True or not, Yukiko does devour Daphne Du Maurier's *Rebecca*. Tanizaki draws on Western storytelling models, but he juxtaposes them with gorgeous set-piece scenes of Japanese ritual: the spring pilgrimage to view cherry-blossom, that fleeting vision "treasured for a whole year"; or the summer hunt for fireflies, with all "the world of the fairy-story in it". If this milieu must fade, it has not lost any of its sculpted grace. Sachiko remembers her mother's death, and its "sadness divorced from the personal, with a sort of musical pleasure in it, at the thought that something beautiful was leaving the earth".

For all its epic delicacy, *The Makioka Sisters* piles danger on disaster. Mortal illness stalks the family. That icon of freedom, Itakura, sickens and dies. In a spectacular scene, freak floods turn the river into a "black, boiling sea". In Tokyo, a typhoon brings "real terror" to Sachiko. Offstage, the international crises alluded to in euphemism – Imperial Japan's brutal invasion of Manchuria becomes the "Chinese Incident" – edge ever closer to home. The plot closes in spring 1941, with Yukiko finally hitched to the illegitimate son of a decayed noble house. But "the cherry blossoms are beginning to fall". Taeko has a stillborn baby: a lovely girl. Neither Tanizaki's first, nor later, readers need to be told of the evils that await offstage. As the horizon of the future inexorably darkens, that "musical pleasure" in fugitive beauty endures to the end.

Translation: Edward Seidensticker's residence in Japan and friendship with its writers informs his long-lived, still deeply affecting, translation (1957).

See also: La Fayette, *The Princesse of Clèves* (1678); Cao, *Dream of the Red Chamber* (1792); Sōseki, *The Gate* (1910); Lampedusa, *The Leopard* (1958)

Selected works by the same author: *Some Prefer Nettles* (1929)*; In Praise of Shadows* (1933)*; The Key* (1956)

59 | Fortress Besieged (1947) by Qian Zhongshu.

Chinese

Translated by Jeanne Kelly and Nathan K Mao (Penguin Modern Classics)

In the strife-torn Shanghai of the late 1930s, a hapless young drifter with pretensions bigger than this talents is asked to lecture about "the influence of Western civilisation on Chinese history". In the first of this novel's wickedly funny scenes of academic folly and hubris, our hero Fang Hung-chien decides to stir up his listeners with a dose of cultural nationalism. The two most enduring Western influences? "One is opium, and the other is syphilis." This from a would-be scholar draped in Western fashions of all sorts whose recent spell as a student in Europe has won him what little status he now has. He wangles a lecturing job on the strength of a phoney "doctorate" bought from a degree-by-post outfit called "Carleton University".

Frequently hilarious, just as often poignant and acerbic, *Fortress Besieged* swarms with artfully sketched characters who float in a restless emotional and intellectual limbo between China and the West. Meanwhile, much of their country succumbs to the "primitive brutality" of Japanese occupation. It is at once a magnificent comic novel, a campus satire, a subtly assured study of romantic delusions, and a high-spirited, sharp-witted account of a group of marginal poseurs who cling on to "provincial cosmopolitanism" as their world hardens into rival armed camps. Hung-chien agonises that the gods have quit "the vast and lofty blue skies above", leaving them in place "exclusively for the sake of dropping bombs". Looking back from the late 1940s on a period of disorder, massacre and upheaval, standing on the brink of another revolutionary age, Qian Zhongshu somehow manages to snatch joy, wit and laughter from the bleakest of times.

An accomplished scholar of both Chinese and Western literature (with an Oxford degree), Qian in the 1940s twin-tracked his academic studies with satirical fiction. Yet, soon after this masterpiece appeared, the victorious Communists began to shut down the kind of open, hybrid intellectual life that Hung-chien and his trend-conscious colleagues ape. Deeply committed to the Chinese classics, Qian retreated into pure scholarship, was forced to work as a janitor during the Cultural Revolution, but survived to achieve high honours in the 1980s. *Fortress Besieged*, then, stands as the glorious swan-song of a fast-disappearing world. It offers an exuberant mash-up of Chinese poetry and learning (a true "scholar's novel") along with romantic mishaps and comic episodes that may put readers in mind of Evelyn Waugh in one chapter, Jane Austen in another.

Qian will cite Dr Johnson, and then show his aspiring literati swapping slick pastiches of Tang dynasty poets. When Hung-chien and his comrades set out from Shanghai to take up jobs at an obscure college in distant Hunan, they put up, aptly enough, at a bedbug-infested establishment known as the "Grand Eurasian Hotel". Qian plays a delightful double game. He mocks European or American affectations, down to the brash businessman Jimmy Chang, forever saying – in English – "Make it snappy!" or "Have a look-see". But the entire novel revels in its nimble to-and-fro between China and the West. Hung-chien scoffs at students who call themselves "Byron" or "Alexander"; these fancy foreign names "reminded him of the British sow and cow. As soon their meat got on a menu, they went under a French name". With mischievous élan, Qian practises what he satirises. He has his cake (or dim sum) while eating it.

Beneath the cross-cultural comedy, Hung-chien's search for love deepens, and darkens, the tone. His fiancée, a banker's daughter, has died during his absence in Europe, but the benevolent Mr Chou still treats him as a son-in-law. On the boat back from Europe, as a clerk in Chou's Shanghai bank, then a shambolically ill-prepared teacher in the ramshackle San Lu University, he falls for a succession of young women – Miss T'ang, Miss Su, Miss Pao – before stumbling into an unwise marriage with Sun Jou-chia. Qian's closing chapters entwine the "besieged fortresses" of wedlock with that of China itself. The couple's relationship fractures into rancour and suspicion while Shanghai collapses under the Japanese onslaught. Even here, the "haphazard, mixed-up feeling" that comes from thinking and feeling between two worlds has its effect. Hung-chien sighs that modern partners who fall in love "conceal their true faces" until they cohabit. "It's the old-fashioned marriages" – arranged by matchmakers as pacts between clans – "that are more straightforward".

Remorselessly, Qian teases the hand-me-down fads of his semi-

Westernised youngsters. Heavily ironic, he suggests that Hung-chien only read "children's literature" such as the *Romance of the Three Kingdoms* – in fact, one of the canonical "Four Great Novels" of China – because he didn't know foreign masterpieces such as *Snow White*. But he shares their fascinated curiosity with life and thought beyond the Middle Kingdom. After another turn of history's wheel, the cult of foreign studies and imported fashions that he sends up here would spread en masse among Chinese millennials. In a final irony, this acidic, elegiac novel, which memorialises a buried culture with such verve and zest, now serves as a mental map to China's present as much as to its past.

Translation: Jeanne Kelly and Nathan K Mao (1979) keep pace with Qian in his many moods: slapstick, droll, caustic, learned and melancholy.

See also: Cao, *Dream of the Red Chamber* (1792); Tanpinar, *The Time-Regulation Institute* (1962); Salih, *Season of Migration to the North* (1966); Toer, *Buru Quartet* (1980-1988)

Selected works by the same author: *Patchwork: Seven Essays on Art and Literature* (1984); *Humans, Beasts and Ghosts: Stories and Essays* (2010).

60 | Dirty Snow (1948) by Georges Simenon.

French (Belgium/France/United States)

Translated by Marc Romano and Louise Varèse (New York Review Books)

From the time of Poe and Dostoyevsky, the greatest fiction of crime, guilt and punishment has felt no need to invoke upright, or even competent, police agencies. Towards the end of *Dirty Snow*, the worthless crook and cheat Frank Friedmaier faces yet more torture at the hands of the (unnamed) Nazi occupiers of France. He no longer fears blows from the brass ruler that has wrecked his features, or any other torments. After all, "no one could ever make him suffer the way he had made himself suffer" when he tricked a girl who loved him and let a crony rape her. In this state, under the brutal thumb of an invading power, never specified as France after 1940 but despoiled and besmirched in just the ways that the Germans had devised, this petty criminal, pimp, cheat and bully makes no political protest against the regime. In his own words of self-condemnation, "I am not a fanatic, an agitator, or a patriot. I am a piece of shit."

No just authority stands over him; merely a gang of thugs, swindlers and sadists in uniform. His mother runs a brothel for the occupiers and their stooges; his mates are thugs and hoodlums, large and small. The military have picked him up not because of the gratuitous slaying that felt like "another loss of virginity", nor for his small-scale scams and heists; still less for his casual brutality towards the country girls hired and broken in his mother's bordello. He happens to have got mixed up in a high-value theft, and murder, that implicates a senior officer in corruption. Soon the "perfect civility" of his early interrogation sessions turns to terror. As Simenon writes, with all his bravura understatement, "From this point on they bothered him."

Yet from the depths of his grubby soul (if he has one), this most obnoxious of anti-heroes – this "piece of shit" – dredges enough of a conscience to understand, and to indict himself. Two people above all show him that something better might exist than the oppressors' whorehouse, the black market deal, the armed robbery and the cynical exploitation of cold, hungry young women. One is Holst, the father of his principal victim Sissy. He is a man of culture and integrity, sacked by the regime, now a streetcar driver. The other is Sissy herself. An icon of goodness and redemption, she surpasses even Graham Greene's comparable heroines in her almost-mystic virtue. After she visits Frank in the school now requisitioned as a detention centre, she gazes at him "with an expression that he had never seen in human eyes".

Notoriously prolific, Georges Simenon interspersed his Inspector Maigret mysteries with "*romans durs*": hard novels. Bleak, stony, immaculately carved, these stories of passion, transgression and retribution glow in the deepest shades of noir. These books convinced Simenon's contemporaries, André Gide prominent among them, that the hyper-active bestseller also ranked among the finest modern writers of French prose. Simenon's language has a limited scope but he deploys his chosen tools with ferocious force and precision. His storytelling has a glacial efficiency, an elliptical drive and focus. A few words do the work that in other hands takes pages. He conveys the winter chill and dread of this corrupted city in phrases impacted with dark energy. That dirty snow rests in filthy heaps along accursed streets, "rotting, stained black, peppered with garbage". When new snow comes, it drifts down in tainted handfuls, "like plaster falling from a ceiling". Above all, he makes us see, never to forget the sight: after Sissy has fled the scene of her betrayal, Frank picks up her black wool stockings, neatly darned at the toes, "the way young girls were taught in convents".

Simenon had stayed in occupied France: neither a collaborator, nor a resister. After the liberation, however, he left for the US; *Dirty Snow* belongs to a fertile phase of voluntary exile. The pre-existing toughness of his style acquires an even harder, American edge. Critics often bracket the greatest *romans durs*, this one above all, alongside the work of Camus as granitic landmarks in the literature of the absurd. Frank does have his moments of philosophical nihilism: his eyes can blaze "as though he hated the whole human race", and he experiences his second murder as "an act whose necessity he had felt for a very long time". Yet, for all the lack of topical references, Simenon roots this nullity more explicitly than Camus does in a toxic soil of national humiliation and enslavement. In the torture cell, Frank plunges into this "world without boundaries". Here, individuals suffer at the whim of arbitrary power, with its "entities, names, numbers, signs that changed places and values every day". Frank too has acted in his own small realm as a vicious and capricious tyrant. In this domain of utter darkness, personal and political, a few tiny pinpricks of light may still shine – if only in Sissy's unearthly eyes.

Translation: In 1951, Marc Romano and Louise Varèse captured Simenon's terse poetry and savage swiftness in shades of noir that still feel more European than American.

See also: Dostoyevsky, *The Brothers Karamazov* (1880); Céline, *Journey to the End of the Night* (1932); Camus, *The Outsider* (1942); Némirovsky, *Suite Française* (1942-2004)

Selected works by the same author: *Maigret and the Yellow Dog* (1931); *Tropic Moon* (1933); *The Man Who Watched the Trains Go By (1938); Pedigree* (1948)

61 | The Moon and the Bonfires (1950) by Cesare Pavese

Italian

Translated by RW Flint (New York Review Books)

The motif of the traveller's or emigrant's return has attracted writers since the homecoming to Ithaka in Homer's *Odyssey*.

Although it dates from the fast-modernising post-war Italy of 1950, and stems from the imagination of an author who felt the lunar pull of both American modernity and Communist revolution, *The Moon and the Bonfires* possesses a classical, timeless solidity. That lapidary quality makes this compact novel feel like an epic etched into stone. It is beautiful; it is brutal; and it creates a mood of contested inevitability that pits choice and freedom against the gravitational force of "destiny", social and natural. When the (unnamed) narrator considers the harsh, "animal-like" life of the poor sharecropper Valino, who has never left the valley of his youth, he thinks that "if I hadn't escaped twenty years ago, this would have been my fate". However, he has opted to return, to bond again with this gorgeous, pitiless landscape, with its hardships, secrets, horrors. "A bonfire seen on a distant hill" could once make him cry out in ecstasy "because I was poor, because I was a boy, because I was nothing". Now, across half a lifetime of experience in distant lands, "I was missing those times and wanting them back."

Cesare Pavese both celebrates that nostalgia for a broken past, and counts its cost. The narrator, an adopted foundling and always an outsider, has left the lonely region of Langhe in Piedmont (Pavese's own birthplace), first as an army recruit and then, after the Fascists hound him, as a penniless migrant. He boards a ship bound from Genoa to the US. Pavese never wandered through America but he did translate its literature (brilliantly), from Melville to Faulkner. In this novel, the recollected California where the narrator makes his fortune has the aura of a waking dream: hard-edged, super-realistic, uncanny (Kafka's unvisited *Amerika* comes to mind). In this "big country", wide open and yielding to drive and ambition, "nobody had enough". The restlessness that impelled him into this hard-boiled wonderland also pulls him back, but to a village and a valley that – by 1945 – has suffered hideous scarring from Fascism and war.

From the outset, we sense that hatred and violence have smashed whatever was idyllic here, although Pavese never idealises the neo-feudal drudgery and resentment of the traditional hierarchy. More recently, "Blood had flowed in the hills like juice from the wine-press," as Partisans, Fascists and Germans slew one another. The narrator's childhood friend Nuto, a charismatic local hero, has for all his anti-Fascist credentials failed to press for reform as conflict ended, when the Partisans had "the power and the push". Now new kinds of injustice harden into habit while, in the woods and on the hills, villagers still uncover the slaughtered corpses of the combatants. The old order, with all its charm and its cruelty, can never come back: "America's already here."

Yet the narrator rows back into his past, enraptured by the scenes and scents of youth. He has this place in his bones "like the wine and the polenta". The past reawakens to radiant life with "the squeak of a cart going downhill", "the swish of an ox's tail", "the taste of thick soup" or simply "a voice heard on the piazza at night". With a clean-limbed, fuss-free lyricism all the more beguiling for its simplicity,

Pavese conveys the enchantment of landscape and labour in a time when "Everything was done by season"; "grape harvests and haymakings and cornhuskings".

He exposes the idyll's shadow-side as well: the ignorance, the servility, the abuse of children, women, animals. We hear how Valino murders his wife, and kills himself, in one of the eerie conflagrations that burn through this book: beacons of a pagan idea of godhead beyond reason or politics. Shock by shock, revelations of family tragedies at the Mora – the wealthier estate where the narrator worked as a farmhand – tarnish the bucolic reverie. The "scent of lime trees in the evening" never forfeits its magic, but, ever stronger, the scent of blood joins it. At the finale, the fate (or choice?) of ill-starred Santa, rebel daughter of Sor Matteo at the Mora, yokes the deathly, double-dealing rivalry of Partisans and Fascists to some ancient cult of sacrifice. Although she gathered information for the Resistance, Santa, we learn, has been shot as a Fascist spy. In awe of her goddess-like allure, her executioners have burned the body to leave an ashen patch "like the bed of a bonfire". "The world," Nuto likes to say, "is badly made and you have to remake it." Neither he, the narrator, nor the purgatorial fires of war, have yet done so. Paradise will not be regained. The pastoral bliss that Pavese conjures with such flawless artistry feels quite as remote as Virgil's, or as Homer's, world.

Translation: RW Flint (2002) balances the "American" swiftness and suppleness of Pavese's prose with a rugged, hard-won lyricism.

See also: Papadiamantis, *The Murderess* (1903); Rulfo, *Pedro Páramo* (1955); Lampedusa, *The Leopard* (1958); Schwarz-Bart, *The Bridge of Beyond* (1972)

Selected works by the same author: *The Beach* (1941); *August Holiday* (1946); *The Devil in the Hills* (1948); *Among Women Only* (1949)

62 | Trilogy: Molloy, Malone Dies, The Unnamable (1951-1953) by Samuel Beckett.

French (Ireland/France)

Translated by the author (*Molloy* in collaboration with Patrick Bowles) (Everyman's Library)

From first breath to last gasp, Beckett's three inter-linked monologues decline towards nothingness and silence without ever quite reaching that state. "Having nothing to say," as the narrator of *The Unnamable* informs us, "no words but the words of others, I have to speak." From the two, comparatively action-packed, parts of *Molloy* through the terminal yarn-spinning of *Malone Dies* and the ever-narrowing horizons of *The Unnamable*, these three works send the resources of fiction spiralling down towards a vanishing point that never arrives. "No more stories from this day forth" we hear, and yet "the stories go on, it's stories still".

For all their sorrow, despair and bewilderment, these stories pulse with laughter, grief, tenderness and yearning. Malone – most explicitly, the novelist among Beckett's three narrators – might write all that off as a sentimental fraud. Still, the monologues flow with exacting but exquisite prose. Phrase by beautifully modulated phrase, it glows with the joy of creation even as the words deny it. Beckett's wicked, pitch-black humour lurks in ambush on every page. At Year Zero for European literature, in the aftermath of a genocidal war in which Beckett himself had with quiet courage resisted the Nazi occupation of France, he both digs the grave of conventional fiction – and midwives it into squealing, bawling re-birth.

Their composition interrupted by the first text of *Waiting for Godot*, Beckett's trilogy of minimal, depleted and yet torrential fictions were written in the late 1940s. They represent the expatriate Irishman's most ambitious raid on his adopted language of French. Its very limits as a second tongue, so Beckett thought, would streamline thought and style. Within a few years, he had converted them into English (with *Molloy* alone, he worked with a collaborator). The relative status of the French and English versions has filled shelves with academic studies. When he Englished other works composed in French, notably the novel *Mercier and Camier*, Beckett's rewriting did amount to a fundamental reinvention. Not so with the Trilogy, although self-translation restored much of the colloquial swing and sting the original had shunned. With its bicycles weaving through a distinctly Irish countryside, not to mention the ever-merging cast of Molloys, Morans, Malones, Macmanns and Murphys, the cultural landscape of the monologues feels Anglophone, even in French.

From the start, these narratives mislaid the "mother tongue" – just as Molloy has lost his actual mother, and goes hunting for her on a bicycle in the first half of his story. Then Moran, a sort of savage detective, searches for Molloy in a section that can feel as much like a parody of hard-boiled crime fiction as an existential pilgrimage. In *Malone Dies,* the slowly expiring Malone spins stories that recount the fate of young Sapo, later known as Macmann. His picaresque adventures lead to the asylum, the sinister keeper Lemuel, and a jolly outing arranged by Lady Pedal ("a huge, big, tall, fat woman"). Like his patron James Joyce, Beckett fuels his innovation with a bonfire of traditions, or habits. One clapped-out genre after another goes up in parodic smoke. A compulsive storyteller, Malone blurs into Molloy and the protagonist of *The Unnamable*, but also presents himself as the artist who has sired this whole pack of characters. When he dies, "it will all be over with the Murphys, Merciers, Molloys, Morans and Malones, unless it goes on beyond the grave".

In *The Unnamable*, arguably, it does just that. The harbinger and template for Beckett's truncated and vacated later work, in both drama and fiction, this novel shrinks its consciousness into an empty room seemingly devoid of co-ordinates in space or time. "Where now? Who now? When now?" it begins. The "I" who speaks still spins stories – about Malone, the alter ego Mahood and his stricken family, the amorphous Worm. More and more, however, their setting contracts to the confines of a single skull, or mouth. "Rid at one glorious sweep of parents, wife and heirs", the narrator dwindles into a lone voice in darkness. Still, "my horror of silence" ensures that the yarn should unspool further. "I must really lend myself to this story a little longer, there may possibly be a grain of truth in it." Indeed, "Perhaps I still have a thousand years to go."

With its random acts of violence, its fearful fugitives and solitary hideouts, the ambience of the Trilogy recalls – as does *Waiting for Godot* – the war-ravaged Europe of its time. These abstract texts have a visceral, corporeal directness beyond the reach of most "realistic" fiction. From Absurdists to Deconstructionists, theorists have sought to recruit Beckett into their armies. But "The thing to avoid", we learn, "is the spirit of system". Meanwhile, the author – then only in his forties – gave an almost prophetic voice to the stranded old, the infirm, the abandoned: those legions of the lost, left with nothing but memory that fades towards fantasy, then oblivion. As *The Unnamable* insists, "I was always aged, always ageing, and ageing makes no difference". Life outlasts hope. Yet words still drip or gush, and "you must go on, I can't go on, I'll go on".

Translation: Patrick Bowles was named as the translator of *Molloy*, although Beckett worked closely with him. With Beckett's versions of the two later novels, the complete *Trilogy* (1959) writes a second masterpiece, attuned to all the resources of English, over the original.

See also: Machado, *Epitaph of a Small Winner* (1880); Proust, *In Search of Lost Time* (1913-1927); Svevo, *Zeno's Conscience* (1923); Bernhard, *Correction* (1975)

Selected works by the same author: *Murphy* (1938); *Waiting for Godot* (1953); *Endgame* (1957); *How It Is* (1961)

63 | The Hive (1946; published 1951) by Camilo José Cela.

Spanish

Translated by JM Cohen, with Arturo Barea (Dalkey Archive Press).

Impersonal, alienating, yet throbbing with hope and desire, the modern city both excites novelists and appals them. Out of that ambivalence, and the new vistas of style and structure opened by the hurry and variety of urban life, a canon of metropolitan masterpieces has grown. Some of the greatest – from Joyce's *Ulysses* to Bely's *Petersburg* and Döblin's *Berlin Alexanderplatz* – depict cities in flux or in crisis, dying or being born, rather than the impregnable centres of empire and culture. In urban fiction, innovation bloomed on the margins, not in the heartlands of power.

Cela set his busy, almost centrifugal, fictional fresco in the Madrid of 1943. The Spanish capital is locked in the immobilising grip of Franco's triumphant nationalist regime and its allies in the Church. Always a maverick, Cela had fought for the Franco's Falangists in the Civil War that ended in 1939. In 1942, he had scandalised the Spanish authorities with his trail-blazing novel *The Family of Pascal Duarte*: the confession of a rural murderer bred by the misery and backwardness of tradition-bound "black Spain", and a tale of seemingly random violence often bracketed with Camus's near-contemporary *The Outsider*. In *The Hive*, Cela comes to town but finds humankind in an equally demoralised condition. He draws a densely shaded and contoured map of a defeated city, and a world "in which everything has gone wrong bit by bit". Usually poor, even destitute, often jobless or reduced to prostitution or beggary, tormented by anxiety even when well-off, the human swarm that buzzes through the multiple short sections of *The Hive* dreams and strives and suffers. All the while, "A kind of sorrow floats in the air and sinks into men's hearts."

Usually taken as a critique of metropolitan solitude and squalor, a view that Cela himself did little to oppose, *The Hive* can read like a different brand of book. True, the customers and staff who congregate at Dona Rosa's cafe, all trailing families, lovers, pick-ups, victims, friends and enemies, suffer hard times in this climate of dismay. Around 160 separate characters (some critics tally many more) flow in and out of Cela's labyrinthine narration. It forks, branches, loops and doubles back on itself at a dizzying pace. From the worried rich to the frantic poor, from the bourgeois Moises and their three daughters to the street-walker Elvira, the barman Celestino and the print-shop worker Victorita, they navigate a city that stalks, plagues and devours them. Mentioned almost in passing, the Civil War and its aftermaths of punishment, tyranny and hunger intensify their woes. Purita, another girl driven to walk the streets by penury, is an orphan with five siblings. "Their father was shot against wall, for one of those things, and the mother died of TB and under-nourishment in 1941."

So it goes in Cela's accursed Madrid. Yet *The Hive* does not have a desolate or depressing atmosphere. The story darts with foxy agility from one strand to another. Cela knits them all together with a virtuosic panache. His dialogue crackles with a rueful gallows wit. Each character, however briefly glimpsed, grabs the limelight for her or his ephemeral star turn. A few can even feel, and enjoy, the hidden beauty and liberty of the humming metropolis. Martin Marco, the high-minded would-be writer whose fate unites many of the cast, loves his "lonely walks, long, weary tramps through the wide streets of the city", which every day suddenly fill with smells, sights and sounds "by something like a miracle".

Each of Cela's people is a small piece in a vast, mobile mosaic. They hardly have the time or space to develop the kind of roundedness and perspective we would have expected from the characters in a classic novel of the previous century. His form matches his setting. *The Hive* is fragmentary, short-winded, marked by rapid montage rather than long, static shots. Significantly, many of these Madrileños spend their brief leisure hours at the cinema. Movie allusions stud the book. Yet modernity may baffle the new art as it does the old; we hear of "films with beautiful poetic names, posing tremendous human riddles which they do not always solve".

Cela, and his creations, can never quite solve the human riddle of the city. Moreover, Franco's rule of silence and dread has made even the naming of its pain a crime. Like the street benches that Martin observes on his strolls, his novel collates "a sort of anthology of every form of trouble".

The Hive hums with energy. In this prison-like society, however, nothing can substantially change. Mere survival substitutes for self-development. This guarded labyrinth has no exit towards maturity and achievement, of the sort that would drive the traditional heroes of fiction in their quests. Published first in Argentina after Franco's censors had refused it a licence, *The Hive* helped shape later novels of the seething metropolis in Latin America as much as in Europe. All its citizens are in motion; none can truly move. Except, perhaps, for the little Gypsy boy – a flamenco singer – whom we spot at intervals. Homeless, penniless, outcasts of the city, his despised clan alone can enjoy "complete freedom and autonomy".

Translation: With advice from the exiled Spanish author Arturo Barea, JM Cohen produced a colloquial and readable version in 1953.

See also: Bely, *Petersburg* (1916-1922); Döblin, *Berlin Alexanderplatz* (1929); Cabrera Infante, *Three Trapped Tigers* (1964); Pamuk, *The Black Book* (1990)

Selected works by the same author: *The Family of Pascual Duarte* (1942); *Journey to the Alcarria* (1948); *San Camilo 1936* (1969)

64 | Memoirs of Hadrian (1951) by Marguerite Yourcenar (Marguerite de Crayencour).

French (Belgium/France/United States)

Translated by Grace Frick, with the author (Penguin Modern Classics)

In her scholarly note on sources appended to *Memoirs of Hadrian*,

Marguerite Yourcenar argues that, although "History has its rules", so too does literature. "The two are not necessarily irreconcilable." Novelists had plundered and cannibalised the documentary records of the past since the Romantic heyday of Scott and Manzoni. By the mid 20th-century, however, a more exacting kind of historical storytelling had evolved. No longer content with travesty, pantomime and melodrama, informed by up-to-date research, sensitive to changes in the literary and social weather, this renovated fiction of the past would seek to avoid both anachronism and pastiche. It would keep faith with its sources, refuse to make up or modify significant events, while at the same time knowing and showing that human lives, and minds, forever change. We can never entirely shed the present when we travel back into the past. The fiction of history, though, might come to resemble the philosophy of "eroticism" that Hadrian sketches. It would become a "form of approach to the Other, one more technique for getting to know what is not ourselves".

The Roman emperor Hadrian (AD 76-138) did write an autobiography, now lost. In Yourcenar's version, he is slowly dying "of a dropsical heart". Facing death with clear-eyed equanimity, he composes a testament for the heir who – after the reign of Antoninus – would rule as Marcus Aurelius. This "written meditation of a sick man who could hold an audience with his memories" surveys Hadrian's career as warrior and governor. The "Pax Romana" holds across an expanded empire, from his wall in northern Britain to the desert frontiers of Syria. Hadrian interrogates his principles and values, remembers his gains and losses in love and politics, and reflects with stoic – but never cynical – modesty on "how ephemeral a shadow man throws on this abiding earth". Ironic and wistful, sophisticated and intimate, Hadrian's voice seduces and commands the reader even as he tells us not to trust seducers or commanders. Fate and happenstance rather than will or virtue have ruled his, and every, life. Although "the landscape of my days" boasts a few "granite peaks of the inevitable", "all about is rubble from the landslips of chance". In contrast, deluded historians fabricate tidy systems of cause-and-effect "too perfect for explaining the past".

Writing in the age of genocidal tyrants, Yourcenar presents a benign emperor but not a modern democrat. Hadrian supports or initiates repressive campaigns in Dacia and Palestine. But she paints a finely shaded portrait of a governor with deep self-knowledge, humane ideals and a respect for the limits of authority. He claims "to have sought liberty more than power, and power only because it can lead to freedom". Completed in the post-war US, the *Memoirs*, for all their scepticism, have a Utopian tinge. Hadrian improves the lot of slaves, frees women from the "legalised" rape of forced marriage and dreams, on a visit to Britannia, of "a hypothetical empire, governed from the West, an Atlantic world". Rooted, like every historical novel, in its own times, the *Memoirs* envisage a NATO – or perhaps EU – model of liberal order, with the just state merely as "a machine to serve man".

Hadrian attracts us for his selfhood more than his statecraft. A gay woman writer, voicing an emperor who loved men, Yourcenar transforms the memoirs into a demonstration of the depth and dignity of same-sex relationships. She did so at a moment when such a stance still amounted to heresy, even in the liberal democracies of the West. Hadrian's whole existence has pivoted around his brief but intense relationship with the youth Antinous, that "graceful hound" from the Black Sea, "avid both for caresses and commands". Antinous' suicide in Egypt, jealous and insecure, becomes in its way an "extraordinary masterpiece". The death turns his imperial lover – always the aesthete – into the heartbroken witness to another's pure act of freedom. *The Memoirs* share their cultural origins, if not their sensibility, with the contemporary works of Sartre and Camus.

Hadrian's confessions still charm and convince thanks to the emperor's dealings not with philosophers, generals, even lovers – but with himself. His quizzical, amused inspection of his shortcomings and divisions ("Different persons ruled me in turn") recalls not so much any Roman source as the sceptical self-scrutiny of Montaigne's *Essays*. He reveres Greek art, and thought, for its humanistic modesty and clarity: "the human contents me; I find everything there, even what is eternal." In this perspective, Hadrian's "eroticism" leaves behind private gratification to become an ethics of respect and solidarity. Yourcenar not only glances sideways to a time eager to rescue ideals of civilised government from the ashes of dictatorship and war. She looks forward to the liberation movements of the later 20th-century. Her reforming, self-critical emperor yearns to banish injustice, "dire poverty and brutality" not as abstract evils but offences against the person: as "insults to the fair body of mankind".

Translation: Collaborating with her life partner Grace Frick, Yourcenar helped to produce a fluent, subtle and serene English text in 1955.

See also: Manzoni, *The Betrothed* (1827-42); Lampedusa, *The Leopard* (1958); Fuentes, *The Death of Artemio Cruz* (1962); Vargas Llosa, *The Feast of the Goat* (2000)

Selected works by the same author: *A Coin in Nine Hands* (1934); *Oriental Tales* (1936); *Coup de Grace* (1939); *The Abyss* (1968)

65 | Pedro Páramo (1955) by Juan Rulfo.

Spanish (Mexico)

Translated by Margaret Sayers Peden (Serpent's Tail)

One of the ghostly figures who drift through the dreamscape of *Pedro Páramo* is a land surveyor named Toribio Aldrete. He has been lynched – left hanging in a locked room, so that he "turns to leather". His measurements have threatened to diminish the estate of the rough and ruthless landowner who gives Juan Rulfo's oneiric tale its title. Hence, "The charge is falsifying boundaries." Over this novel's brief span, *Pedro Páramo* suspends and erases every conceivable boundary: between dream and waking; the living and the dead; illusion and reality; the present and the past. Its narrative shifts from voice to voice, period to period. The storyteller who sets out to find Pedro, his already-deceased father, dies midway through the novel. People, and deeds, from the past haunt the present; conversely, future occurrences erupt into history. This parched backwater of southern Mexico becomes a stony limbo, a scorched purgatory where times and identities forever blur. "On windy days I can see the wind blowing leaves from the trees," says the spectral housekeeper Damiana, "when anyone can see that there aren't any trees here."

Soon after its publication, this first novel by Rulfo – once a travelling tyre salesman, later an editor for Mexico's Indigenous Institute – became a Latin American legend. Its mysterious, even sinister celebrity eclipsed any tale told about its titular rural patriarch. For Gabriel García Márquez, the book unlocked the door in his imagination that led directly to *One Hundred Years of Solitude*. No sketch of that mythical literary city, "magical realism" fails to place *Pedro Páramo* at the entrance gate. Yet there is nothing exotic, nothing flamboyant, nothing luxuriant in Rulfo's scrambled and shattered account of a rustic tragedy in the Mexican badlands. The bare bones of the narrative, as the first narrator Juan Preciado returns to the abandoned village of Comala, depict a process of desertification and depopulation. The violence of the Mexican Revolution in the 1910s has aggravated ancient sufferings – a history that becomes explicit in the final chapters. In this "town full of echoes", set in once-fertile countryside now coated in "ruined, sterile earth", political convulsions have intensified local disputes over lands, brides, and ranks. Strife has fragmented families and cursed communities. Thefts, raids, rapes and frauds disfigure this burning wasteland ("Páramo" means "barren plain"). Each crime is a bid to snatch and hold property: ranches, wives, mistresses, mines, troops. So far, so almost naturalistic. The hallucinatory mood of Rulfo's prose reshapes a place of peasant rivalries not so remote from Thomas Hardy's Wessex or Giovanni Verga's Sicily.

From the material of a lurid provincial melodrama, Rulfo fashions a story both thoroughly ancient and extremely modern. The ghostly voices that Juan encounters in forsaken Comala, murmuring and buzzing "like a swarm of bees", serve as a Greek tragic chorus. Fragmentary memories of Páramo, the seductive tyrant who "flourished like a weed" on his estate at Media Luna, grow patch by patch into a collective chronicle. This impersonal, almost epic style also resembles some sun-bleached documentary film. Broken shards of voice-over narration interrupt a series of, often conflicting, witness statements. Rulfo once wrote that he sought to build "a structure made of silences, of hanging threads, of cut scenes".

Grief – and mourning – splice these scenes together. We share the angry nostalgia of Juan's dying mother for the man and place that formed and then expelled her; the unresolved anguish of the ghostly informants in Comala, each one "a soul wandering like so many others, looking for living people to pray for it"; the priest's lament that, here, "everything that grows is bitter. That is our curse." Pedro himself, towards the finale, rises from backwater despot to tragic protagonist thanks to his unappeasable longing for Susana San Juan – the miner's daughter he loves from childhood, virtually imprisons, but can never marry. Yet a retrospective shuffling of each piece into a clear mosaic of passion and murder, bereavement and separation, can betray the experience of reading *Pedro Páramo*. In this heat that chills, Rulfo lends to family tragedy and social catastrophe the weird enchantments of a ghost story. "I felt," says Juan on his arrival in Comala, "I was in a faraway world and let myself be pulled along by the current." That current still feels utterly irresistible.

Translation: Rulfo's near-mythical stature in the Hispanic world once reached Anglophone readers merely as a rumour; in 1993, Margaret Sayers Peden made it blazingly real.

See also: Kleist, *Michael Kohlhaas* (1810); Fuentes, *The Death of Artemio Cruz* (1962); García Márquez, *One Hundred Years of Solitude* (1967); Han, *A Dictionary of Maqiao* (1996)

Selected works by the same author: *The Burning Plain and Other Stories* (1953)

66 | The Cairo Trilogy (Palace Walk, Palace of Desire, Sugar Street) (1956-57) by Naguib Mahfouz.

Arabic (Egypt)

Translated by William Maynard Hutchins, Olive E Kenny, Lorne A Kenny & Angele Botros Samaan (Everyman's Library)

Al-Sayyid Ahmad Abd al-Jawad is a prosperous merchant, a pillar of the community and the stern but devoted father of three sons and two daughters. He has toiled to make his fine house in an ancient neighbourhood of Cairo into a fortress and an enclave. Here, private virtues and family duties may flourish, unimpeded by the doubts and dangers of the world beyond. His own (frequent) adventures with mistresses and alcohol must no more threaten this little domestic empire than the Egyptian uprising of 1919 against Britain's quasi-colonial rule. After all, "His children were meant to be a breed apart, outside the framework of history." In principle, Al-Sayyid Ahmad as a respectable patriot supports the nationalist Wafd party and backs the revolution, which "should rage on outside… But the house was his and his alone". When, as the *Cairo Trilogy*'s first part ends, his middle son Fahmy dies under a hail of British gunfire during a peaceful mass demonstration, we know that the wall that the patriarch of *Palace Walk* has sought to build between family and history will crumble. It proves as futile as the trench dug by protestors to interrupt troop movements, which Al-Sayyid Ahmad and his neighbours must then fill up at gunpoint, "exhausted, humiliated and afraid". In truth, that imaginary trench around the household never existed at all. Through the years to come, the jealous father's fears that he will "lose control of his family" will be fully realised, not in isolation but as one chapter within this epic of transformation as it ripples in widening circles from the individual mind out to the home, the city, Egypt and – by extension – the world itself.

The patriarch himself does not open and close the *Trilogy*. His wife Amina occupies that role: shrewd, loving, pious, a traditional Muslim homemaker but equally a woman of vision and wisdom who moves through a "living, intelligent world". When she breaks free of her husband's control to visit the nearby Al-Hussein mosque and imbibe "the sweet spiritual waters of the shrine", her defiance has all the drama of some hair-raising battlefield ordeal. Mahfouz imparts suspense and even grandeur to each critical domestic episode with an unflagging artistry that brings Tolstoy to mind. The daughters, beautiful Aisha and clever Khadija, marry and so bind other clans into the Jawads' destiny. The sons, wayward Yasin (whose mother was Al-Sayyid Ahmad's discarded first wife), idealistic Fahmy and equivocal, indecisive Kamal, both resent and reproduce the mixed-up morality of their father. Yasin shares the paternal weakness for affairs with musicians from Cairo's *demi-monde*, but times are changing. As political nationalism and Islamic fundamentalism dig new troughs, Al-Sayyid Ahmad's genial double standards, his knack of living happily in two moral and social spaces at once, no longer hold. Yasin "did not have this ability to reconcile his piety and his practice".

In *Palace of Desire* and *Sugar Street*, Kamal's divided consciousness becomes the principal lens through which Mahfouz observes the end of an era. As self-rule comes to Egypt in the 1920s, the grace of custom and the balm of hypocrisy can no longer keep these contradictions in check. Kamal falls for Aida Shaddad, the Westernised daughter of a family from the "top echelon" of the bourgeoisie. His thwarted passion is nurtured by meetings in the gazebo of the Shaddads' paradisal garden, that "joyous vision of a happy dream". As a modern-minded teacher, he also feels the pull of scientific rationalism, and revolutionary socialism. Family and tradition, however, never quite lose their grip, leaving him "teetering uncertainly between East and West". Firm commitment, either to marriage or ideology, eludes him. At the finale, the patriarch's two grandsons face arrest during the Second World War – one as a Communist, the other as an Islamist. We grasp that this period of interregnum – as the old world dies, and the new struggles to be born – will close amid world-changing upheavals.

As he chronicles the fall, or perhaps the fragmentation, of the house of Jawad, Naguib Mahfouz tells the story of a century by knocking on a single Cairo door. This mansion has many, richly furnished rooms: the family saga that miniaturises the fate of a whole society; women's struggle for dignity and freedom within a tenacious patriarchal order; young men's journeys to maturity through love, career or politics; not least, the complex interaction of private and public time. The rifts and shocks of history disrupt the cycles of the day, the year, the human lifespan. From the muezzin's call to prayer to the eternal vigilance of Sphinx and Pyramids, different frames and spans of time converge on individual lives.

Yet when Mahfouz composed his peerless fresco, between 1946 and 1952, the modern novel in Arabic was hardly older than the author (born in 1911). Both the hallowed narrative styles of the *Thousand and One Nights* and the legacy of Egypt's ancient history meant much to Mahfouz – a tense picnic at the Pyramids supplies the context for a key scene in *Palace of Desire*. But the *Trilogy* itself reads not so much like a hybrid form as an astonishingly confident raid on a non-native genre. Mahfouz adopts, and commands, the panoramic fiction of emerging selfhood within a changing society that he so admired in Mann and Proust. So these novels enact a dialogue between Egyptian ways of being and European ways of knowing – the same encounter we share in the hesitations of Hamlet-like Kamal, with his "infernal vacillation". They do so with a grand architectonic vision, and a bountiful prodigality of human and social detail, that have few equals in any time or place.

Translation: In 1990-1992, William M Hutchins and his collaborators brought both the *Trilogy*'s big pictures, and its local colours, to captivating life in English.

See also: Tolstoy, *War and Peace* (1869); Proust, *In Search of Lost Time* (1913-1927); Mann, *The Magic Mountain* (1924); Tanpinar, *The Time Regulation Institute* (1962)

Selected works by the same author: *Midaq Alley* (1947)*; Children of Gebelawi* (1959)*; The Thief and the Dogs* (1961)*; Arabian Nights and Days* (1979)

67 | That Awful Mess on the Via Merulana (1946-1957) by Carlo Emilio Gadda.

Italian

Translated by William Weaver (New York Review Books)

Detectives and other police officers play a smaller role in the standard histories of literature than they do in the imaginations of ordinary readers around the world. True, major cultural critics – from Borges to Gramsci to Umberto Eco, who found popular acclaim with the genre – have frequently written with insight and respect about mystery stories. Tales of crime, investigation and (less often) punishment blossom on every branch of the 20th-century novel. Yet no book brings a mould-breaking creative ferment to the protocols of the whodunnit with such spectacular results as Gadda's one-off masterpiece. Our stolid sleuth Officer Ingravallo, who acts "like a person fighting a laborious digestion", probes two potentially connected crimes in the same apartment block at 219 Via Merulana in Rome. In this "palace of gold, or of sharks", old and new money uneasily co-habit around the grand staircase. The time is 1927, five years into Italy's "New Order" under the dictatorship of "the Ass on high", that "Death's Head in a frock coat", Benito Mussolini, never named, endlessly mocked, the champion of harmony who brings only chaos, confusion and lies.

In one apartment, the elderly Contessa Menegazzi has had her family jewels stolen. Close by, the wealthy Liliana Balducci is found with her throat viciously cut. Detective Ingravallo, "Don Ciccio" – a Southerner from Molise, ill-at-ease amid the secrecies and snobberies of the Eternal City – must link and resolve this "unwanted double of a pair of crimes". With his partners and rivals in the Carabinieri, he appears to clear up the jewel theft. As for the almost-ritual murder, Gadda left his novel tantalisingly unfinished just before a final reveal

– although readers have often deduced a culprit. This incompletion feels apt. Gadda insists that "unforeseen catastrophes" never follow the simple logic of cause-and-effect. Rather, "a whole multitude of converging causes" will produce "a whirlpool, a cyclonic point of depression". This is detective fiction according to Einstein's rather than Newton's physics. Policemen, like politicians, might try to exercise "the objective clarity of ratiocination". Always, below the surface of mind and world alike, "the unreason of the powers of darkness" threatens to break through and take over.

In Gadda's world, relativistic forcefields mock Fascist fantasies of top-down control and discipline. No single style or language can describe or explain everything. So Gadda presides over a glorious, often ecstatic carnival of parody and pastiche, comedy and burlesque. Seamlessly, he dons and discards every verbal disguise from the police report and the scientific paper to the classical epic and the dialect melodrama. In the original, the "mess" Don Ciccio must sort out is actually a "pasticciaccio". In a period of phoney, coercive order, Gadda's language breaks free of all chains. Wonderfully inventive flights of literary fancy disrupt every stage of the investigation.

During a crucial interrogation in the Alban Hills outside Rome, a defecating chicken catches Gadda's attention, as it deposits "a green chocolate drop twisted alla Borromini [the great Roman architect] like the lumps of colloid sulphur in the Abule water". Phrase by dancing, glinting phrase, Gadda compresses all his learning in arts and sciences (he was an engineer by profession) into these impacted gems of description and allusion. They sparkle like the jewels that Ingravallo hunts – or, perhaps, like closely-observed hen dung. The colours and textures of his people, their surroundings and their stories change, in the manner of the "bad-luck piece". This is a watch-fob once adorned with an opal but now with a jasper: the Hitchcock-style "McGuffin" that helps Gadda's plot to twist.

Ever the intuitive cop, Don Ciccio understands that "the world of so-called verities" is merely "a tissue of fairy tales – and bad dreams". This underworld of myth, often voiced as a mock-heroic homage to Virgil, Ovid or Homer, erupts throughout the investigation. Gadda associates it with the domain of women: the childless Liliana and her brood of "nieces" or wards; and the archetypal figure of La Zamira, the "Oriental Wizardess". At her country workshop of poor seamstresses, Zamira the "priestess of abominable spells" fuses the roles of bawd, fence, sorceress and sibyl. At the outset, Gadda dubs Italy "a kind of great fertile womb". Ideas of barrenness and fecundity, even of sacrifice to the ancient chthonic powers, bubble away not far below the crust of the police procedural. The novel's women, feared and revered, scorn and subvert the masculine parade of reason embodied most absurdly in the bald phallus of Il Duce himself. In a pregnant image, Gadda suggests that each person possesses a "uterus" of reason. However, it only takes "a kneading of the fingertips" for this womb of thought to revert to the dark side, where "the most enlightened certainties are poisoned". *That Awful Mess on the Via Merulana* itself commands a sort of magical prowess. As Ingravallo's cases lose the thread of reason, a tangle of sinister, delightful doubt ensues.

Translation: William Weaver's heroic and hilarious quest to find Gadda's voice in English (1965) is a high point of his illustrious career.

See also:Manzoni, *The Betrothed* (1827-42); Kafka, *The Trial* (1925); Perec, *Life A User's Manual* (1978); Pamuk, *The Black Book* (1990)

Selected works by the same author: *The Philosophers' Madonna* (1931); *The Castle of Udine* (1934); *The Experience of Pain* (1963)

68 | The Leopard (1958) by Giuseppe Tomasi di Lampedusa.

Italian

Translated by Archibald Colquhoun (Vintage)

Don Fabrizio, Prince of Salina and the patriarch of a fading dynasty

in the Sicily of 1860, is astonished at the pace with which his nephew's courtship of a wealthy, low-born, heiress moves. The marriage suit reminds the narrator of *The Leopard* of the difference between "one of those easy-going old planes pottering between Palermo and Naples" and a speedy "Super Jet". This sudden jolt into the present recurs later, with allusions to Freud, to scientific medicine and – most shockingly of all – to an aristocratic ballroom fated to destruction in 1943 by "a bomb manufactured in Pittsburgh, Penn". The only published novel by Giuseppe Tomasi, Prince of Lampedusa, *The Leopard* lavishly recreates the interior and exterior scenery of his great-grandfather's semi-feudal society. The story summons this lost world with such ravishing beauty and sympathy that it often feels – a certain frankness about sexual passion aside – less like a novel about, than one from, the mid 19th-century. However forgivable, that impression misses the originality that makes it so much more than a supremely elegant pastiche. The writer, like his presumed reader, understands Freud and flies on jets.

Lampedusa punches at times through the veil of verisimilitude to indicate that he knows, and we know, the impossibility of resurrecting this culture. The Prince registers the irreversible changes in Sicily and Italy that have led to "the decline of his prestige" with an alloy of nostalgia, fatalism and even relief. Equally, the reader understands that an abyss far deeper the Straits of Messina divides us from the lost island of the past. Far from being a backward-looking exercise in repro- or retro-fiction, *The Leopard*, with unequalled craft and grace, inaugurates a new epoch for historical novels. "Post-modern", critics might call it. It is marked not only by scrupulous, authentic detail but a sophisticated awareness that the whole enterprise amounts to a splendid but illusory performance. Lampedusa at first planned, on Joyce's model, to tell the Prince's story within a single day. He found that he couldn't "do a *Ulysses*". In the form he eventually chose, with the bulk of the action confined to 1860-1863 and codas reaching up to 1910, his brilliantly etched and tinted set-pieces proceed like the hang of heirloom pictures in a noble drawing-room. Time in his Sicily runs according to a clock both more ancient and more contemporary than the linear tick-tock of realistic fiction. Chevalley, the rationalistic bureaucrat from mainland Italy who voices an antique-sounding "progressive" ideology, condescendingly thinks of Sicily as "this lovely country which is only now sighting the modern world". Chevalley's one-dimensional version of modernity went extinct long ago. Whereas the Prince's – and his author's – ironical location within both space and time endures.

In 1860, Garibaldi's revolutionary troops land in Palermo to dragoon backward Sicily into the great campaign of Italian reunification. Don Fabrizio, the Prince, plots his survival strategy within the new, increasingly bourgeois status quo. No diehard reactionary, he enjoys and upholds his role as "a member of the old ruling class" like a star actor with a solemn duty to his part, the play and to the public that applauds it. His dynamic nephew, and favourite, Tancredi sees more explicitly that "If we want things to stay as they are, things will have to change". That maxim applies on the romantic as much as the diplomatic battlefield. Tancredi's alliance with Angelica, daughter of the self-made Calogero Sedara, promises at a stroke to assure him "an ephemeral carnal satisfaction and a perennial financial peace". Around the marital and political intrigue, Lampedusa weaves his exquisite tapestries of Sicilian life in its drawn-out twilight. "The wealth of centuries" has now "transmuted into ornament, luxury, pleasure". Through radiant frescos of hunting, dancing, worship, courtship, politics and business, the Prince leads us through this "Utopia thought up by a rustic Plato". Like some gorgeous mirage or hologram, this dreamland is "apt to change any second… or even not to exist at all".

If *The Leopard* does rank as a "conservative" masterpiece, as some champions claim, that conservatism entails unremitting self-awareness. It mandates incisive irony, a delicious sense of the absurd, and a brisk refusal to sanitise a hidebound social order. For the Prince, Sicilian sensuality and nostalgia reveal "a hankering for oblivion", even for death itself. The islanders fail to "improve" their ossified customs because "their vanity is stronger than their misery". A keen amateur astronomer, Don Fabrizio finds in the eternal stars a certainty unknown in human lives. He belongs to "an unlucky generation, swung between the old world and the new", but "ill at ease in both". Lampedusa, just as torn as the hero modelled on his own ancestor, fashions the Prince's disappearing realm as lovingly as he evokes the ballroom of the Ponteleones, that "superb jewel-case shut off from an unworthy world". Then he slips in the provenance of the high-explosive device that will smash the "jewel-case" once and for all. Even the Prince's beloved Great Dane Bendicò, canine mascot of the clan, will in time become no more than a mangy, glass-eyed rug, thrown into the garbage "in the hope of final riddance". Lampedusa's art gloriously rescues Bendicò and his people from that "final riddance". It also shows that they cannot, perhaps should not, live again.

Translation: Urbane, courtly, lyrical and wistful, Alexander Colquhoun's prose (1961) splendidly matches the sunset ironies of its source.

See also: Turgenev, *Fathers and Sons* (1862); Tagore, *Home and the World* (1916); Laxness, *Independent People* (1934–35); Mahfouz, *Cairo Trilogy* (1956-57)

Selected works by the same author: *The Professor and the Siren* (1961)*; Lessons on Stendhal* (1977)*; Letters from London and Europe* (2010).

69 | The Tin Drum (1959) by Günter Grass.

German

Translated by Breon Mitchell (Vintage)

At a Nazi rally in Danzig, little Oskar Matzerath takes a good look at the local party luminaries – from behind the rostrum. The view from behind, or beneath, will always tell the truth about power. Inspect a podium from the rear and you will be "immunised" against "any magic practised" at its front.

This perspective on history from below, irreverent and even scurrilous, defines not just Oskar's viewpoint and the timbre of *The Tin Drum*: it marks the entire span of Günter Grass's career as maverick and mischief-maker. Appearing in 1959, just as the frozen post-war silence over the years of the Third Reich began to thaw in divided Germany, this raucous, picaresque novel showed that an alternative future of free inquiry and expression might beckon for a culture still immobilised by grief, guilt, or else nervous denial.

Both complicit and defiant, Oskar laughs, mocks, dreams and – above all – screams his way through the era of madness and cruelty, "a little demigod whose business it was to harmonise chaos and intoxicate reason". We encounter him in a psychiatric hospital in the 1950s, scribbling his story and insisting that heroes can thrive even if fashionable novels assume that "individuality is a thing of the past". An amoral trickster and small lord of misrule, Oskar manages to drum a nation's buried trauma into the light of day with his talent for disruptive, cathartic merriment.

Aged three, Oskar decides to stop growing. That is the fantastic fulcrum for a novel otherwise tangily flavoured with the earthy, salty realism of Baltic farmers and seafarers. Unsure of his parentage, growing up at this coastal crossroads between Poland and Germany, "the eternal three-year-old drummer" beats out on his lacquered instrument all the deceits and impostures of his place and time. The Nazis seize power, Blitzkrieg and invasion come to Danzig, and Oskar joins a travelling band of dwarf performers to entertain German troops in France. Yet his progress never feels like the unfolding of some omniscient author's top-down plan.

Canny, slangy, sensual, his first-person voice keeps the wisdom of the body and the senses always close at hand. For Grass, this visceral and instinctive life offers a precious armour against the sledgehammer abstractions of history and politics. Oskar's passion for his lover, and step-mother Maria; his memories of infant bliss hiding under his grandmother's wide skirts; the fatty, greasy Baltic food that oozes through his narrative: all of this outranks the bullying headlines of totalitarian autocracy and catastrophic war. Roast goose, smoked eel and lard-smothered potatoes matter more than the "special communiqués" that history blares "at the top of its lungs".

Perhaps Oskar made such an apt hero for post-war Germany because his rebellion takes on a privatised, self-seeking guise. "For as long as I sang glass to pieces, I existed." His screaming bafflement at a lunatic system co-exists with cunning, even ruthless ruses that enable him to make the best of it. As with millions of Germans, this indecipherable protest brands him not as an active resister but a sort of "inner emigrant". When, on Kristallnacht in November 1938, Nazi thugs wreck the shop of the toy merchant Markus, "I was worried about my drums."

As readers, we can sympathise with Oskar's naïvety and selfishness, but still gaze past his story towards the grisly truth it half-conceals. His stunted growth comes to stand for the semi-voluntary infantilisation of a whole society. The comic exuberance of Grass's prose, with all its artisan's delight in the sheen and grain of words, makes its own kind of protest against the inhuman rhetoric of genocidal ideology. As much as George Orwell, he turns honest, concrete language into a weapon of freedom. Like a northerly gale off the Baltic, this breezy vernacular idiom blew the cobwebs off literary

German. Unlike Orwell, however, Grass had to negotiate the moral minefield of growing to manhood under the Nazi yoke.

Opinion still divides over Grass's six decades of silence about his two teenage months of conscripted service in an SS Panzer division in 1945. Our knowledge that this consistent, courageous, champion of truth-telling and account-settling in post-war Germany carried a burden on his own conscience may lend Oskar's survival stratagems an extra piquancy. Oskar even shares some of his author's movements after the German defeat in 1945: as a stonecutter in Düsseldorf, then as a habitué of the city's art school – though as a model rather than a student.

In Düsseldorf, Oskar also finds acclaim as a jazz drummer in a night club called the Onion Cellar. Onions, like eels, rats and flounders, often recur in the earthbound ecology of Grass's work. Here, patrons can at last recover from the icy sorrow of "the tearless century" and learn to cry again. As, for a small fee, customers chopped up onions, "The tears flowed and washed everything away". Manic and haunted, *The Tin Drum*'s laughter lies very close to tears – the tears that would flood through post-war European literature as it opened the cellars of memory.

Translation: The first English translation, by Ralph Manheim in 1961, still grips and strikes hard. However, Breon Mitchell's in 2009 – which had the benefit of Grass's collaboration – improves on that achievement.

See also: Hašek, *The Good Soldier Švejk* (1923); Roth, *The Radetsky March* (1932); Agnon, *Only Yesterday* (1945); Kadare, *Chronicle in Stone* (1971)

Selected works by the same author: *Cat and Mouse* (1961); *Dog Years* (1963); *The Flounder* (1977); *The Rat* (1986)

70 | Life and Fate (1959, published 1980) by Vasily Grossman.

Russian

Translated by Robert Chandler (Vintage)

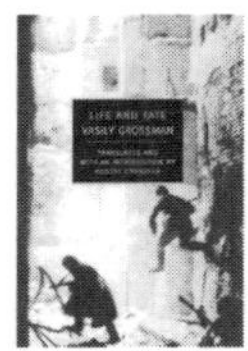

Like his literary forefather Tolstoy, Vasily Grossman sometimes dares to put the titans of history into his fiction – if only to cut them down to size. Hitler and Stalin both make cameo appearances in *Life and Fate*, surely the greatest novel of the Second World War in any language. The latter has a nightmare vision in which his millions of victims – the slaughtered peasantry, the ranks of purged rivals, the dead armies of the Gulag – come "crawling out of the earth" to judge him. In a sense, Grossman's masterpiece itself delivers that verdict. It was composed in isolation in the 1950s, by a former war correspondent who had reported on the front lines from Stalingrad to Berlin and exposed the death-camp at Treblinka. Yet the manuscript of *Life and Fate* proved so incendiary that a Soviet ideologist told Grossman that two or three centuries would have to pass before its publication. Seldom has "the might of the State", which Grossman dissects in its power both to shape the present and "construct a new past", offered such a thunderous tribute to a work of literature.

Grossman's multi-layered epic marshals a crowded cast of scientists, doctors, officers, Old Bolsheviks and political prisoners. All are caught up in the defence of Stalingrad against the Nazi advance and in the mass evacuation of threatened Russian cities. The novel swarms with the sort of characters who, even under artillery fire or in a concentration camp, will stop to argue whether the chaos and cruelty of the present serves any purpose or reveals any pattern. Viktor Shtrum, the theoretical physicist whose extended family supplies many of the novel's principal figures, wonders if the world itself might not be "a reflection of mathematics".

If so, then only chaos theory might properly apply. Episodes of intense drama, terror and tenderness multiply at this turning-point in global war, lit by military flares on the battlefield, the bulbs of the interrogation cell, or the dim lights of freezing apartments in hungry cities. But even in the corpse-strewn outpost of House 6/1 at Stalingrad, pounded by German guns and bombs, we feel that "life's grace and charm can never be erased by the powers of destruction". What higher unity – the march of history, the progress of humanity, or even the arbitrary fate which in the dire winter of 1942-43 seems alone to have "the power to pardon and chastise" – can possibly make sense of this random collision of human particles under the bombardment of tyranny and war?

In its form, as well as its ideas, *Life and Fate* answers that challenge. Against the idealists, the system-builders, the bloody breakers of human eggs to make a theoretical omelette, it insists that "the only true and lasting meaning of the struggle for life lies in the individual". So, as beautifully marshalled scenes move from battlefield to forest idyll, from scientific institute to prison camp – even into the gas chambers – Grossman shows us why we should put the restless hunt for an over arching "big picture" on hold.

That big picture ought to lie in the minute particulars of love, fear, hope, despair and simple kindness. The old Tolstoy disciple Ikonnikov, who dies in a German camp, believes that human history amounts to "a battle fought by a great evil struggling to crush a small kernel of kindness". True, in this dialectical novel, every action finds its reaction, every point its counterpoint. A committed supporter of the Bolshevik revolution in his youth, Grossman can feel the ethical weight of those actors – the Red Army officers, the power-plant managers, the healers, the teachers, the ordinary workers – who sincerely think that human solidarity requires the scaffolding of centralised power. Yet at pivotal moments, it's the tiny gesture of "everyday human kindness" that catches his acute eye – not the quest for "the terrible Good with a capital 'G'". During their evacuation to Kazan, Viktor's historian friend Madyarov champions the arch-individualist Chekhov as the true pathfinder of "Russia's freedom". "Let's begin with respect, compassion and love for the individual," he urges, "or we'll never get anywhere." Theory becomes heart-rending practice when Grossman – shockingly – takes us through the doors of the gas chamber with the army doctor Sofya Levinton and David, the little boy she cares for in the jaws of hell. Her final thought is to comfort him and then, as life slips away, she feels "pity for all of you, both living and dead".

Grossman's indictment of "the power of the State" that "reared up like a cliff of basalt" takes multiple forms. Bravely, for a Soviet writer, he equates Stalin's and Hitler's autocracies. He scrutinises the Soviet apparatus of terror in an age when "murder had become the basis of everyday life". Alert to the virus of anti-Semitism in every variant, he shows how the lie-machine of totalitarian systems gathers scapegoats and outsiders as its fuel. And, in Viktor's final surrender of "inner freedom" after Stalin grasps the strategic value of his nuclear physics, he demonstrates that moral choice persists under extreme duress. Even for the Nazi camp commandant Kaltluft: "A man may be led by fate, but he can refuse to follow". Under the winter ice of dictatorship and war, a spring of freedom still awaits.

Translation: Robert Chandler performed epic feats in his 1985 version, with a stylistic range – from world historical grandeur to domestic intimacy – that matches the novel's enormous sweep and scope.

See also: Tolstoy, *War and Peace* (1869); Platonov, *The Foundation Pit* (1930); Némirovsky, *Suite Française* (1942-2004); Vargas Llosa, *The Feast of the Goat* (2000)

Selected works by the same author: *Kolchugin's Youth* (1940); *An Armenian Sketchbook* (1962); *Forever Flowing* (1970)

71 | SOLARIS (1961) by Stanisław Lem.

Polish

Translated by Bill Johnston (Premier Digital Publishing); Joanna Kilmartin and Steve Cox (Faber & Faber)

The true masterpieces of science fiction, as its champions often maintain, explore not outer space but inner space. Among the topmost peaks of a genre that still too often lacks critical respect, *Solaris* seems to bear out that premise. Kris Kelvin, the inter-planetary psychologist who tells this story, laments that "Man has gone out to explore other worlds…without having explored his own labyrinth of dark passages and secret chambers, and without finding what lies behind doorways that he himself has sealed." Lem's multi-dimensional fable of a near-deserted space station in orbit around the enigmatic planet Solaris does indeed probe the shrouded interior of its human protagonists. But it also asks vast and unsettling questions about the world beyond the reach of their puny brains.

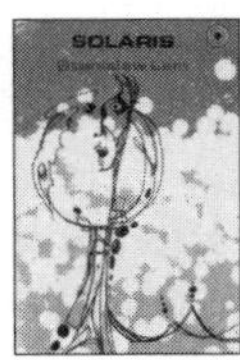

What if "life" existed elsewhere in forms that bore no remote, or even metaphorical, relationship to the organic processes we know? The Earth people's dream of "contact" with alien beings "means the exchange of specific knowledge". What, however, if the nature of alien existence rendered all exchange impossible? "Where there are no people," or even entities comprehensible to humans, "there can be no motives accessible to people." Utter loneliness within the universe, which is the fate or fear that haunts so much classic SF, may be less terrifying than the thought of co-existence with many kinds of "life" that we will never understand.

During the Cold War, just as many conventional critics judged the novel either dead or moribund, the leading figures of scientific and speculative fiction fashioned an extraordinary corpus of philosophical tales. They are unequalled in intellectual zest and range since the age of Voltaire, Diderot and the storytelling sages of the Enlightenment. Whether Philip K Dick and Ursula Le Guin in the US, JG Ballard in Britain or Lem himself in Poland, many of the most original figures worked at a tangent to the dominant culture of their time. Never a political exile, or even a straightforward "dissident", Lem stood so far outside the loop of official Polish literature during the Warsaw Pact years that his very separateness won him a relative freedom. Although *Solaris* does give us glimpses of power politics back on Earth, for the most part it hunts intellectual game of a size to dwarf the petty wrangles between 20th-century ideologies.

Solaris shares with the modernist mainstream the sense that an era of decadence can become the breeding-ground of innovation. Research aboard the space station, which circles above the giant island-studded "ocean" of Solaris, has come to a dead end. One of its scientists, Gibarian, has killed himself. The discipline of "Solaristics", which for decades has thrown up competing theories about the planet's "ocean", has quarrelled itself into exhaustion. Is this gelatinous sea a sort of sentient being, "an organic structure, extraordinarily evolved"? Or does its "plasmic mechanism" defy every definition of life that humans can devise? Perhaps it mutates with all the ineffably advanced intelligence of a quasi-animate "computer". Lem shows a startling prescience about the debates that now surround artificial intelligence, virtual reality and the planetary "brain" sought by digital Utopians in cyberspace. On one reading, the ocean of Solaris acts like a massive, colloidal internet. In some unknown fashion, it turns maths into mind. The "symmetriad", one of the organic-seeming forms that heave and seethe around its ocean, "represents a spatial analogue of some transcendental equation".

One of the ocean's powers is to mine human consciousness and manufacture phantoms, replicants or simulacra from it. These embody the deepest fears and desires of the humans orbiting the planet. Thus, aboard the station, Kelvin meets a version of his lover Harey, who committed suicide after their separation. Real feeling flowers again even though one partner has the status of an idea, a memory or a longing. Thanks to the oceanic intelligence, that phantasm has "become flesh and blood". Does the ocean wish the reunited lovers well or ill? Lem raises such questions but then insists that, thanks to the anthropomorphic cast of human thought, such assumptions can make no sense. The mighty oceanic plasma consists of "a library where all the books are written in an indecipherable language". Still, its capacity to materialise human desire means that "it knows us better than we know ourselves".

Solaris plants the human, or pseudo-human, tenderness of Kelvin and Harey's second-chance romance amid Lem's soaring speculations. They circle around the mysteries of consciousness. Memories

– or fantasies – of intimacy with one being of the same species forever trace the horizon of our understanding. But our own minds defeat us. "We think of ourselves as Knights of the Holy Contact," says Kelvin's colleague Snaut. "This is another lie… We have no need of other worlds. We need mirrors." *Solaris* holds up a mirror to human need and dread. It also invites us to think, impossibly, about what may lie on the other side of selfhood.

Translation: Ironically, this novel of broken or flawed contact for long existed in English thanks only to a two-stage translation from Polish via French (1970) – a text Lem disliked. Bill Johnston's digital remix of 2011 may prove elusive, whereas Kilmartin-Cox remains easy to find.

See also: Voltaire, *Candide* (1759); Bioy Casares, *The Invention of Morel* (1940); Buzzati, *The Tartar Steppe* (1940); Murakami, *Hard-Boiled Wonderland and The End of the World* (1985)

Selected works by the same author: *Eden* (1959); *Memoirs Found in a Bathtub* (1961); *The Invincible* (1964); *The Futurological Congress* (1971)

72 | The Time Regulation Institute (1962) by Ahmet Hamdi Tanpinar.

Turkish

Translated by Maureen Freely and Alexander Dawe (Penguin Modern Classics)

For Halit Ayarci, "Progress begins with the evolution of the time-piece." Halit has founded the time-keeping and time-managing agency that gives a focus to this gorgeously melancholic satire of modernisation and development. Respect for, and obedience to, the uniform time maintained by clocks and watches in sync with one official source has opened "a rupture with nature itself". Freed from the dubious data imparted by sun and moon, modern man can stride into the future with an accurate watch in his pocket and an eye on the public clock tower. After all, organised work itself, in the office, workshop or factory, requires "a certain conception of time". As for modern woman, she may well end up working in Halit Bey's bustling headquarters in Istanbul, in a regimented typing pool conducted by a baton-wielding time-beater.

Decades before the career of Orhan Pamuk, who has acknowledged the older writer as his master, Ahmet Hamdi Tanpinar transformed the inner and outer turmoil of Turkey into gloriously eccentric novels. They move with a pace and rhythm all their own. Dragged into secular modernity under the leadership of Ataturk after the Ottoman Empire's fall, Turkey fast became – and arguably remains – the national prototype for breakneck development. As it lurched between tradition and innovation, country and city, Europe and Asia, the state Ataturk created has for almost a century stood on the perilous front line of "progress" and weathered the backlashes it brings. In his two great novels, *A Mind at Peace* and *The Time Regulation Institute*, Tanpinar traces the marks left by this uneasy metamorphosis. They inscribe not only social relations but, above all, the consciousness of newly-minted modern people. Fallible, divided, fearful, wistful, his heroes feel that humans were not designed for that "relentless march towards progress" decreed by politicians. Their desires, their fantasies, their phantoms, throw endless spanners in the efficiently time-managed works. As our narrator often notices, not least from observing his own behaviour, "if we examine how we manage our affairs, we are hard-pressed to find any trace of reason at all".

Hayri Irdal, who tells this story, is writing his memoirs. The vicissitudes of his career in Istanbul have flung him from a warm, squabbling clan through a variety of jobs that left him poised insecurely on the cusp between old and new societies. Finally, he landed a top post at the hallowed Institute itself. He has even written a book – never mind that it was a biography of the entirely fictitious "Ahmet the Timely", supposedly a 17th-century horologist and patron saint of time-keepers. Picaresque and often farcical, told by Tanpinar with immense charm and cunning, Hayri's adventures tumble him through Turkey's years of transition. Everything seems to change – government, language, professions, customs – while the people themselves cussedly refuse to get up to 20th-century speed.

Hayri learns the skill that will fix his fate while an apprentice to the clock and watch repairer Nuri Efendi. He "equated people with clocks" but still sees mechanical horology as, above all, a pious aid to the Muslim routines of prayer and fasting. Tanpinar's spry and droll storytelling bounces his perplexed hero around this world in flux. Hayri tangles with ancient arts – an alchemy scam practised by the sinister Seyit Lutfullah, "more evil dijnn than human being" – and ultra-modern ones. The pioneer Turkish psychoanalyst Dr Ramiz (a splendid comic creation) struggles to fit his patient's florid symptoms into the latest one-size-fits-all model of the mind imported from Vienna. For Ramiz, the family's patriarchal, phallic grandfather clock – the "Blessed One" – has much to answer for. Hayri marries twice, first to traditional helpmeet Emine then, when widowed, to the Hollywood-mad Pakize. Some of his Istanbul circles – the Spiritualist Society or the rumour-packed coffee house where gossip coalesces into "collective memory" – unite the habits of ancient and modern worlds.

Halit Ayarci's grand design for an institute that will keep all Turkey up to the minute, and even impose fines for laggardly timepieces, thrusts modern greatness on Hayri. Outwardly, he becomes a prophet and a paladin of the "age of bureaucracy", in which every second counts. Within, he drifts in an emotional limbo, attached to the leisurely, time-defying friendships and formalities of his youth, but compelled to don one "mask" after another. A sense of absurdity bedevils him: "I was living in a world without connection…

in a fairground torn asunder by a violent tornado that had come out of nowhere". Yet, beyond this existential plight, Tanpinar peppers the institute with superbly piquant satire. As a burlesque of corporate pomposity, paranoia and deceit, it echoes far beyond Ataturk's Turkey – not least via the PR machine that erases complexity to write "the film version of our lives". Like some hi-tech headquarters today, the office even has a ping-pong room for "relaxation". Hayri, "a man poisoned by words", enjoys instead the time-honoured, time-squandering games of conversation, storytelling, reminiscence and nostalgia. For Halit, that wasteful wordiness makes him hopelessly "old-fashioned". From this man out of time, and in a style defiantly rich in the hybrid subtleties of old Ottoman Turkish, Tanpinar constructed a book that mocks, and stops, the clock. It still chimes for the wound-up souls of every mega-city.

Translation: Maureen Freely and Alexander Dawe (2013) sustain an expressive and engaging English idiom that honours the wit, inventiveness and grace of Tanpinar's voice.

See also: Svevo, *Zeno's Conscience* (1923); Arlt, *The Seven Madmen* (1929); Qian, *Fortress Besieged* (1947); Pamuk, *The Black Book* (1990)

Selected works by the same author: *A Mind at Peace* (1949)

73 | The Garden of the Finzi-Continis (1962) by Giorgio Bassani.

Italian

Translated by Jamie McKendrick (Penguin Modern Classics)

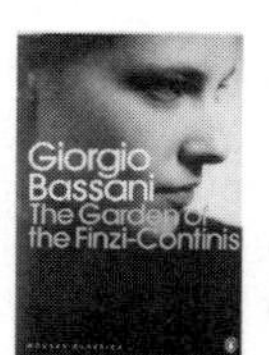

In April 1939, the narrator of Giorgi Bassani's novel for once leaves his home in the northern Italian city of Ferrara. He visits his brother, a student across the Alps in Grenoble. There, this dreamy young man with vague ambitions for a literary career consults the manuscripts of Stendhal. He finds within them a stray note written in English: "All lost, nothing lost". It could almost serve as a motto for Bassani's wistful, lyrical but quietly devastating love story set within Ferrara's Jewish community on the eve of the genocide that would consume so much of it. If this novel counts as a record of first love, it also offers last rites for a people robbed by mass murder not only of their lives but their memorials.

A prologue, set two decades after the main action, sees the narrator return to Ferrara from Rome. A detour takes in ancient Etruscan tombs, where this refined people, soon to be conquered by "stronger and more warlike" tribes, could rest in peace. Here, perhaps, "eternity did not appear to be so much of an illusion". In contrast, in Ferrara's Jewish cemetery, the grand mausoleum built by the Finzi-Contini family in their tolerant, late 19th-century heyday stands almost empty – save for a son who died of natural causes. Otherwise, "no one knows whether they have any grave at all". Their true sepulchre, arguably, consists of Bassani's flawlessly shaped and phrased novel. It is one of six books in his "Romanzo di Ferrara". This fictional cycle found in his home city, and above all its long-established Jewish community, a small world as complete and satisfying as the Renaissance cityscape he maps with loving precision.

"All lost, nothing lost": apart from that elegiac preamble, and a mournful postscript, the only direct allusion to the catastrophe looming for Ferrara's Jews comes when the narrator recalls the unhappy passover dinner of 1939. It takes place soon after the enactment of Mussolini's Racial Laws. Those edicts showed that Fascist Italy had forsaken its habits of relative tolerance to curry Hitler's favour. The storyteller scans the faces of his kinsfolk and, with hindsight, recognises that many would be "swallowed up by German crematoria ovens". In defiance of this utter loss, Bassani's story restores these people and this place to life. He makes that life as sensually rich and luxuriant as the foliage in the Finzi-Contini family garden: a coveted Eden that, for all its secret beauties, has a "wild and dark and rather melancholy" aspect.

The narrator does not belong in the garden. In the snobbish hierarchy of Ferrara's Jews, he and his family dwell among the down-to-earth, well-integrated majority, almost "banal in our normality". Hence the visceral shock when, in the cinema, the library or at the tennis club, neighbours curse "filthy Jews". The Finzi-Continis have always kept themselves a little apart, hidden behind the dark gates of their grand mansion just inside the city walls. Their "aloofness and seclusion" are perpetuated by their wealth as landowners, their Spanish (rather than Italian or German) forms of worship, and an aura of aristocratic cultivation that both vexes and fascinates the rest of the community. As a child, the narrator has fallen under the spell of Micol, daughter of Professor Ermanno Finzi-Contini and Signora Olga. He and Micol's childhood expedition into an underground chamber by the city walls retains a super-charged erotic allure. A decade later, such memories stoke his desire for this bright, worldly but inscrutable young woman. The exclusion of Jews from the tennis club means that, as the fine weather of 1938 stretches into a "luminous Indian summer", the narrator can play on the Finzi-Continis' hallowed private courts. So he edges closer to Micol. Their games stretch deep into the gathering twilight, an idyll all the more precious for its transience. The "good times" still lie within their grasp, "while the season lasted".

These "excessively beautiful" days nonetheless feel "undermined by the approaching winter". From the closed circle of Ferrara's walls to the threatened Eden of the garden and the slow waning of the autumn light, Bassani – a poet before he wrote fiction – builds a discreet but haunting symbolism into the fabric of his story. Meanwhile, the narrator proves over-zealous in his pursuit of Micol. He spars with the genial but brusque Communist chemist Malnate – his rival, he suspects, in her affections. Next year he finds himself "chased out of Paradise" by his beloved. Micol fears that a sexual relationship with him would feel like incest, and spoil their "lovely memories of a shared childhood".

In every sense, the summer ends. The shades darken around the family, the city and its lovers. As he cycles past entwined bodies under the walls at midnight, the narrator thinks of himself as "a kind of strange driven ghost, full both of life and death, of passion and compassion". Those vacant tombs glimpsed at the outset tell their own story of a known horror. Bassani has no need to elaborate. In the elegance of its architecture, and the finesse of its execution, his novel erects their lasting monument.

Translation: The poet Jamie McKendrick brings grace, suppleness and strength to his exemplary version (2007).

See also: Némirovsky, *Suite Française* (1942-2004); Gadda, *That Awful Mess on the Via Merulana* (1957); Lampedusa, *The Leopard* (1958); Sebald, *The Emigrants* (1992)

Selected works by the same author: *Within the Walls* (1956); *The Gold-rimmed Spectacles* (1958); *The Heron* (1968); *The Smell of Hay* (1972)

74 | The Slave (1962) by Isaac Bashevis Singer.

Yiddish (Poland/United States)

Translated by the author and Cecil Hemley (Penguin Modern Classics)

The finest historical novels never try to escape the present. Often,

they must revisit past ages in order to grasp events that, viewed close up, might defeat all understanding. In hands as artful as Isaac Bashevis Singer's, a fictional time-shift can also explore the evergreen – and unanswerable – perplexities that vex the human mind. In *The Slave*, the learned Jacob teaches his wife Sarah – formerly a Polish peasant girl called Wanda – about Jewish law and ethics. She raises one question more than any other:

"why did the good suffer and the evil prosper?" By the time he wrote *The Slave*, Singer, who had emigrated from his native Poland to the United States in 1935, had already begun to mine that bottomless mystery. He pursued it in stories and novels set both in the Jewish shtetls of Poland, and among the diaspora communities of the New World. He wrote in Yiddish, and re-engineered the richly allusive idiom of the Jewish rural and provincial past as an agile language of urban modernity.

The Slave returns to the Cossack massacres of Jews during the mid 17th-century. This "time of upheaval" saw Poland overrun and wasted by the rival armies of the Thirty Years War: the period of Singer's first novel, *Satan in Goray* (1933). Since that work, however, sorrow and affliction beyond any historical precedent had visited the Jews of Europe. We hear in *The Slave* that the rapacious invaders, with the anti-Semitic Cossacks under the rebel leader Khmelnytsky, have reduced Poland to "one vast cemetery". Singer spares us no details of their tortures, rapes and murders during these pogroms. Jacob, who after the mass slaughter that killed his family has become the informal "slave" of a Polish farmer, struggles to comprehend the calamity. "It was beyond the power of any man to contemplate the atrocities and mourn them adequately." The Jewish survivors of the Second World War in Europe, and their families overseas, knew just such a state of frozen bafflement. Although a richly evocative and wholly credible portrait of a distant epoch, *The Slave* also ranks, albeit obliquely, as one the greatest Holocaust novels.

Yet, in its early sections, Singer inhabits the lovely wilderness of the highlands near Krakow with a rhapsodic delight. The "slave" Jacob, a studious timber trader's son with a rabbinical career in prospect, now herds cows for Jan Bzik. His summer bed is a barn, his winter berth the granary. Jacob strives to remember the Law he learned and inscribe it on the rocks. Meanwhile, the beauty around him writes a scripture of its own, and "one clearly discerned God's hand among the flaming clouds". Nominally Catholic, the Polish peasantry still cherish pagan customs. Imps, sprites and demons lurk in every hill and wood, while "werewolves and trolls swarmed the roads".

In this folk tale landscape, enchantingly described, Jacob falls in love, and in lust, with Jan's daughter Wanda. Smart, curious, capable, she yearns to share his Jewish faith. Passion conquers piety, as often with Singer. The couple's loving, indeed erotic, wrangles over "the freedom of the will, the meaning of existence and the problem of evil" come to an end when Jacob is ransomed and re-enters the Jewish community. Yet he dares to return to fetch her. With Wanda now the supposedly dumb "Sarah", they live as husband and wife when Jacob becomes an estate manager for the erratic and volatile nobleman Adam Pilitzky – sometimes an anti-Semite, sometimes a sympathiser. For Catholics and Jews, conversion is utterly taboo; the pair risk not just exposure but execution. Jacob laments that persecution has not elevated his "tortured people": envy, malice and bigotry still plague them. A solitary "branch torn from its trunk", he has to forge his own code of ethics, rooted in the Torah and Talmud he reveres but shorn of narrow prejudice and pedantic literalism. Especially after Sarah dies in childbirth and he becomes a wanderer in the Holy Land, the woes of the innocent gnaw at him: "Not death, but suffering was the real enigma. What place did it have in God's Creation?" For Jacob, as for the vegetarian, animal-loving Singer, that urge to share the pain of the powerless extends beyond humankind to every living being. The animals deserve not just respect, but "At the end of days, they too must have salvation." Jacob even "silently blamed the Creator for forcing one creature to annihilate another".

Singer taps into every resource of the traditional tale but without kitsch, without nostalgia. Deeply affecting as a transgressive romance, *The Slave* also satisfies as a pastoral idyll, an adventure yarn, a village comedy and, above all, as a philosophical investigation conducted with candour and compassion in the shadow of unspeakable crimes. Through all its charms, and its griefs, Singer never ceases to challenge his unfathomable God. The divine riddle remains, although Jacob's answer – typically, in the form of a question – must suffice for us. "What does a father want from his children but that they should not do injustice to each other?"

Translation: In collaboration with Cecil Hemley, Singer's self-translation has the pace, colour and mood of a folkloric legend mapped onto dark modern times.

See also: Manzoni, *The Betrothed* (1842); Dostoyevsky *The Brothers Karamazov* (1880); Agnon, *Only Yesterday* (1945); Grossman, *See Under: LOVE* (1986)

Selected works by the same author: *Satan in Goray* (1933); *The Family Moskat* (1950); *The Magician of Lublin* (1960); *Enemies, A Love Story* (1966)

75 | The Death of Artemio Cruz (1962) by Carlos Fuentes.

Spanish (Mexico)

Translation by Alfred MacAdam (FSG Classics)

Super-sized monsters of pride and ambition have always stalked the pages of fiction. Their amoral charisma may burn with a brilliant flame that few conventionally virtuous heroes ever match. For the Latin American novel, so avid to do justice to the continent's history, and geography, of excess, these seductive rogues can attain Andean heights and Amazonian intricacy. In Fuentes's deathbed portrait of a Mexican titan, Artemio Cruz insists he has always lived in a "zone of ambiguity" – between and beyond the blacks and whites, angels and demons of everyday morality.

The "dictator novel'" practised by authors such as Augusto Roa Bastos, Miguel Ángel Asturias and Mario Vargas Llosa took devilishly attractive political leaders as the model for this species of New World superman. Often the genre built stories around the careers of actual autocrats. Fuente's Cruz does, indirectly, wield political power. Above all, however, he is a wheeler-dealer entrepreneur. Cruz makes fortunes as a rapacious landowner, exploiter of Mexico's mineral resources, press magnate, hotelier, railway investor and – not least – local agent and fixer for predatory corporations from the United States. A trail-blazing book in many ways, *The Death of Artemio Cruz* pivots on the privatisation of power. These days, most of his region's political strongmen have gone, replaced by more-or-less fragile democracies. Artemio's billionaire successors – in Fuentes's Mexico, as elsewhere – still reign unchecked.

As he lies in intermittent agony in Mexico City, Artemio is plagued by the "long cold dagger" of pain in his terminal illness and harassed by family, employees and priests. He looks back in anguish on his own and his nation's past. Like several other stellar talents of the Latin American "Boom" in fiction, Fuentes later sought to roll vast tracts of history, culture and thought into an encyclopaedic novel of the region's development: in his case, *Terra Nostra* (1975). This book also crosses epic distances, but at a brisker pace. The novel covers not only its flawed hero's spectacular progress from poverty and soldiering in the Mexican Revolution to wealth and influence. It embraces almost a century of the country's history – not to mention an evolutionary, even cosmic, dimension that ties human life-span to the fate of the stars. "You are, you will be, you have been the universe incarnate. For you galaxies will flame and the sun will burn." Yet it does so at a moderate length, each intensely realised scene flashlit and then swiftly cut. In his technique, as much as in his glamorous ogre of a protagonist, Fuentes drew on Orson Welles's *Citizen Kane*.

These flashbacks from the deathbed do not unroll in strict biographical order. For Artemio, "Desire will send you back into memory." His delirious return to episodes of triumph and calamity takes the form of a subjective jigsaw rather than a step-by-step chronicle. The great path-breaking novels of the "Boom" shine with a sense of almost limitless freedom: of form, of voice, of subject. Fuentes makes a wonderful nonsense of previous critical distinctions between the psychological and historical novel; between stream-of-consciousness and social realism; between interior and exterior space. Artemio's rhapsody of memory encompasses all of those elements and more, from the tender wartime romance with his lost love Regina to the blazing vision of Mexico's mingled and scrambled past as "a thousand countries, with a single name", and to high-society dialogue at soirées where the nation's "new order" does its crooked business. Fuente's prose inherits literature's old world and enriches it with the new. Nothing seems off limits. In stylistic terms, he can feel as much like a swaggering plunderer and extractor as his hero.

Artemio's power has grown out of violence. Whether nakedly obvious or held in reserve, that threat of force also underlies erotic and family relationships in this patriarchal society. Catalina is the reluctant "trophy wife" won by his military prowess and political manoeuvring: an intimate enemy for the rest of Artemio's life. Daughters and mistresses inspire love, need and the will to domination. From the first, conflict-ridden miscegenation of Spanish conquerors and Indians, Fuentes suggests, the politics of bedroom, battlefield and boardroom have replayed in cycles of strike and counter-strike. "Viva Mexico… Born of fucking, dead from fucking, living fucked: pregnant belly and winding sheet, hidden in the word. " The assertive machismo of a poor man from a dominated culture spreads outward into Artemio's military and financial conquests. Above all it moulds his pleasure in outwitting the slick, rich but naïve "gringos" from the north: "you imposed your will so they would admit you are their equal". Injustice breeds injustice; corruption seeds corruption.

As his death nears, Artemio builds into more than the tainted sum of his memories and his desires. Behind these "vulgar facts and events" lies the unique being with his love of fresh quinces, his "youth of dark horses" and a childhood of wonder and dread only revealed at the finale. His innocence will expire, we learn, not at the hands of guilt but from "enormous surprise". Beyond the struggle, cruelty and grief of its setting and its epoch, Artemio's testimony never loses that surprise.

Translation: Alfred MacAdam's 1991 version restores some structural idiosyncrasies of Fuentes's text that the original translation by Sam Hileman (1964) had smoothed away. Hileman's ventriloquism retains a striking early-Sixties flavour, truculent and transgressive.

See also: Beckett, *Trilogy* (1951-1953); Cortázar, *Hopscotch* (1963); García Márquez, *One Hundred Years of Solitude* (1967); Vargas Llosa, *The Feast of the Goat* (2000)

Selected works by the same author: *Terra Nostra* (1975); *The Old Gringo* (1985); *Christopher Unborn* (1987); *The Crystal Frontier* (1995)

76 | HOPSCOTCH (1963) by Julio Cortázar.

Spanish (Argentina/France)

Translated by Gregory Rabassa (Everyman's Library)

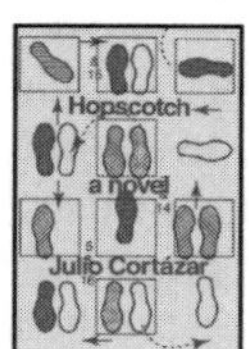

At the close of *Hopscotch*, the protagonist Horacio goes to visit the writer Morelli in hospital. Morelli, whose notebook entries drop not some entirely reliable clues about *Hopscotch* itself, asks Horacio – an erudite Argentinian, adrift in 1950s Paris – and his artist friend Etienne to take care of his manuscripts. He says that "You can read my book any way you want to". Famously, Cortázar invites his readers to find their own path through the main story of this novel. We can either read the chapters in sequence, or in a "hopscotch" pattern of jumps according to a numerical plan that precedes the text. The first fifty-six sections contain the more or less chronological story of Horacio, who acts like an existentialist dandy but works as a "clandestine book-keeper". He loves but loses the mercurial, waif-like La Maga, wrangles with his bohemian chums in the "Serpent Club", and returns to Buenos Aires to work first in a circus, then an asylum, where he suffers a breakdown. Another hundred "expendable chapters" fill in the gaps of Horacio's story, and gather a collage of quotations that illuminate the novel. They also give Morelli's own commentary and manifesto for a free-form style of fiction that would break open the "closed order" of the traditional novel, making the no-longer-godlike author not the master of ceremonies but "an accomplice of the reader, a travelling companion". For Morelli, who is not Cortázar but shares much of his artistic DNA, "the true character and the only one that interests me is the reader."

All of which may have the unfortunate effect of making *Hopscotch* sound like a wilfully abstruse experiment in avant-garde literature that belongs firmly to its period and locale: the post-war Parisian café scene of amateur existentialists, jazz buffs and superannuated Surrealists, spiced with beatnik-era Asian philosophy. The "hopscotch" diagram also becomes a Buddhist mandala ("On top is Heaven, on the bottom is Earth"). It serves as the mystical matrix of a liberation from the Western chains of cause-and-effect that have hitherto imprisoned both people and novels. Against the nostalgia for a fixed order to life, that "anxiety for an axis", *Hopscotch* not only argues but demonstrates that "the world has broken into pieces and it will be necessary to rename it, finger by finger, lip by lip, shadow by shadow". Yet Cortázar's schema, although deeply considered and deftly arranged, would hardly have been enough to install this serpentine maze of a story as the cornerstone of Latin American fiction during the "Boom" years. An inspirational work, it was admired, amended and plundered for decades, from García Márquez to Bolaño.

All trickery aside, the skipping, teasing author hops between his squares in an exhilarating spirit of curiosity, creativity, even joy. The expat life of passion, theory, quarrels and strong coffee in Parisian cafés, "neutral territory for the stateless of the soul", has never felt so sweet, or so sorrowful. Horacio's longing for the vanished La Maga pours buckets of tenderness into the novel's river of cleverness. Along the way, rapt and witty discussions of a new kind of art, ludic, non-linear and improvisatory, blaze with excitement and eloquence – most often, in Cortázar's evocations of his beloved jazz, "the only really universal music of the century". The riffs, runs and syncopations of a Charlie Parker or Oscar Peterson point the way towards a fluid, migratory ideal of art that floats and dances across all barriers, "a cloud without frontiers... an archetypal form". Other post-war Paris-based writers who, like Cortázar, cherished the Surrealist legacy had also worshipped jazz – Boris Vian, above all. None managed to create the ultimate bebop novel. This displaced Argentinian did.

In Buenos Aires, Horacio's adventures with his old friends Traveller and Talita – a married couple – begin in a mood of weird, comic exuberance but gradually darken. Literally, and figuratively, the circus gives way to the asylum. That hopscotch principle of endless chance and choice, "the giddy discontinuity of existence", can push its free-spirited followers towards dread and paranoia. Cortázar here counts the cost of a breakdown in system and reason. Dump the "usual hypocrisy" that allows "an order in thought and life", and demons rather than angels may rush in. Horacio – still pining for La Maga – ends up wrapping threads around his room at the clinic to ensnare potential attackers. For all his unfettered liberty, he ties himself in knots. In this light, the libertarian fiction sketched by Morelli in the "expendable chapters" has its shadow-side. As the putative author admits, a book detached from the usual moorings of psychology and causality would amount to "a kind of disquiet, a continuous uprooting". In an age of "continuous uprooting", Cortázar employs a bulging tool box of avant-garde devices to push liberation – in art, in feeling, in ideas – to the limit. The result thrills and delights, but unsettles too. Morelli's, or Cortázar's, "accumulation of fragments" can never "crystallise into a total reality". Not even the all-powerful reader can reach the last square on the court, and find their way to Heaven – or Utopia.

Translation: Gregory Rabassa's 1966 rendering shows off all the virtuosity, and versatility, of a translator who did so much to bring the "Boom" to Anglophone readers.

See also: Musil, *The Man Without Qualities* (1930-43); Cabrera Infante, *Three Trapped Tigers* (1964); Perec, *Life A User's Manual* (1979); Pamuk, *The Black Book* (1990)

Selected works by the same author: *The Winners* (1960); *All Fires the Fire* (1966); *62: A Model Kit* (1968); *We Love Glenda so Much* (1981)

77 | THREE TRAPPED TIGERS (1965) by Guillermo Cabrera Infante.

Spanish (Cuba)

Translated by Suzanne Jill Levine and Donald Gardner with the author (Dalkey Archive)

In many ways, no novel could feel more "literary" than Cabrera

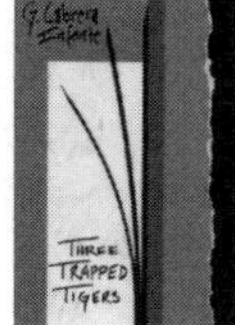

Infante's crazy, learned, reckless and pun-stuffed journey through shady and steamy Havana in the dying days of Fulgencio Batista's dictatorship. Its bohemian drifters and talkers – a press photographer, a journalist-writer, a jobbing actor, a bongo-playing musician – argue, dream, desire and remember their way through the night clubs and street life of a hedonistic, violent city on the eve of Cuba's revolution. Cabrera Infante, who begins with "Showtime!" at the Tropicana club, stages a tropical tribute-act to the James Joyce – or "Shame's Choice" – who wrote *Ulysses* and *Finnegans Wake*. Typically, this polyglot punster cites *Ulysses*, that previous carnival of city life, as both "a milestone" and "a millstone".

Three Trapped Tigers (the title alludes to a Spanish tongue-twister) bursts at its ragged, multi-coloured seams with sparkling parodies of authors both local and foreign, from Ernest Hemingway and TS Eliot to José Martí and Alejo Carpentier. Its layout and typography borrow from Lewis Carroll's *Alice* books and (above all) Laurence Sterne's *Tristram Shandy*. A brutal slaying is rendered as black pages. Empty space appears where we expect "revelations" and a page of reversed type captures consciousness "on the other side of the mirror" – the parallel reality of memory, art and language. The novel's salty, scabrous monologues and dialogues seek to fix in print the passing cloudbursts and rainbows of Cuban street-slang. Beyond all this, the bilingual Cabrera Infante's close involvement with the translation means that the distorting mirror or lens that refracts Spanish into English also takes centre stage. This is a "*Remembrance of Things Past* Translation". In any case, the "original" text was itself but a wan reflection of the torrential talk and intangible thought that nurtured it, since "Ways of speaking are also styles of writing. You'll end up spiking Spunnish".

Sometimes hard work, mostly pure joy, Cabrera Infante's riot of "Spunnish" misadventures both revels in pyrotechnic brilliance and douses it in elegy, grief and nostalgia. *Three Trapped Tigers* neither absolves nor prosecutes the decadent late-1950s demimonde of playboys, hustlers, gangsters, pimps and whores in which its main characters must swim to survive. We glimpse only in snatches the wave of protest against US-funded despotism and corruption that would soon lead to Castro's revolution, as when photographer Codac transfers from the entertainment supplement to the front pages, and takes pictures of "political prisoners and bombs and… dead bodies the police leave". In a parade of festive masculinity, these garrulous lads chase the sirens of Havana and swap erotic anecdotes – or fantasies. But the novel's polyphonic play of voices frames their romantic machismo within scenes that reveal the trapped lives of girls and women. In this time and place, beauty and cruelty always intertwine. From a depressed society lady's sessions with a psychiatrist to childhood memories of abuse and a prostitute's sudden urge to flee her gilded cage, the defiantly "apolitical" author (who would leave Cuba for exile in London) does show how injustice inscribes itself on the bodies and minds of victims. One evening, at an upscale brothel, the writer Silvestre sees his pick-up Magalena fall into a trance, "hypnotised by something that I couldn't see, that I didn't see, will never see".

For all their loquacity, our verbose narrators know that there is much they cannot see – let alone write down. This intensely literary novel dwells on the life that escapes literature, and especially on the experience that verbal memory can never recall. Two remarkable characters show what even the genius of a "wordfinder general" will always miss. One is the black singer La Estrella, enormous, seductive, beautiful, a diva whose charisma no recording can ever catch. For Codac, her style "is a thing that lasts longer than a person or a voice or a revolution". Her premature death leads Codac to admit, as might all the novel's people, that "the one thing I feel mortal hatred for is oblivion".

That oblivion has also engulfed Bustrofedon. He is the barfly prankster, yarn-spinner and parodist who from beyond death inspires his pals, and their creator, to these feats of linguistic acrobatics. The Cuban *flâneurs* know that "We're aerialists more than materialists". Any revolution will bring them crashing to earth. Bustrofedon believed that "literature is no more important than conversation". He never transcribed a line of his high-wire wit and yet he, above all, possessed the gift of conjuring "ordinary clumsy language" into "magic nightwords". Into his own all-star cabaret of "magic nightwords", Cabrera Infante introduces a thudding drumbeat of loss and mourning. The fun must stop, the carnival will be over, and death – that "invisible tiger", we learn, of Burmese myth – will trap us all. Meanwhile, this "Greatest Show on Hearse" deserves a standing ovation.

Translation: Working with Levine and Gardner, Cabrera Infante (1971) pushes the boundaries of translation to fabricate an English text whose dazzling wordplay can match its Spanish cousin.

See also: Bely, *Petersburg* (1916-1922); Döblin, *Berlin Alexanderplatz* (1929); Cortázar, *Hopscotch* (1963); Pamuk, *The Black Book* (1990)

Selected works by the same author: *Mea Cuba* (1968); *View of Dawn in the Tropics* (1978); *Infante's Inferno* (1979); *Map Drawn by a Spy* (2013)

78 | Season of Migration to the North (1966); by Tayeb Salih.

Arabic (Sudan)

Translated by Denys Johnson-Davies (Penguin Modern Classics)

In a remote village "at the bend of the Nile", a Sudanese civil servant gazes at the sturdy palm in his family courtyard. He yearns to be like that tree, "with a background, with roots, with a purpose". Even in this self-sufficient corner of Muslim Africa, however, the age of secure rootedness is drawing to a close. The narrator of Tayeb Salih's audacious and still-shocking novel has written a thesis on English poetry in London (Britain effectively ruled Sudan from 1898 to 1956), and now works as a schools inspector. Back home, immersed again in the time-hallowed routines that he missed during his exile, he meets an unfamiliar neighbour. This older man startles him by reciting a poem of the First World War in English.

Through a patchwork of reported conversations, interspersed with the narrator's entanglements in village life, we hear the story of this learned, troubled figure: Mustafa Sa'eed. The triumph and calamity of Mustafa's long sojourn in England is coupled with the narrator's own experience as a semi-reluctant recruit to the country's foreign-educated elite. Together, their experiences give Salih a double perspective on the human dramas of displacement, migration and return. Beside the northward-flowing Nile, in a place where "things begin and things end", we witness a generational tragedy that knows no frontiers. Although as rooted as that palm tree in the landscapes and traditions of northern Sudan, this novel tells a story in which all the big, bland words that smooth the jagged edges of history – colonisation, dispossession, migration, globalisation, patriarchy – shrink to the dimensions of a cluttered room, and a tormented mind.

Mustafa, as we learn through episodes of his confessions, went to England as a teenage prodigy, an intellectual phenomenon with a mind "like a sharp knife". Brilliant but disengaged, he feels detached both from his gifts and the honours they win in Khartoum's colonial academies: "I was cold as a field of ice." In Cairo, where he studies before moving out of Africa, an Englishwoman – Mrs Robinson – shows him disinterested affection (which he never forgets) as well as introducing him to Bach and Keats. Once in Oxford, and then in the hedonistic Chelsea and Bloomsbury of the 1920s, Mustafa becomes not only a high-flying economist but a seductive "Third World" celebrity: "the handsome black man courted in Bohemian circles". Playing up to every Orientalist fantasy, he bewitches his conquests – political and sexual – with the phoney glamour of the exotic prince. In a demoralised time when "history becomes a pimp, and the jester is turned into a sultan", this act serves his chief aim: "the filling of my bed each night". If Mustafa appears a Nietzschean superman, taking revenge on the inferiors who patronise him, he is also the absurdist hero who can affirm his authenticity only in extreme acts. Poor and posh alike, the English women who want and even love him are prey not only to his desire, but to the mutually reinforcing fantasies that underpin colonial-era subordination. Three of Mustafa's lovers (whom Salih dignifies with credible characters and histories) commit suicide; one, Jean Morris, he marries but then kills. He insists that he did not become Othello on this "night of truth and of tragedy". Still, the fate of Shakespeare's Moor casts its shadow over him. We grasp that a jury's manslaughter verdict – prompted by Jean's alleged infidelities – has saved him from the gallows and allowed his eventual homecoming. Questions of nation and faith aside, masculine privilege has favoured him in the London courts.

In the village, Mustafa vanishes, presumed drowned in the Nile. Forced into marriage to a much older man, his widow Hosna will – in a grisly reprise and reversal of Mustafa's story – kill the husband, then herself. By the Thames as by the Nile, Salih attends to the gross inequalities of gender as much as race. Indeed, this outspoken work still runs foul of censors in some Arab states. The narrator, who has come to love Hosna, laments that "There is no justice or moderation in the world." Although his official role mandates an optimistic view of progress in newly-independent Sudan, he feels the tug of despair, as irresistible as the river's flow. His quest for an authentic life in this uprooted world seems doomed, just as, for all his talents, Mustafa sank into bad faith. At the book's close, the narrator sets out to drown in the Nile but then repents, crying for help "like a comic actor shouting on a stage". Even in the face of death, the mask distorts the face. For him as for Mustafa, for shop girls and surgeons' wives in England, or the maidens and matrons of a Nile village, the "poison" that oppressive power has injected into "the veins of history" toxifies their lives. Every figure here is, in some sense, the victim of that poison. Only during an impromptu night-time festival beneath the desert stars does the narrator glimpse a world in which "we are all brothers", united by a sympathy that knows no race or nation "under this beautiful, compassionate sky".

Translation: Doyen of Arabic translators, Denys Johnson-Davies (1969) conveys all of the novel's tenderness and violence; its poetry, and its fury.

See also: Camus, *The Outsider* (1942); Pavese, *The Moon and the Bonfires* (1950); Bâ, *So Long a Letter* (1972); Toer, *Buru Quartet* (1980-88);

Selected works by the same author: *The Wedding at Zein* (1962).

79 | ONE HUNDRED YEARS OF SOLITUDE (1967) by Gabriel García Márquez.

Spanish (Colombia)

Translated by Gregory Rabassa (Penguin Modern Classics)

Among the extravagant tales recounted in *One Hundred Years of Solitude*, we hear about an eating contest in which one of the teeming Buendía clan challenges a voice teacher: a lady known as The Elephant. For their heroic breakfast, each contestant consumes "the juice of forty oranges, eight quarts of coffee, and thirty raw eggs". Notice the accountant's exactitude with which Gabriel García Márquez modifies his hyperbole in this most globally influential, most riotously inventive, carnival of so-called "magic realism" in fiction. In fact, documents, records and even statistics, rather than super-sized legends, often prove the novel's most precious means of holding on to memory and history – an abiding obsession for the Buendías. The numbers count, from the three thousand striking workers murdered in a massacre ordered by banana company bosses (an episode rooted in Colombia's real history) to the forlorn military tally of Colonel Aureliano Buendía, who "fought thirty-two civil wars and lost them all", and the biblical deluge that washes away the dynasty's home town of Macondo ("It rained for four years, eleven months, and two days"). This family's story enlists the magic of fact as often as fancy to wrest a shared past from "the voracity of oblivion".

García Márquez's first full-length novel was frequently devoured by readers with an unbridled greed worthy of The Elephant herself. After years of "death-of-the-novel" obsequies from critics, and a generation of austere fictions that scarcely moved beyond the shrunken consciousness of their protagonists, here was narrative abundance beyond measure. Within a single humid century, this hothoused tropical scripture races from Genesis to Apocalypse. Macondo rises, flourishes and falls in its doomed "paradise of dampness and silence". The Buendías labour, love, fight, dream and, across six generations, strive but fail to escape the curse of their "solitude". Both saga and vision, the novel opened the gates to a new Eden of prodigal storytelling. But this Eden crawls with serpents. Despite the fairy tale ambience that so delighted foreign readers, Macondo expresses – albeit in a fantastic key – the actual experience of provincial Colombia, indeed, of Latin America as a whole. In this "city of mirrors (or mirages)", the Buendías' tumultuous chronicle adds up to no more than "a machine with unavoidable repetitions". Each generation claws at the jungle walls of isolation. Progress, riches, freedom: all will arrive, and all will depart.

The cascade of near-identical given names – José Arcadio, Aureliano, Amaranta – signifies a calcified state of social (and sexual) relationships that no bewitching yarn can shift. A recurrent incest theme hints at Macondo's plight of self-consuming isolation. The entropic force of history – and social hierarchy, even of nature itself – will reduce the town to the warm swamp whence it arose, "a bog of rotting roots". From the moment of its foundation by the "youthful patriarch" José Arcadio Buendía, Macondo understands, and grieves for, its loneliness. At the outset, the Gypsy alchemist Melquíades – who annually brings "the wonders of the world" to the settlement – sets up his telescope and proclaims that "Science has eliminated distance". Yet railways, telephones, cinemas, "progressive" ideologies and international capital will never save the minds of Macondo from their solitude. Rather, the Gypsy's news of a world elsewhere only robs the town of its happy sense of immortality and marks it "with a small black dot on the motley maps of death".

For all the ravishing imagery of wonder that García Márquez strews across the book, he makes us view this "magic" not as exotic decoration but as another symptom of under-development. Each charm carries a curse, from the priest who levitates "by means of chocolate" to the "light rain of tiny yellow flowers" that falls when the founding patriarch dies, the trickle of blood from a slain son that snakes across town to reach his mother, the matriarchal Ursula, and the clouds of yellow butterflies that attend the mechanic Mauricio's passion for Meme Buendía. From the legacy of Spanish colonialism through the bloodily pointless wars of Liberal and Conservative elites to the short-lived prosperity (and plunder) brought by the "gringo" fruit corporation, Macondo never takes its irrevocable step out of solitude. It never enters into the history where real change – and equal love – takes root. Those bewitching stories of miracles and metamorphoses speak of oppression, not liberation. In Macondo's state of "permanent alternation between excitement and disappointment, doubt and revelation", no one knows for certain "where the limits of reality lay". Not for nothing does one of the most memorable images take the form of a Spanish galleon, stranded far inland, occupying its own space of "solitude and oblivion" and carpeted within by "a thick forest of flowers". Generations later, it survives, an encrusted relic of conquest and command, richly garlanded but utterly inert.

Beauty and immobility, wonder and sorrow, entwine in Macondo like the blooms around that petrified hull. Honoured everywhere as a daringly hopeful leap into the future for the novel, *One Hundred Years of Solitude* nonetheless dwells in a suffocating past. It clings and strangles like a rampant jungle vine. For García Márquez, his prodigious ability to conjure this "world of shadows" serves as a sort of exorcism. In imagination, at least, the boundless liberty of literature can lay the troubled ghosts that still haunt, and harm, his country, and his continent.

Translation: Gregory Rabassa's version (1970), with its matter-of-fact voice and luxuriant language, swiftly established the novel's canonical status for English- as much as Spanish-speaking readers.

See also: Rulfo, *Pedro Páramo* (1955); Fuentes, *The Death of Artemio Cruz* (1962); Cortázar, *Hopscotch* (1963); Han, *A Dictionary of Maqiao* (1996)

Selected works by the same author: *Leaf Storm* (1955); *The Autumn of the Patriarch* (1975); *Chronicle of a Death Foretold* (1981); *Love in the Time of Cholera* (1985)

80 | The Quest for Christa T (1968) by Christa Wolf.

German (German Democratic Republic)

Translated by Christopher Middleton (Virago Modern Classics)

As a discontented young vet's wife in the East German provinces of the 1950s, Christa Wolf's elusive heroine attends a fancy dress ball in the guise of Sophie von La Roche. Sophie was a novelist of the Enlightenment, and friend of Goethe's, whose best-known work tells of a young woman torn between the contrasting destinies offered by two titled English suitors. Christa T wants to "step back" in time the better to understand her own predicament. After all, "In a hundred years, no, in fifty, we too shall be historical figures standing on a stage."

Half a century after Wolf published her second novel, and sixty or seventy after its events, author and characters have settled down, as Christa fears, into different levels of history. One kind will view Christa Wolf chiefly as a great descendant of Sophie von La Roche: as a pioneering woman writer who, under a regime that paid rhetorical lip-service to gender equality but remained thoroughly conservative, had to build her own lonely road towards the authorship of innovative fiction. Another type of historical scrutiny will ask how she registered – or else overlooked – the social and political climate of her time. How did she manage to keep up a literary career as an insider-outsider in the German Democratic Republic, sometimes acclaimed and sometimes marginalised? And how in this authoritarian surveillance state did she speak up – or stay silent – about disillusion and dissent as socialist faith waned and "the role of the iron believer was now defunct"?

All those histories matter still. For readers of *The Quest for Christa T*, they can wait. The fugitive life that the novel so beautifully, and sadly, records blooms in the cracks left when history, or ideology, or psychology, fail to explain the mystery of our conscious existence. Anglophone readers cannot but think of her near-namesake, Virginia Woolf. Christa T, whose early death we learn about in the novel's first pages, pursues "her experiments with various forms of living" – as student, teacher, writer, lover, mother, housewife, patient. Yet she knows that each role hides or denies something essential about her, and her unique path through life. She "carried many lives around with her" but never found a lasting rest on "this long and never-ending journey towards oneself".

Crucially, Christa does not tell us her own story. Rather, the friend who acts as narrator pieces together the vanished woman's voyage via the personal writings – notebooks, diaries, poems – that she left behind. "Writing means making things large," we learn, though as the quest continues, its quarry often shrinks into a vanishing point or else fragments into facets that never quite cohere. History, in the sense of great public events, does have a role in this sense of fractured selfhood.

The two girls meet at school during the last phase of the Second World War. Allied bombing reduces nearby Berlin to rubble, while the Nazi fantasy of absolute order and single meaning falls apart in and around the Hermann Göring School. Later, history again intrudes in jagged fragments. The narrator glimpses Christa as a student in Leipzig, a country school-teacher, a would-be writer, and a romantic siren who attracts rival suitors of her own. Even under a system that licensed overt political debate, Wolf would surely have written with the oblique, quicksilver lyricism that slips only these broken shards of public life into her heroine's mind. In East Germany, the narrator says, "we were fully occupied in making ourselves unassailable", immune to denunciation and persecution. At the same time, genuine idealism still conjures visions of the socialist "paradise on whose doorstep we were sure we stood". After all, "One must, once in a lifetime… have believed in the impossible".

As for Christa, she increasingly seeks her paradise within. "We must have big thoughts about ourselves," she tells her pupils. Her own writing tries to "make things large". For a spell, the provincial idyll of marriage and children with vet Justus in a "picture-book town" in Mecklenburg glows with a beauty and dignity of its own. It cannot last. When Christa falls for a young forester, the narrator-friend blurts out "Madame Bovary". Of course, "that was no news to her". As dreams of freedom fade into the prospect of hackneyed intrigue, "She saw herself melting away in an endless welter of deadly banal actions and clichés". Then mortal illness imposes its own rusted plot-lines. She fights their tedium with a final pregnancy – she will live to give birth safely – and the joyful re-discovery that "it was wonderful to be in this world". Christa T has made a strange kind of "star child" – but then "one has heard of difficult stars, with a changing light, disappearing, returning, not always visible". Not simply a "historical figure", Wolf's difficult star still lights up other lives.

Translation: Poet and scholar Christopher Middleton does subtle, graceful justice to the mysterious intimacy of Wolf's voice in his 1970 translation.

See also: Flaubert, *Madame Bovary* (1857); Rilke, *The Notebooks of Malte Laurids Brigge* (1910); Lispector, *Near to the Wild Heart* (1943); Kundera, *The Book of Laughter and Forgetting* (1978)

Selected works by the same author: *Divided Heaven* (1963); *Patterns of Childhood* (1976); *Cassandra* (1983); *Medea* (1996)

81 | I Served the King of England (1971) by Bohumil Hrabal.

Czech (Czechoslovakia/ Czech Republic)

Translated by Paul Wilson (Vintage)

No, he did not serve the English king. Ditě, the waiter and hotelier who embroiders this gilded yarn of his rackety life in pre-war, wartime and then Communist Czechoslovakia, has certainly received a medal and sash for his exemplary service to Haile Selassie during the Emperor of Ethiopia's visit to Prague in the 1930s. "Barbecued camel" was the highlight of the menu – if we can believe Ditě. But it was the august Mr Skrivanek, his mentor in the fine art of waiting at the luxurious Hotel Paris in Prague ("If you want to be a good headwaiter, never sit down"), who had "actually served the King of England". How typical of Ditě, who embellishes his life-story just as he loved to strew flowers around the naked laps of his girlfriends, shamelessly to steal another's glory.

Power tends to corrupts, Lord Acton's dictum states. So can its lack. Worse: an absolute lack of power may corrupt absolutely. Viewed through one lens, *I Served the King of England* ranks as one of the wittiest, most enchanting novels of the later 20th-century in Europe. Told in a cheeky, confiding voice, sensuously alert to the look, taste and feel of everything Ditě encounters, Hrabal's novel traces the adventures of this canny little scamp and rogue. Starting as a lowly busboy, he becomes a hotel servant, a waiter, a hotel-keeper, a prisoner, a wood-worker and a road-mender while his Czech homeland passes from bourgeois democracy through Nazi occupation to the post-war Soviet bloc. From his youthful exploits onwards, overcharging travellers for sausages on station platforms, Ditě rips off his wealthy clients. He seduces merry wenches and fine ladies alike, slips smartly through the cracks in every social hierarchy, and has a whale of a time: "If life works out just a tiny bit in your favour it can be beautiful, just beautiful." Ditě skims a tasty profit from every transaction, professional or sexual. He has witnessed, from his close-quarters observation of the rich, that "money could buy you not just a beautiful girl, money could buy you poetry too". His escapades update the stock figure of the clever, cocky valet who charms and tricks his way through the fiction, drama and opera of the 18th-century.

Now change the filter. Right from the get-go of his adolescent scams, Ditě's picaresque progress takes him along a track of deepening depravity. It moves from the procuring of defenceless girls for lecherous businessmen at his hotels through passive support for the German invasion of his native land and active collaboration with the Nazis as a staff member at a mountain resort repurposed as an SS "breeding station" for "a refined race of humans". Worst of all is the purchase of his country hotel with the proceeds from rare stamps plundered by his German wife from a Jewish family in Lvov. After the Communist take-over, Ditě spends a comfortable couple of years in detention as a "millionaire", and therefore a foe to the proletariat. Yet this "war profiteer" who usually gets off lightly ("I was always lucky in my bad luck") might equally be branded as a war criminal: a vulture of the Holocaust. Ditě chooses to call his own post-war establishment the "Hotel in the Quarry" not just from its location but because "something inside me had been broken and crushed and carted away".

Hrabal achieves an extraordinary, bittersweet triumph of tone and voice in this book. Ditě makes us utterly complicit in his ploys and ruses. Especially in the 1930s episodes of life behind the scenes in grand hotels, the waiter's-eye view satirises the follies of the rich not just with high-spirited bemusement but a true tenderness for the plight of his fellow toilers. Ditě enjoys a thrilling freedom from the cant of well-heeled opinions. "All that stuff about happiness in poor country cottages," he twigs, has been concocted by his plutocratic guests. So steal some more champagne, and sweet-talk another girl. His romance with the German Lise begins in genuine rapture. Only at the mountain hotel, where they must have "National Socialist intercourse" under strict medical supervision to replenish the Aryan stock, does reality begin to bite. Slowly, fitfully, conscience and understanding awaken. Their son Siegfried turns aggressive, perhaps autistic. Lise dies, decapitated, in an Allied air-raid.

After his release from the cushy prison-camp, Ditě retreats to the eerie forest highlands – now emptied by expulsion of their German-speaking inhabitants – to work, to think, to rebuild himself. As he repairs the tracks, he pursues "the maintenance of my own life". With his horse, dog, goat and cat for company, he learns that "my own best friend and companion would be that other self of mine, that teacher inside me". Gloriously funny, immaculately voiced, this supremely evocative crook's tour of mid-century Central Europe morphs into, of all things, a spiritual pilgrimage. "Beauty," discovers Ditě, "always points to infinity and eternity." Hrabal, the deadpan lord of misrule whose art of irony and mischief made him a jester-hero to his Czech compatriots, saves this most gob-smacking of punch lines for the end.

Translation: Pitch-perfect, Paul Wilson (1989) implicates us in Ditě's subversiveness – and selfishness – with unflagging fluency and wit.

See also: Diderot, *Jacques the Fatalist* (1796); Hašek, *The Good Soldier Švejk* (1923); Grass, *The Tin Drum* (1959); Kundera, *The Book of Laughter and Forgetting* (1978)

Selected works by the same author: *Dancing Lessons for the Advanced in Age* (1964); *Closely Watched Trains* (1965); *The Little Town where Time Stood Still* (1974); *Too Loud a Solitude* (1976)

82 | Chronicle in Stone (1971, revised 1997) by Ismail Kadare.

Albanian (Albania/France)

Translated by Arshi Pipa,
Revised by David Bellos (Canongate)

A "slanted" Balkan city, set "at a sharper angle than perhaps any other city on earth", endures waves of occupation during the Second World War. Italians give way to Greeks, who yield to the Italians again, then the Germans, while Communist partisans prepare to take over. Meanwhile, British planes rain bombs nightly on a place that endures its "winters of blood". Within, civil war threatens a fresh hell of suffering, in which "brothers kill each other" and "The son slays the father". Matter-of-factly, a boy observes this rotation of conquerors and flags. His extended family summon the ghosts, the legends, the yarns that anchor them to this abode of past and present strife. The boy finds parallels with his people's plight in the human and supernatural drama of Shakespeare's *Macbeth*. His escapades alternate with fragments of a collective "chronicle" of city life, which sound almost like a tragic chorus.

Deadpan, ironic, even genial in its recounting of violence and terror, Kadare's early masterpiece draws on his wartime childhood in the Albanian city of Gjirokastër. His level-headed, unemphatic narration – an "epic" voice in the ancient sense – only intensifies the impact of the bizarre, often horrific episodes that multiple invasions bring. At the finale, the post-war Communist dawn begins to break: a joy to the partisans but to Sheikh Ibrahim, the local mosque's imam, a catastrophe. He climbs the minaret and tries to blind himself: "Better no eyes at all than to see Communism!" The Italian authorities have tried to hunt down "the dangerous Communist Enver Hoxha": Albania's future dictator, also a native of Gjirokastër, and Kadare's persecutor in decades to come.

Chronicle in Stone witnesses all the chaos and carnage of total war through its wide-eyed young protagonist. This studied impassivity, which allows for comedy as much as terror, served Kadare well when he channelled the despotic absurdity of Hoxha's regime into later novels such as *The Concert*, *The File on H* and *The Successor*. Always a subtle heretic, Kadare refuses to portray the partisans' triumph in the stone city as a heroic finale. Their advent simply joins the endless flow of tales that make up its identity. Grandparents, aunts and resilient "crones" act as the sibyls and seers who watch the ephemeral victors, from Ottomans to Fascists, come and go. Bearers of ancient secrets, grudges and tales, these womenfolk – Xhexho and Kako Pino, Aunt Xhemo and Grandmother Selfizhe – situate the shocks of modern warfare in a landscape of myth.

The boy learns that, while power always crumbles, stories endure like stone. He even meets a labourer called Omer, who shares his name with "a blind poet of ancient Greece". Reading *Macbeth* drives him into a state of delirious excitement caused by nothing more than "little black marks" on a page. Even as "the world was falling apart" in external assaults and internal feuds, "the power of words was at its peak".

A novel of all-consuming war seen through a child's eyes, *Chronicle in Stone* also paints a portrait of the fledgling artist. Rich in idiomatic dialogue, in eccentric minor characters and tragi-comic anecdotes, its storytelling brings an offbeat, folkloric quality to apocalyptic Europe in the early 1940s. The view from this seemingly marginal vantage point in southern Albania looks – as so often in modern fiction – clearer than from the metropolitan centres. Kadare has always relished the role of the oracular outsider, a suspect cosmopolitan in Albania but a provincial interloper "along wide lighted boulevards in foreign cities". There, as a postscript tells us, "I somehow stumble in places where no one ever trips."

Like much of his work, this fast-flowing novel feels both ancient and modern. Kadare's "cool" narration has an antique detachment. It also carries a contemporary sense of power, and history, as an arbitrary pile-up of chance and circumstance rather than the expression of some grand design. Neither respected nor especially resented, the British bombers rain death and mayhem on the city almost as an earthquake or an avalanche might. The battle-strewn chronicle bears witness to no moral or ideological destiny. These people's fates feel Homeric, but the gods – if they are still watching – merely shrug. Kadare takes the tragic grief as read, and gives prominence instead to the surreal side-shows of war, such as the downed airman's detached arm that somehow drifts around the city. Both intimate and objective, the storyteller shows us that states will rise and fall; governors arrive and depart. What survives is the timeless realm the "crones" rule and the boy yearns to enter: "the kingdom of words".

Translation: Until recently, much of Kadare's work reached English from Albanian via French. *Chronicle in Stone*, however, was translated directly by Arshi Pipa in 1987. In 2007, the excellent David Bellos revised this translation.

See also: Andrić, *The Bridge on the Drina* (1945); Grossman, *Life and Fate* (1959); Grass, *The Tin Drum* (1959); Márquez, *One Hundred Years of Solitude* (1967)

Selected works by the same author: *The General of the Dead Army* (1963); *The Siege* (1970); *Broken April* (1978); *The Palace of Dreams* (1981)

83 | THE BRIDGE OF BEYOND (1972); by Simone Schwarz-Bart.

French (Guadeloupe)

Translated by Barbara Bray (New York Review Books)

After her second husband dies of burns when sugar factory bosses turn jets of scalding steam on striking workers, Telumée Miracle finds that, in spite of herself, her neighbours in rural Guadeloupe treat her as a wise woman, a "seer and first-class witch". In her own mind, she's no more of a witch than she is the Virgin Mary, even though her old friend Ma Cia did command occult powers and seems to have transformed herself into a dog. In these tropical forests and on these Caribbean shores, the island's natural bounty and beauty provides magic aplenty. No spell or charm can match the fulfilment of "a satisfied belly visited by all the fruits of the earth". Yet not only flood, drought and tempest but, above all, the legacy of slavery – in the world and in the mind – conspire to snatch these everyday treasures from the reach of the poorest, darkest inhabitants.

On this "volcanic, hurricane-swept, mosquito-ridden, nasty-minded island", that final epithet hints at the historic chain of wounds that poisons paradise. The dead Amboise, who had lived for seven years in France and suffered all the hurts of racism there, has told Telumée that "enemy hands had gotten hold of our soul and shaped it to be at war with itself".

Across three generations of family history in the French West Indies, Simone Schwarz-Bart dramatises her heroine's stubborn journey towards a fulfilled life not only as a struggle with fate, but a war within the self. *The Bridge of Beyond* (in the original, *Rain and Wind on Telumée Miracle*) is often a gloriously lyrical and sensuous novel. Every sumptuous paragraph channels the prodigal splendour of woods, seas, flowers, fruits and trees. Her grandmother, who raises Telumée, finds in a luxuriant garden "permanent joy and richness, as if Indian poppies, Congo canes, hummingbirds and orange trees were enough to fill a woman's heart with complete satisfaction". They never can be. We follow Telumée's long labour to overcome the social, and psychological, barriers that still fence off the black people of the Caribbean from the enjoyment of this natural wonder. With "a blue-black skin and a face not overflowing with beauty", she must fight for every patch of ground that, literally and figuratively, she wants to occupy. Like other Caribbean authors, Schwarz-Bart shows that slavery and colonialism have not only segregated black from white but stratified people of colour themselves, the better to divide and rule. Resigned villagers tell her that "the only place on earth that belongs to a Negress is in the graveyard" – and if the terminology now disconcerts, than maybe it should. Telumée will, despite all obstacles, claim her own cabin and stake out her patch, even when it means exile among the mavericks and rejects of the "Brotherhood of the Displaced".

Beyond endemic poverty and racism, some of the snares she has to dodge are brutally straightforward. As a resourceful maid and cook in service with an old plantation family, descendants of the patriarch known as "the White of Whites", she has to fend off a sexually predatory master. Even when treated as a chattel, however, "I beat a special drum in my heart". That drum must also thump when her beloved Elie, the romantic carpenter who once made her feel "no longer a stranger on earth", yields to his inner demons and beats her savagely. If Elie loses himself and starts to "sleep in the arms of darkness", we never forget the history that has scarred the men and women of this isolated underclass. Without any sermonising, Schwarz-Bart lays bare "the curse of being a master, the curse of being a slave". With the arrival of the thoughtful, travelled Amboise, political themes begin to shade her pastoral lyricism without ever swamping it. In Elie's violence, as in Amboise's chosen path of activism and martyrdom, we witness the islanders "dying silently of slavery after it is finished".

The women endure, and flourish, better than the men. Grandmother, known in later life as Queen Without a Name, spreads a suitably regal influence over her family and community. Telumée learns from her that "Sorrow is a wave without an end. But the horse mustn't ride you, you must ride it". With Elie, then with Amboise, then blissfully alone, Telumée does taste happiness, even serenity. For all its sorrows, this novel – Schwarz-Bart's defiant tribute to the lowliest, least-privileged of her fellow islanders – touches a level of unsentimental, bucolic ecstasy that the fiction of Europe had lost. It finds a voice for beauty, and a language for pain. Both ring absolutely true. Telumée has no need to mimic Ma Cia's sorcery and turn herself into some kind of "flying succubus". In the cane fields, amid the forests and along the shores of this island "swept alternately by winds from the land and winds from the sea", the earth and its people spawn monsters, and miracles, enough.

Translation: In 1975, Barbara Bray rose magnificently to the lyric heights, and sombre depths, of Schwarz-Bart's prose.

See also: Zola, *Germinal* (1885); Deledda, *Reeds in the Wind* (1913); Rulfo, *Pedro Paramo* (1955); García Márquez, *One Hundred Years of Solitude* (1967);

Selected works by the same author: *Between Two Worlds* (1992)

84 | CORRECTION (1975) by Thomas Bernhard.

German (Austria)

Translated by Sophie Wilkins (Vintage)

The narrator of *Correction* tells us that "everyone has an idea that kills him in the end". For Roithamer, the scientist and thinker whose lifelong urge to go "some different way" leads to an obsessive pursuit of purity and originality, the idea ruins not only its inventor but the only person that he loves. Roithamer, a solitary perfectionist whose fictional career shares several features with the life of the philosopher Ludwig Wittgenstein, spends years designing and building a cone-shaped house for his fragile, much-loved sister. It stands in the dead centre of an Austrian forest: an "inhuman location". Roithamer plans this logical, innovative and mathematically precise "edifice as a work of art" in order to give her "supreme happiness". (Wittgenstein himself designed a meticulous Modernist house for his sister in Vienna.) Yet its completion pushes her into a terminal illness. After she is "destroyed by the creation of the perfect Cone", Roithamer takes his own life. The novel's narrator, his executor, occupies the paper-filled garret in a mutual friend's house where the late genius cogitated, his "thought-chamber". He endeavours, amid this mass of manuscripts, to rescue Roithamer's scrambled legacy and make sense of an inspired, yet catastrophe-filled, life.

Known as a vitriolic, misanthropic satirist, as an uncompromising experimentalist in fiction, Thomas Bernhard trails a reputation as chilly and forbidding as that of Wittgenstein himself. Certainly, *Correction* – his fourth novel – makes few concessions to convention. It consists of two single paragraphs, both more than a hundred pages long. The prose, supple and agile, flows, eddies and tumbles like the rushing waters of the Aurach Valley where Roithamer, and later the narrator, work. Bernhard's perennial scorn for the "congenital imbecility" of his native Austria spits and crackles; this land of lies, hypocrisy and mediocrity has "corrected" its Nazi past into oblivion and now squats amid the debris of the past, a "rummage sale" of history. Roithamer worships the purity of music and maths, but like his creator detests the "intellectual vomit" of a "totally decrepit" civilisation. He despises much of his family, his butcher's-daughter mother above all, and recalls his childhood on the estate at Altensam as a prison of loneliness and chastisement, with revolt punished by "deadly injuries to the psyche". As for the blinkered architects, those "intellectual charlatans" with "brains of cement", he spurns their profession in favour of his own plans for the Cone. Cambridge, where he works as a university scientist during term-time (and where Wittgenstein, originally an engineer, taught), is a dull place of exile. Fear, even loathing, of others frames this "shut-in, solitary life", while Roithamer acts on the principle that "A man approaches another only to destroy him". Suicide appeals as the ultimate means "to correct our entire existence".

Yet, in spite of all this, *Correction* delights, exhilarates – even entertains. To begin with, the process of "correction" – as the narrator takes control of Roithamer's papers, perhaps to manipulate him – inserts an element of mystery or suspense that readers of Henry James might recognise. The reader becomes a detective, challenged to disentangle Roithamer's voice and thought from the posthumous interference of this disciple who may become a Judas-like betrayer. As the vehicle of choice for his splenetic invective, Bernhard chooses comedy. Granted, this is laughter black as midnight in the Kobernausser woods. Still, the antics of the eccentric, single-minded genius acquire an edge of hilarity. Besides, our human drive to "correct the corrections, and correct again the resulting corrections" in our botched and bungled lives itself has a risible side.

A gifted playwright as well as a great novelist, Bernhard manages this torrential monologue (or perhaps dialogue) with absolutely mastery. The voice tugs us along in its hypnotic grip, credible and compelling even when it rises to the Alpine heights of philosophical speculation. Very few novels convey as this one does the excitement, and the risk, of pure thought. For Roithamer, "the lack of ideas is death". Yet his unyielding cerebration will kill the one being he reveres; he immures her in the idea of the Cone as in the blocked-off chamber of a pyramid. Glimpse by glimpse, a harrowing family drama – almost a soap-opera – comes into view: the insecure mother, transplanted into the gentry and compelled to act the snob; the bitter rivalries between brothers; the psychologically incestuous devotion to the sister whom he slays with love; the fate of the estate, bequeathed to the rebellious "foreign element" Roithamer rather than his conformist siblings. He will spend his fortune on the Cone and then donate the rest to ex-convicts; he loves outcasts and rejects, and befriends the poor miners and foresters of the neighbourhood.

As with Wittgenstein himself, humility and practicality balance a mind that loses and finds itself alone, in the darkest woods of thought. The anguish of Roithamer, who goes crazy in his ascetic quest for "mysteries of meanings" but always cherishes the yellow paper rose he once won at a country fair, becomes a common human tragedy rather than the destiny of some hyper-intellectual freak. In Bernhard's words, an echo of Wittgenstein's own, "Everything is what it is, that's all."

Translation: Sophie Wilkins's 1979 version marvellously conveys both Bernhard's cascading fury, and his ripples of tenderness and awe.

See also: Mann, *The Magic Mountain* (1924); Céline, *Journey to the End of the Night* (1932); Beckett, *Trilogy* (1951-1953); Sebald, *The Emigrants* (1992)

Selected works by the same author: *Frost* (1963); *Wittgenstein's Nephew* (1982); *The Loser* (1983); *Extinction* (1986)

85 | LIFE A USER'S MANUAL (1978) by Georges Perec.

French

Translated by David Bellos (Vintage)

Bartlebooth, the eccentric English multi-millionaire whose grand design anchors the teeming stories that multiply across this novel, had a great-uncle called James Sherwood. This neurotic magnate, who made a fortune from cough-lozenges in Boston, found solace only in collecting what the antiquarian book trade calls "unica": "an object which is the only one of its kind". If ever a work of fiction ranked as an incomparable "unicum", it must be *Life A User's Manual*. Over ninety-nine chapters, grouped and linked according to an authorial programme of mind-boggling, self-imposed complexity, it recounts the lives of a score of major characters – along with dozens more ancillary figures – who live in the same apartment block in the XVIIth arrondissement of Paris.

Perec's scheme captures this human termitary of tales and memories as it exists at a single moment, that of Bartlebooth's death, on 23 June 1975. However, his swarming encyclopaedia of humankind stretches back across a century. It covers all manner of professions, passions and adventures, and spreads out from Paris to locations from the Wild West to Cameroon, Mexico to Australia. As for the Harrow-educated monomaniac Bartlebooth, his life-long obsession reflects the ambition of "a man of exceptional arrogance who wishes to fix, to describe and to exhaust not the whole world" but "a constituted fragment of the world", and so defy "the inextricable incoherence of things". His fifty-year programme begins with a decade, after 1925, spent learning the art of watercolours. Then, for twenty years, he tours the world's ports to paint scenes which are converted, back in the apartment-block at 11 rue Simon-Crubellier, into five hundred fiendishly complicated jigsaws of 750 pieces. Each is fabricated by a demon puzzle-maker called Gaspard Winckler. Bartlebooth will then spend two further decades testing his skill against the "cunning, trickery and subterfuge" of Winckler's jigsaws, only to have them scrubbed bare at their original sites to leave "a clean and unmarked sheet" behind. This infinite toil, this life-devouring artifice, will consume itself.

Perec took part in the literary games and puzzles practised by the post-war French writers of the Oulipo group. With its intricate mathematical ground-plan, its ramifying cross-connections, its fractal generation of lists, inventories and catalogues, this fictional edifice pushes to extremes their frantic playfulness. In summary, the entire project can sound like Bartlebooth's own gloomy verdict on his enterprise when stymied by the crafty Winckler: "a wretched madman's obsessive and sterile musings". Nothing could be further from the truth. For all its secret rooms, its hidden passageways, *Life A User's Manual* is a not only a mansion of mystery but a house of fun. Each of the resident's biographies opens the door into a colourful scene, an entertaining story. Perec tells them all with untiring brilliance and panache, although nostalgia and melancholy darken his picaresque comedy. We jump to and fro in knight's moves from storey to storey, downstairs to the bourgeois dynasties and up into the eaves among the servants, the pensioners, the students. We meet the former Australian child star Olivia Rorschach and the DIY tools tycoon Madame Moreau, a troubled banking family, the Altamonts, and the Polish Jewish migrant Cinoc, who works for the dictionary as a "word-killer" of outdated terms. Perplexed readers can always consult the appendices: a comprehensive sixty page index, a meticulous chronology of events, and Perec's plan of the block and its inhabitants.

Artists of different sorts loom large in the buzzing activity of number 11: the celebrity painter Hutting, but above all the much poorer Valène. In a parallel endeavour to Bartlebooth's, Valène intends to paint in microscopic detail a cross-section of the block and so capture this "grotesque mausoleum" of human joy and pain. He will give the shape of art to "this unordered massing of stories, grandiose and trivial". As Valène ponders the deaths, the losses, the partings that the house has already seen, and the inevitable destruction to come, he feels "unbearable sadness". All this teeming life must pass. Then we move, with Perec's riddling wit and mischief, to the next room, the next dream, the next puzzle.

Memories of traumatic violence – double murders, suicides, abduction and torture during the Nazi occupation – echo among the apartments and across the floors. Crime stories, actual or literary, turn up behind almost every door. The threadbare scholar Monsieur Jerôme "liked only detective stories with a mystery to solve". *Life A User's Manual* stacks mystery upon mystery, most bound up with family secrets and sorrows. The reader, like Bartlebooth with his jigsaws, must sometimes sweat to make the picture fit. Shadows of exile, of persecution, fall over the house: it is never irrelevant with the orphaned Perec to note that his mother died in Auschwitz, his father as the Germans invaded France. *Life A User's Manual* abounds with anecdotes about polymathic and autodidactic scholars – figures a little like Perec himself. One of these, Carel van Loorens, is dubbed "one of the oddest minds of his time". Perec's magnificent oddity, though, comes fully furnished with endless humour and humanity; with an almost worshipful attention to the tiniest scraps of our death-haunted world. Sometimes, as he cracks Winckler's jigsaw codes and intuits the whole picture behind the knotty fragments, Bartlebooth glimpses "a kind of ecstasy", an "intimation of grace". Behind the street-door of 11 rue Simon-Crubellier, just such a vision awaits the reader.

Translation: In 1987 David Bellos, also Perec's biographer, matched the novel's exuberance and erudition step by step, story by story, in his tremendous English version.

See also: Proust, *In Search of Lost Time* (1913-1927); Némirovsky, *Suite Française* (1942-2004); Gadda, *That Awful Mess on the Via Merulana* (1946-57); Cortázar, *Hopscotch* (1963)

Selected works by the same author: *Things: A Story of the Sixties* (1965); *A Void* (1969); *W, or the Memory of Childhood* (1975)

86 | The Book of Laughter and Forgetting (1978) by Milan Kundera.

Czech (Czechoslovakia/France)

Translated by Michael Henry Heim (Penguin)

The novels that deserve to endure rewrite themselves as their readers, and their contexts, change. A political refugee in France, Milan Kundera composed his first great work of exile during the late 1970s. At that point, the worst "massacre of culture and thought" since the 1620s had sought to wipe out the Czech people's collective memory and let their nation perish in "a desert of organised forgetting". Husák's puppet regime in Czechoslovakia, Kundera notes, had fired 145 historians. The vision of Franz Kafka, "prophet of a world without memory", had materialised in Prague.

However, two decades after the Soviet invasion of Prague in August 1968, which deprived the free-thinking writer and professor of cinema of his voice and livelihood, the Communist empire itself expired. A few years later, his compatriots' new freedom from the totalitarian war on memory would lead to the break-up of Czechoslovakia itself. In spite of these upheavals, this riddling, fractured compendium of stories and ideas – once feted as a vital weapon in the intellectual Cold War – has kept its freshness, its mischief, even its capacity to shock. In the kitsch, fraud and sentimentality of state socialism, Kundera shrewdly diagnosed symptoms, not causes. That history-denying quest for "paradise regained" had already, as he wrote, moved on from Communism towards other Utopian desires. We still yearn to sacrifice the lonely, critical, embarrassing adult self and pursue "an idyll of justice for all".

The Book of Laughter and Forgetting reflects the fragmented, disrupted life of the literary exile. Theme rather than plot glues its loose patchwork of tales. Kundera shuffles essays, anecdotes, yarns and dreams into a set of fictional variations in homage to Beethoven's late piano sonatas – so beloved by the musician father he recalls here. A disciple of Sterne and Diderot, Kundera treats the heretical capacity of fiction to digress, meander, mix its genres, as a sign of the freedom it celebrates. His "novel in the form of variations" cherishes "the infinity of internal variety concealed in all things". In contrast, the single-minded fantasies of utopians and totalitarians insist that everyone's story must be identical in its innocence and happiness. These interchangeable units dance merrily in a "magic circle" of togetherness. Our solitary storyteller, though, has fallen from the charmed circle of uniformity "like a meteorite broken loose from a planet", and has "been falling ever since".

Almost all his stories tie the power-politics of the bedroom to the lies and fantasies of the repressive state. One after another, he studies couples bound by lust, love or remembrance – Mirek and Zdena, Karel and Marketa, Tamina and Hugo, Kristyna and the student – in a sort of Kremlinology of desire. Bright and playful in his words, but often heavy in his heart, the narrator shows how public deceptions or delusions distort their intimate lives. Yet within erotic relationships, the will to power, or the drive to fulfilment, can create its own burden of "legends and lies".

Tamina, the exiled waitress and the book's moral heart, longs to remember her dead husband by rescuing his notebooks from Prague. She finds herself invaded by her lover Hugo's controlling fantasies. Sometimes censured for presumed anti-feminism, Kundera resists not the autonomy of his female characters but any attempt by utopian ideologists to kidnap the search for freedom. In a set-piece café debate among boozy poets, the one nicknamed "Boccaccio" provokes his fellow-bards by claiming that the male "gynophobe" will make a lover happier than an idoliser of women. Why? Because he "prefers the woman to womankind". Kundera's method seeks to puncture every windy abstraction. That goes as well for the post-1960s libertarian chimera of jealousy-free sexual experiment. In a threesome with his wife and mistress, Karel "felt more like a diplomat than a lover". Free love, it turns out, is hard labour.

In this, and many other scenes, Kundera practises what he preaches. He foments the "devil's laughter" that mocks power, punctures delusions, and shows us the muddled truth behind the shining lie. Its antithesis is the false, "angelic" laughter of dogma, propaganda and advertising: the sort of fake bliss peddled by publicists for "their religion, their product, their ideology, their nation, their sex, their dishwashing detergent". True laughter, according to the poet "Petrarch", breeds not jovial solidarity but the "frigid solitude" of understanding reality: "A joke is a barrier between man and the world." Besides, Kundera's ironic take-down of every artificial paradise hunts bigger, more contemporary game than Soviet-era Stalinism alone. His acerbic sketch of a narcissistic epoch of "mass graphomania" in which everyone clamours for attention, but no one pays any, predated the internet's invention by a decade. It could hardly sound more timely. "We are in," he warns, "for an age of universal deafness and lack of understanding." The roar of total communication may threaten human memory, and human love, as much as the secrecy and silence of dictators.

Translation: Michael Henry Heim honours Kundera's mischief, irony and gravity in his trail-blazing 1980 rendering. The later, authorised version from the French text has not displaced it.

See also: Diderot, *Jacques the Fatalist* (1796); Hašek, *The Good Soldier Švejk* (1923); Kafka, *The Trial* (1925); Hrabal, *I Served the King of England* (1971)

Selected works by the same author: *The Joke* (1967); *Life is Elsewhere* (1969); *The Unbearable Lightness of Being* (1984); *Immortality* (1990)

87 | If on a Winter's Night a Traveller (1979) by Italo Calvino.

Italian

Translated by William Weaver (Vintage)

For all its tantalising trickery, Italo Calvino's magical labyrinth of a novel never loses its thread of sheer fun. One of its many writer characters is a blocked Irish bestseller named Silas Flannery. Opposite his desk hangs a poster of Charles Schulz's "mythomane dog" Snoopy, at his typewriter. The cartoon beagle can never move beyond his opening words, "It was a dark and stormy night…" before "the void yawns on the white page". Enthralled by "the potentiality of the beginning", Calvino, Snoopy-like, opens *If on a Winter's*

Night a Traveller over and over again. He presents the initial chapters of ten different novels, which then swerve and branch into the next narrative. Interspersed with these centrifugal tales, a more unified plot develops. A Reader ("you"), frustrated after buying a novel bound together with a separate book, hunts down the missing story.

In search of his next chapter, the Reader falls in love with another bookworm named Ludmilla. They uncover a global novel-tampering conspiracy that involves a conniving translator, a Middle Eastern princess, a militant sect that splinters after a literary-critical dispute, and Silas Flannery himself. If, like Ludmilla, Calvino's reader happens to be the sort who likes "to live several lives simultaneously", then the stacked and nested stories in this fiendishly smart puzzle book amply reward that urge. But the romantic convergence of "Reader" and Ludmilla on the trail of an outlandish publishing swindle satisfies our itch for solid ground. It passes beyond the "trap-novel designed by the treacherous translator", with its carnival parade of false starts, wrong turnings, dead ends.

In summary, *If on a Winter's Night a Traveller* can sound like a coterie high-wire act, more an acrobatic display than a truly involving narrative. Certainly, Calvino – whose own literary progress had taken him from the neo-realism of post-war Italy through fable, fantasy and avant-garde experiment – enjoyed the meta-fictional games of his French colleagues in the "Oulipo" group. And his book does star in literary histories as a textbook specimen of European post-modernism. Yet its humour, its humanity, its spiralling ingenuity, and the piercing insight of its reflections on how readers read and authors write, burst the bounds of any academic category. As the Reader and Ludmilla tumble from one story to another, Calvino teasingly invites us to ask, if not answer, the deepest, child-like questions about stories, their construction and consumption. Who is the author, that "ghost with a thousand faces"? How can "the voice of that silent nobody made of ink and typographical spacing" capture our hearts, sway our moods, even change our lives?

With a wit and warmth beyond the reach of literary theory, he lets us inspect the strange transaction that binds writer and reader through words on a page. The first ten chapters themselves comprise a sort of encyclopaedia of genres, each crafted with consummate skill, from existential murder-mystery to Japanese erotic lyricism, Latin American saga, high-finance thriller and Eastern European revolutionary intrigue. Needless to say, the mysteries of literature preoccupy the characters in these interpolated chapters, as it they do the Reader and Ludmilla in the frame tale. One narrator admits to spinning "too many stories at once", so that we feel "a saturation of other stories I could tell". Ludmilla yearns for a novel that has "as its driving force only the desire to narrate, to pile stories upon stories, without trying to impose a philosophy of life on you".

With its cellular division into swarming, seething tales, *If on a Winter's Night a Traveller* often feels like that sort of book. At the same time, Calvino sets up a dialogue between two kinds of work, two kinds of reader. One glories in endless invention, in fiction made up of masks and performances, "of imitations and counterfeits and pastiches". The other hunts, among "the false books flooding the world", for the few (or the one) bearing a hidden truth, "perhaps extrahuman or extraterrestrial". Hence those rival factions split, as does every reader at different moments, between a "Wing of Shadow" and a "Wing of Light". Should authors aspire to create, and readers to devour, a "unique book" of timeless wisdom. Or should they revel in the multiple truths of "all books", and so "pursue the whole through its partial images"? Through its joyous multiplicity, this particular novel seems to side with the forces of prodigality and pluralism. Yet the recurrent figure of "the woman who loves reading for reading's sake" suggests that pure immersion in the story has a transcendent value. It can lead us to understand the "two faces" behind each tale: "the continuity of life, the inevitability of death". Whatever we decide about the metaphysics of literature, Calvino fashions a work that tugs and grips like one of the opening chapters we enjoy: "once you have got into it, you want to go forward without stopping."

Translation: William Weaver (1981) negotiates every one of Calvino's stylistic shifts with supreme skill.

See also: Diderot, *Jacques the Fatalist* (1796); Cortázar, *Hopscotch* (1963); Perec, *Life A User's Manual* (1978); Murakami, *Hard-Boiled Wonderland and The End of the World* (1985)

Selected works by the same author: *The Path to the Nest of Spiders* (1947); *The Baron in the Trees* (1957); *Cosmicomics* (1965); *Invisible Cities* (1972)

88 | BASTI (1979) by Intizar Husain.

Urdu (British India/Pakistan)

Translated by Frances W Pritchett (New York Review Books)

"Houses never stay empty," Basti tell us. "When those who lived in them go away, the time lives on in the houses." The Urdu word "*basti*" means a settlement of some sort, from a hamlet to a city. Intizar Husain's novel of the change – and damage – wrought by time and power dwells in many kinds of houses, from the memory-laden mind of his protagonist Zakir to the villages and cities shaken by strife at critical moments of Indian and Pakistani history. But in this richly freighted, densely wrought story, which achieves an epic scope within its two hundred-odd pages, language itself becomes the splendid mansion occupied by one tenant after another. First a journalist in the newly-created state of Pakistan, then a short story writer, Husain brought to this first full-length novel the vast poetic and narrative resources of Urdu – that great linguistic bridge between Indian cultures and the Persian and Arabic traditions. Echoes of legend, scripture, formal verse-forms and ancient tales (such as those of *The Thousand and One Nights*) resonate through a novel that never drops the golden thread that binds "now" to "then". Fast-moving, episodic, compressed and imagistic in a strikingly modernist vein, *Basti* also shows in style as much as theme that "the merciless present pushes us back again toward our history".

Zakir experiences two waves of upheaval: first, as a child, when the British Raj collapses and his Muslim family moves to the fledgling Pakistan during the chaotic violence of Partition in 1947. In 1971, as a teacher in Lahore, he endures the war with India – and its terrifying riots, air-raids and blackouts – that accompanied the division of Pakistan and the blood-washed birth of Bangladesh. Husain also time-slips back to Delhi during the Uprising of 1857, when the North Indian revolt against British rule ended in the brutal eradication of the last vestiges of Mughal civilisation. From Zakir's childhood in the idyllic town of Rupnagar ("lovely city") onwards, we also drop back into "the lampless time of the forest". (In Rupnagar, the arrival of "the age of electricity" marks a decisive break with the old order.)

In this forest-time, passages from the ancient Sanskrit epics, from Persian poetry, from Hindu myths, Buddhist parables and Islamic lore combine into an eclectic story-world. Its wisdom, humour and diversity voices an enchanting reproach to the sectarian passions of the present. Leaving the child's earthly paradise of Rupnagar, growing up amid the protests and repressions of (fictitious) Vyaspur and then Lahore, Zakir has had to abandon "the remote, mythic era" of his youth. Reluctantly, he must breathe "the air of his own time". Still, that precious legacy of undivided stories joins the "dense clouds of memory" that both burden and console him – "Zakir", indeed, means "he who remembers".

For all its sedimentary layers of legend, poetry and scripture, *Basti* moves at an urgent pace. During and after Partition, then amid the perpetual tumult of Lahore, events unfold against a backdrop of riots and speeches, fire and gunshot, protest and persecution: "a roar of slogans and a rain of bricks". Zakir's dialogues with his friends Afzal and Irfan twist and leap between hope, nostalgia and despair. Their idealism for the new nation is forever thwarted not just by the cruelty and corruption of its rulers – "this land has grown oppressive" – but a corrosive sense of fate. His childhood companion Surendar, a Hindu who has stayed in India after their symbolic parting of the ways, laments in a letter from Delhi that "We're all in the power of time". Zakir longs for news of his boyhood sweetheart Sabirah, now part of India's Muslim minority, but we understand that "the vanished days never came back". In waves of expulsion and migration, the people move, but the dwellings remain, though rendered desolate by hatred. In one of the elegiac passages set in Delhi in 1857, the narrator, amid a patchwork of quotations from Urdu verse and the Qur'an, confesses that "I myself am the ruined city". Husain interleaves these historical fragments with Zakir's anxious diaries of the 1971 war: a mirror of catastrophes.

Amid the ravages of time, memories glide through Zakir's mind "the way a snake would raise its head from the grass, then vanish again in an instant". Husain alternates first- and third-person narration, adding another strand to the richly woven textures of the novel. Amid the "Doomsday-chaos" of Lahore in 1971, Zakir visits his parents' graves in the burning cemetery and regrets that "everything around me is in pieces. Time too". Yet Husain gathers these shattered pieces of memory and culture into a deeply satisfying mosaic, which fashions through its inclusive vision a harmony denied its characters, and their age. From that Muslim cemetery on a night of apocalypse we slip back to the forest-time of Buddha's parables. The teacher tells his monks that "when jackals speak, then tigers fall silent". In an era of jackals, *Basti* gives the tigers back their voice.

Translation: Frances W Pritchett's magisterial rendering (1995) navigates *Basti*'s shifts of tone, register and genre with ingenuity and elegance.

See also: Tagore, *Home and the World* (1916); Mahfouz, *Cairo Trilogy* (1956-57); Grass, *The Tin Drum* (1959); García Márquez, *One Hundred Years of Solitude* (1967)

Selected works by the same author: *A Chronicle of the Peacocks* (2002); *The Death of Sheherzad* (2014)

89 | So Long a Letter (1979) by Mariama Bâ.

French (Senegal)

Translated by Modupe Bode-Thomas (Heinemann African Writers Series Classics)

"Tonight I am restless. The flavour of life is love." Ramatoulaye, who

writes her long epistle to an old friend in America, has recently buried her husband. After a quarter-century of marriage, he wrecked their home and her peace of mind by taking the second, younger wife that local tradition allows. She has many children, and enjoys respect as an outstanding schoolteacher. Yet the just-completed rituals of Muslim mourning have shown Ramatoulaye that she counts for less than her glamorous but hapless rival Binetou: "A victim, she wanted to be the oppressor… she wanted her prison gilded."

Ramatoulaye addresses her childhood friend Aissatou, who unlike her, has left the husband who sidelined her for a second bride to build a new life abroad. Writing her letter, she summons the wisdom of the past and the reason of the present. She reflects on her own condition, and that of every African woman who must consent to become "a thing in the service of the man who has married her". At fifty, however, and with her own brood prey to all the pitfalls of adolescence and young adulthood, from fighting to pregnancy, she is not ready to vanish into invisible old age. A throng of suitors, "that greedy pack of hounds", plague Ramatoulaye. She brushes them away, even Daouda: the dapper doctor and parliamentarian, surely a worthy match. For her, in spite of "thirty years of harassment" with the treacherous Modou, marriage remains "an act of faith and love". A friend gently mocks her: "You speak of love instead of bread. Madame wants her heart to miss a beat. Why not flowers, just like in the films?".

Old modes of fiction may lie dormant and then bloom without warning in distant soil. The epistolary novel, long defunct in Europe, flourished unexpectedly again when the Senegalese writer, educator and reformer Mariama Bâ found in it the perfect vehicle for this compact but profound first-person story of African women trapped between two worlds. Although a single missive from Ramatoulaye to Aissatou, *So Long a Letter* incorporates other pieces of correspondence, dialogues, political and ethical debates, and jewelled fragments of memory – along with an epigrammatic flair that brings to mind the genre's French originals. Bâ explores the relationship between the European culture she had absorbed and African ways of belief and expression. Ramatoulaye attends a college with a French syllabus intended to drag the local elite out of "the bog of tradition", but – for all the humiliations heaped on her by Modou's taking of a "co-wife" – she never renounces the Islam of her upbringing. In her grief, she insists that "My heart concurs with the demands of religion".

Likewise, the shape of Bâ's novel unites local and foreign elements. It folds oral storytelling and the didactic tone of the teacher into a courageous scrutiny of women's roles in a transitional generation, one poised between colonial "domination" and a new era of independence. Ramatoulaye remembers of her fellow-students that "We were full of nostalgia, but we were resolutely progressive". In spite of the "assimilationist" policies of the colonial regime, the past will not die. Bâ sprinkles Ramatoulaye's testimony with "the salt of remembrance". It vivifies every argument and proposition, right from her earliest memories of bonding with Aissatou in "the procession of wet young girls chattering on their way back from the springs".

Professional women such as Ramatoulaye may rank among the "messengers of a new design" in the fledgling republic of Senegal. Their menfolk, though, have yet to grasp that principles of equality apply on the home front. Modou, an influential trades union leader, has a French law degree and talks the talk of liberation. But after twenty-five years he shunts Ramatoulaye into a limbo of scorn and neglect while Binetou and her avaricious mother ("Lady Mother-in-law") scoop up his care, and cash. Ramatoulaye can sympathise with her rival's plight, as "a lamb slaughtered on the altar of affluence". She chooses to stay in the family, trying vainly to determine how "the break in the thread" of her marriage occurred. Aissatou, in contrast, has divorced the aristocratic husband whose snobbish relatives, consumed by "the fierce ardour of antiquated laws", had never accepted this mere goldsmith's daughter into their proud clan. Bâ dissects prejudices of rank as well as race and gender. Like the author, who stayed in Senegal as an activist to help channel "the irreversible currents of women's liberation" into her own society, Ramatoulaye refuses to fall silent, or to flee. Now a widow, this "fluttering leaf that no hand dares to pick up" will, through work and children, persist in her pursuit not only of justice but of fulfilment. Meanwhile, "My heart rejoices each time a woman emerges from the shadows."

Translation: Modupe Bode-Thomas (1981) lends to Ramatoulaye's voice both a formal restraint, even stateliness, and an aphoristic bite.

See also: La Fayette, *The Princesse de Clèves* (1678); Lampedusa, *The Leopard* (1958); Salih, *Season of Migration to the North* (1966); Wolf, *The Quest for Christa T.* (1968)

Selected works by the same author: *Scarlet Song (1981)*

90 | Buru Quartet (This Earth of Mankind; Child of All Nations; Footsteps; House of Glass) (1980-1988) by Pramoedya Ananta Toer.

Indonesian

Translated by Max Lane (Penguin Australia)

Surely no epoch-defining epic has had to fight so fiercely for its life

as the *Buru Quartet*. Affronted by his "seditious" writings, the colonial Dutch government of the East Indies imprisoned Pramoedya Ananta Toer for two years in the late 1940s. In independent Indonesia, the state whose genesis he chronicles across this sequence of novels, he soon fell foul again of authoritarian regimes. From 1965, Pramoedya spent fourteen years on the prison island of Buru; his research materials and manuscripts for the *Quartet* had been burned after his arrest. So, in an ironic reprise of his great theme of clash and convergence between Asian tradition and European modernity, he began his epic again as oral narrative told to his fellow inmates. Only after 1975 could he begin to write the stories down. For years after his release in 1979, censorship and persecution by the Indonesian authorities still dogged these books and their advocates.

Pramoedya, who remained under house arrest until 1992, vaulted over these obstacles and privations. In the *Quartet*, he created a classic account of the long, fitful and roundabout process of liberation, both for the individual colonial subject and any society in the grip of a foreign power. With a panoramic sweep and intellectual breadth that really does merit the adjective "Tolstoyan", the novels place their Javanese hero Minke not only in the richly elaborated context of his family, his island and his culture. He also joins the fast-moving history of both Europe and Asia: the continents whose diverse peoples the books show as inseparable "links in a chain". Yet, especially in the first two volumes set in and near Minke's home city of Surabaya, intimate domestic drama fuels the plot as much as the hubbub of great events, whether in Batavia (now Jakarta), Amsterdam, Tokyo or Manila. During the first phase of globalisation – the action takes place, mainly in Java, between 1898 and 1918 – not even the most hallowed of customs and relationships can withstand this "age of the triumph of capital". Political and economic turmoil engenders crises at home, even in the soul. Imperial rule shapes the colonised mind, while for Minke and many of his compatriots, "European ideas have changed the way we look at things." Even though "the colonial world is a world of terror", as his birth mother laments, history cannot be reversed or erased. Freedom, though, can be pursued, perhaps won.

Minke, whose career as a journalist, reformer and social organiser draws on the life of the anti-colonial activist Tirto Adhi Soerjo, comes from a noble Javanese family. His father serves as a "bupati", a local official in the service of the Dutch overlords. Unusually, Minke attends a high school for the Dutch masters and their mixed-race underlings, although a pure "Native" himself. (Pramoedya traces the toxic effects of these minute gradations, and degradations, of colour and class.) His real breakthrough into free thought comes when he enters the household of Nyai Ontosoroh, his adored "Mama". She has overcome her past as the bought concubine of a Dutch merchant to thrive as a dynamic businesswoman, a "rock of coral" who has freed herself.

The opening novels, *This World of Mankind* and *Child of All Nations*, set Minke's youthful awakening against the early stirrings of the islands' movement for self-rule. They range wider across history, from the exploitative scourge of "sugar capital" to the ascent of Japan. That land becomes a threat to European authority, and a model for Asian nationalists. The cruelties of colonial law rob Minke of his wife Annalies, Mama's daughter. His burgeoning career as a journalist sends him into the countryside to discover his "peasant people". Propelled by debate and dialogue, passions and ideas, crammed with character and incident, the novels have little time for the touristic exoticism that colours much Western fiction of the East. Minke, and his creator, care for and celebrate "this world of mankind", not scenery or folklore. Torn between old grace and new force, Minke rejoices that European modernity has "provided many breasts to suckle me", with Multalili – anti-imperialist Dutch author of *Max Havelaar* – a particular inspiration. At the same time, we detect in him and his educated peers "the loneliness of orphaned humanity".

The two Surabaya novels almost stand alone. In *Footsteps*, Minke moves to Batavia as a medical student, then a campaigning journalist. His exploits as editor and militant introduce more heavily documentary episodes (again, Tolstoy comes to mind). Always, though, the quest for emancipation must begin in the home, and in the heart. Other charismatic women take centre stage. They include his second, Chinese wife Ang San Mei – who compares Japanese and British imperialism to the bacteria that cause syphilis and gonorrhoea – and, after her death, the firebrand Princess Kasiruta. *House of Glass* boldly changes course. Its perspective shifts from Minke to the detective Pangemanann: a guilt-ridden, Westernised careerist charged by the Dutch to investigate the liberator he privately admires. Compromised, conflicted, the embodiment of "a defeated generation", the policeman with his self-doubt shows that the vision of the exiled Minke – "the pioneer of a national awakening" – has opened even his foes' eyes. Like his real-life counterpart, Minke dies as the Great War ends. His defeat will be temporary. We grasp that his cause is gathering strength, and his ideas "spreading like fireflies" in Java and beyond.

Translation: Published from 1983 onwards, Max Lane's idiomatic and immersive English versions keep faith with the grandeur, and intimacy, of the *Quartet*.

See also: Tolstoy, *War and Peace* (1869); Tagore, *Home and the World* (1919); Qian, *Fortress Besieged* (1947); Grossman, *Life and Fate* (1959)

Selected works by the same author: *It's not an All-Night Fair* (1951); *The Girl From the Coast* (1962); *The Mute's Soliloquy* (1995)

91 | The True Deceiver (1982) by Tove Jansson.

Swedish (Finland)

Translated by Thomas Teal (Sort of Books)

In the snowbound coastal village where Katri Kling lives with her brother Mats in the attic above a shop, neighbours distrust her – despite the supernatural skill with numbers she shares with them when they need help with taxes and accounts. This yellow-eyed loner cares, the gossips think, only for herself and the innocent, perhaps "simple" Mats. Besides, her giant German Shepherd has no name, and "all dogs should have names". What kind of a name, then, should we give to *The True Deceiver*? This is a novel as eerily inscrutable as Katri herself, but as streamlined and precise as her unerring calculations, or the drawings of boats that Mats makes with all "the love and care a person devotes to…a single overarching idea". It belongs among the novels for adults that Tove Jansson wrote after the Swedish-speaking Finnish artist-author had moved on from books and cartoon strips about her globally cherished (but subversive, ambiguous) Moomin characters. Like them, it crackles with a timeless, folkloric, mischievous magic. To suspicious villagers in this winter realm of sheet ice and snowdrifts, Katri is a "little witch" – gifted but touched, even cursed. Later she becomes "Cinderella on her way to the castle". When she and Mats go to live with the elderly, wealthy artist Anna Aemelin, it feels to Anna "like having a spirit in the house, one of those magically enslaved and obedient pixies that frequent the castles in fairy-tales…ever-present yet always just vanishing". Katri also reminds Anna of "the Big Bad Wolf", although her dog – whom the old lady tries to tame by giving him the bathetic name of "Teddy" – has his own prior claims on that title.

A fairy story for grown-ups, then? Only up to a razor-sharp icicle's point. In our contemporary Western mythology, the far North now feels like the sacred heartland of mutual trust, caring communities and social solidarity. Yet Jansson delivers a chilly fable about self-interest muffled by self-sacrifice, and cynicism that wears the mask of innocence. First, she presents Katri as the amoral intruder in this cosy nest of right-thinking, like-minded conformists. An illusion-free forward-planner, she pursues money, "as pure as numbers", to secure a better future for herself and the vulnerable Mats. She despises the "sloppy, disgusting machinery" of social hypocrisy, and plots to seize what she and Mats need with a forest predator's efficiency. Informal village accountancy will only take them so far. Katri plans to inveigle herself into the mind, and life, of Anna.

Alone in the mansion bequeathed by her parents ("rich as trolls"), Anna is a much-loved children's author. With each spring thaw, she paints for her books "implacably naturalistic" watercolours of the forest floor – but embellished with cute bunnies sporting flowers on their fur. Her little admirers write to the lady in the house known to the villagers as "rabbit villa". The fans ask how the bunnies got their fancy blooms. When, and why, does genuine art turn into kitsch? The nature of the artistic vocation, and the dividing line between the "true deception" of the real thing and the pretence of fake art, always preoccupied Jansson – even in her Moomin period. Katri moves in with Anna (after a break-in she has staged in order to frighten her) and takes over the management of her career. The novel grows, as well, into a gentle but sophisticated allegory of the creative life.

When not drawing real plants and unreal rabbits, Anna loves to read naïve adventure stories. These two-dimensional romps beckon her into "an honourable world of just desserts, eternal friendship and rightful retribution". Back in the real, imperfect world, Katri – an artist in deeds if not words or images – prefers serious "literature". She gets Mats to read these books about "people with problems", but "they just make me sad". The downside of Anna's problem-free, sentimental bunny world is her "criminally credulous" approach to royalties, contracts, percentages, secondary rights, fan mail and all the other complications of a bestselling author's life. Katri takes charge of Anna's public and financial identities. She skims off a fair commission to help her and, especially, to order a splendid craft for Mats from the village boat builders. Katri, who conceives of every relationship apart from her bond with Mats as "a kind of barter, reciprocal performance in kind", has no trouble mimicking Anna's signature, nor the "awkward kindness" of her replies to child fans.

Soon, as in some Strindberg play transplanted to an icily enchanted backwater, the battle of wills between the two women slides into a disruptive exchange of roles. We grasp that Anna never was that fluffy-bunny innocent. "She eats only grass," concludes Katri, "but she has a meat-eater's heart." Conversely, the "little witch", with her faith in cold-eyed ambitions and clean-edged transactions, will go astray in the woods of human complexity. Meanwhile, the dog rediscovers his feral roots to run wild "under the ominous ensign of the wolf skin". Mats will have his boat – another proper work of art. Anna will absorb enough of Katri's spirit for her to reject those blooming bunnies, which "seemed suddenly silly and quite without charm", and return to her own kind of true deceiving. In the dark earth, when the snow melts, her real inspiration lies, beyond "hypocrisy" but immune to "money" too. "Cluttering the ground with flowery rabbits would have been unthinkable."

Translation: Thomas Teal (2009) finds a perfect pitch for Jansson's voice in English, wry and cool, each deft stroke carried off with unobtrusive artistry.

See also: Staël *Corinne* (1807); Hamsun, *Hunger* (1890); Laxness, *Independent People* (1934–35); Camus, *The Outsider* (1942)

Selected works by the same author: *Comet in Moominland* (1946); *The Book about Moomin, Mymble and Little My* (1952); *Sculptor's Daughter* (1968); *The Summer Book* (1972)

92 | The Lover (1984); by Marguerite Duras (Marguerite Donnadieu).

French (French Indochina, France)

Translated by Barbara Bray (Harper Perennial)

No reader will treat *The Lover* merely as an exotic travelogue. It does, though, offer some hallucinatory descriptions of the Mekong Delta in French Indochina, where Marguerite Duras spent her youth. Under these searing skies, within "the long hot girdle of the earth", the tropical heat obliterates all seasons. The "black slime" of the rivers erases the distinction between solid and liquid, land and water. Likewise, the material of an unforgotten adolescent passion became for Duras an infinitely plastic medium. It flowed through memoir, fiction and then cinema without ever losing its clinging potency. Like the narrator of *The Lover*, Duras did, as a teenage schoolgirl in the colonial Sadec and Saigon of 1930, conduct a scandalous affair with a wealthy young Chinese businessman. From her other writings, we know that he never lost his obsession with "the queen of his desires". Duras herself transformed this exhilarating, mortifying rite of passage into two novels (this one, and the much earlier *The Sea Wall),* while her *The North China Lover* incorporates her screenplay for this work's film adaptation. On the French literary scene of the 1950s and 1960s, Duras had passed through the austere formalism of the *nouveau roman* but never quite left it behind. She went on testing the boundaries of genre as well as theme – in 1960, her screenplay for *Hiroshima Mon Amour* gained an Academy Award nomination. If, as many critics agree, *The Lover* counts as a supremely "transgressive" work, then it breaches the boundaries that divide autobiography from fiction as much as the conventions that forbade love across the frontiers of age and race.

The narrator is fifteen-and-a-half when her future lover offers her a lift in his limousine as she returns to boarding school in Saigon. Her mother is a widowed teacher who has almost bankrupted the family with a rash land investment. Poverty, isolation and emotional instability have reduced her and her three children to the ragged margins of European privilege in this colonial society. Sometimes "we ate garbage, storks, baby crocodiles, but the garbage was cooked and served by a houseboy". Dressed in gold lamé heels and a brownish-pink fedora, the girl intuits that the mother's desperation is pushing her daughter towards a gold-digger's career. Nonetheless, the stolen days of "pleasure unto death" with her lover crackle with an electric charge of bliss, dread and shame. To the outraged French colonists, she becomes that "little slut" who "goes to have her body caressed by a filthy Chinese millionaire". But, like some libertine novelist of the 18th-century, Duras pays meticulous attention to the shifting dynamics of power within their erotic bond. The girl feels that her lover is disempowered, "at her mercy". For him, overwhelming desire collides with the family duties that will, inevitably, steer him into marriage to a suitable Chinese wife. "His heroism is me," she thinks, "his cravenness is his father's money."

However intense, their trysts cannot catch fire in a vacuum. Apart from her breach of decorum on two fronts – age, and culture – the girl also bears the burden of her family's anguish. Her mother (modelled on Duras's own) haunts her every thought. This tormented figure forfeits class, security and status on the fringes of empire. Then she retires to a calamitous old age in the Loire, while seeing every doomed project through "to the bitter end". "It's in this valour, human, absurd, that I see true grace." Two brothers – the elder, a bullying and manipulative "murderer without a gun", the younger a frail soul whom she adores – also mould her memories. We never love, or even lust, in isolation. Beyond the misery and madness of her family, the girl carries into the chamber of desire a cargo of scorn and guilt. It is loaded by the taboos of class, gender and race.

Duras's narrative voice has the tone of a confession: episodic, intimate, discontinuous. In fragments, we glean the course of the girl's later life as a writer in France. On the boat "home", a snatch of Chopin reminds her of their romance through "this moment of music flung across the sea". Beauty and abjection, desire and regret, never feel more than a few words, or heartbeats, apart. Duras, always restless and mercurial, could speak slightingly of *The Lover* and the late fame it won her. On one level, this compacted, explosive story feels wild, bold and free, even formless. Past and present ooze and swirl like that Mekong Delta mud. Yet the narrating consciousness drives fear and desire into a narrow channel where passion flows with hypnotic, disruptive, force. The mother, the brothers, the lover, the girl: this quintet of ghosts, we sense, have determined every step of the narrator's life as a woman and an artist. Eroticism and fatalism intertwine. The illicit affair merely solidifies the aura of doom and ruin that the narrator bears with her from childhood. Long before she steps into the lover's limousine, she has "crossed to the other side".

Translation: Barbara Bray (1985) proves more than equal to Duras's forensic emotional intelligence as well as her lavish sensuality.

See also: La Fayette, *The Princesse de Clèves* (1678); Laclos, *Dangerous Liaisons* (1782); Lispector, *Near to the Wild Heart* (1943); Colette, *Chéri/The Last of Chéri* (1920-26)

Selected works by the same author: *The Sea Wall* (1950); *Moderato Cantabile* (1958); *Hiroshima Mon Amour* (1960); *The Ravishing of Lol Stein* (1964)

93 | The Year of the Death of Ricardo Reis (1984) by José Saramago.

Portuguese

Translated by Giovanni Pontiero (Vintage)

At least since Cervantes framed *Don Quixote* as the translation of an Arabic work by "Cide Hamete Benengeli", fiction has nourished itself on its real or imaginary forebears. From the title onwards, *The Year of the Death of Ricardo Reis* appears to be a book made out of other books; an act of homage, tribute, or maybe downright theft. "Ricardo Reis" was one of the principal literary alter egos – he called them "heteronyms" – of the Portuguese poet, essayist, philosopher and unclassifiable genius, Fernando Pessoa. His prismatic masterwork *The Book of Disquiet* defies every genre classification (that of fiction included). For Pessoa, as for José Saramago in this disciple's novel that devours and transforms its source material, each human being contains multitudes. When Saramago's

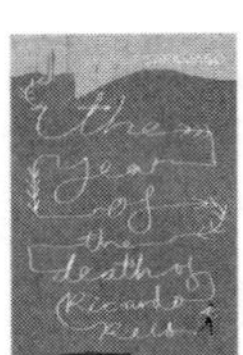

Ricardo Reis contemplates himself "in the depths of the mirror" (a presiding image here), he sees "one of the countless persons that he is, all of them weary". Words, ideas, whole selves multiply, fragment and proliferate: "innumerable people exist within us". Our minds, and works, breed other minds and works. The mirrors reflect to infinity.

The melancholy metaphysics of Pessoa, and the Borges-like atmosphere of dissolving identity that Saramago evokes, might suggest that *The Year of the Death of Ricardo Reis* proceeds like some sort of airless, disembodied experiment in the pulverisation of narrative and character. Not at all. A former journalist in Portugal, and life-long political radical, Saramago wraps satire, romance, social comedy, philosophy and history within the elegant, snaky coils of his sentences. The novel's conceit is that, just as Pessoa himself dies in Lisbon during the sodden early winter of 1935, his invention Ricardo Reis – a morose, becalmed physician and poet – comes home. He returns from a sixteen year period of residence in Brazil to this forgotten capital of a once-great empire. Here he enjoys, or endures, nine months of limbo. He converses with the spectral figure of Pessoa himself, who materialises at regular intervals, has an on-off affair with the hotel chambermaid Lydia, pursues a chaste romance with a lawyer's crippled daughter, Marcenda, and waits for the final dissolution that will unite him in oblivion with the poet who created him. "You are floating, in other words, in mid-ocean, neither here nor there. Like the rest of the Portuguese."

Saramago moves in and out of Ricardo's brooding consciousness, embeds dialogue within monologue, and threads the private and public lingos of the nation and the period through the drifting hero's mind. He builds a novel distinguished by both political and philosophical audacity. Ricardo wanders on every margin: between life and death, present and past, memory and perception, new America and old Europe. He comes to rest on the drizzly borderlines of Lisbon, "where the sea ends and the earth awaits". At this moment, as 1936 dawns, Europe itself hangs suspended between states. The relatively new Salazar dictatorship in Portugal, which Saramago mocks with discreetly wicked wit, acts as an almost comic, though still sinister, reflection of the fearsome might of Hitler's Third Reich. The Portuguese, after all, "play a most humble role on the great stage of the world". That role, though, involves an abundance of bizarre parades and performances. Although an interior journey, the novel also whisks us with panache through marketplaces, shopping streets, newspaper offices, religious rituals and political rallies in a city forever rain-drenched as if "made of absorbent cotton, smoked, dripping".

As Pessoa's own vision proved, as Saramago's novel so artfully confirms, one can often see more from the edge than from the hub. Paradoxically, the wistful, sombre and regretful tones in which Saramago paints Dr Reis and his city still have their appeal. Meanwhile, all the "modern" noise of the 1930s – the slogans, the advertisements, the headlines, the doctrines – stand revealed as quaint curios, or worse. Lydia, Ricardo's casual fling and a hard-pressed worker disadvantaged in this class-stratified world ("The rule is that some eat figs while others watch"), develops into a genuine heroine: courageous, loving, truthful and resourceful. Pessoa's creed of estrangement and disappointment ("a man can never reach the horizon before his eyes") becomes in Saramago's hands the basis for an ethics, and an art, of plucky marginality.

The losers cast aside by life – the poor, the unlucky, the disabled, the dreamers, the declining nations, the just-departed dead themselves – may enter realms that the winners and conquerors never see. So the shade of Pessoa (who did once exist) tells Reis (who never did) that "the wall that separates the living from one another is no less opaque that the wall that separates the living from the dead". Ghostly, eerie, Saramago's Lisbon becomes a place where imagination can breach those opaque barriers that cut people off from one another, and from the other selves hidden within each of us. For all its introspective dives into the abyss, his novel sounds sociable, conversational. It is keen-eyed and quick-witted. This damp abode of the abashed, the defeated, the almost-dead, feels remarkably alive. Or rather, as the phantom Pessoa says, "None of us is truly alive or truly dead". That goes, as Saramago hints, for societies as much as souls.

Translation: Giovanni Pontiero (1992) masterfully catches every flash and twist in the sinuous, quicksilver movement of Saramago's prose.

See also: Eça de Queiróz, *The Crime of Father Amaro* (1875-80); Machado, *Epitaph of a Small Winner* (1880); Rilke, *The Notebooks of Malte Laurids Brigge* (1910); Sebald, *The Emigrants* (1992)

Selected works by the same author: *Baltasar and Blimunda* (1982); *The Stone Raft* (1986); *The Gospel According to Jesus Christ* (1991), *Blindness* (1995)

94 | HARD-BOILED WONDERLAND AND THE END OF THE WORLD (1985) by Haruki Murakami.

Japanese

Translated by Alfred Birnbaum (Vintage)

By the final quarter of the 20th-century, the most contagious genres of Western consumer culture – Hollywood movies; rock and jazz music; sport, food and fashion brands – had wrapped the globe so completely that they evolved into a sort of narrative *lingua franca.* Writers could invoke this all-purpose lexicon of myths as their ancestors had summoned the heroes of epics or scriptures. Arguably, Haruki Murakami counts as the first great novelist to embed these elements into his work not as local colour but as a guiding principle. At the same time, this former manager of a Tokyo jazz bar remains more indelibly "Japanese" than the critics who scorned him as a copy-cat pseudo-American novelist could ever admit. Movie- and music-mad like so many Murakami narrators, the protagonist of *Hard-boiled Wonderland and The End of the World* regrets that he will never resemble the actor Ben Johnson, a star of John Ford's Westerns often seen "riding across the landscape, swift as an arrow, our hero forever in frame". The inability of Murakami's solitary, questing young or young-ish men ever to occupy with confidence the role of settled hero, "forever in frame", ties them not only to European fiction (Kafka inevitably, and also Stendhal). It makes them kin to a tribe of melancholy Japanese outsiders that stretches back to the novels of Sōseki and beyond.

*Hard-Boiled Wonderland...*bursts with such a dazzling display of genre fireworks that its admirers often miss the simple loneliness of the narrator – his yearning for intimate contact, but also his hunger for a state of self-contained withdrawal. One story, set in a "hard-boiled wonderland" of a near-future Tokyo, frames another. In the second, the same character (or at least his avatar) finds himself in a timeless Town guarded by an impenetrable Wall at "the End of the World". Gritty, wise-cracking urban noir, in the Raymond Chandler manner; high-concept science fiction in the vein of Philip K Dick; a quasi-medieval fantasy with a Tolkienesque tinge; an eerie fable of confinement à la Kafka: Murakami, the magpie virtuoso, packs all these strands into his twin-track story. He transforms them all into something rich, new and achingly sad. As ever in his fiction (and this novel marked a breakthrough into the artful, genre-mashing mayhem of his mature work), pulp and profundity intermesh. Mysticism and melodrama can mingle in a style that collapses all distinctions between "high" and "pop" forms. Dostoyevsky, Turgenev and Stendhal rub shoulders with Lauren Bacall, Star Trek – even the pop group Duran Duran. Murakami's mode has much in common with the boundary-breaking eclecticism of his beloved jazz musicians and movie directors.

Our narrator is a super-gifted "Calcutec". He makes a good living as a data security specialist on the fringes of an all-powerful hi-tech corporation ("the System"), but looks forward in retirement to "an easy life of cello and Greek". In the "hard-boiled" plot, our Calcutec is targeted by thugs who may work for the rival "Factory". This is a gangster outfit whose "Semiotecs" hack into the data that the Calcutecs encrypt. (Murakami imagines in detail commercial cyber wars that did not yet exist). The Calcutec escapes into the underground laboratory of a rogue Professor – another lone wolf – who, it transpires, has experimentally programmed our hero's brain with a signature story that represents the core of his unconscious mind. This story, or "encephalodigital conversion", concerns the parallel reality of *End of the World.*

Here, in alternating chapters, the narrator discovers the Town beyond time and change. In this "clean slate of eternity", pain and grief do not exist – but neither do memory and love. We see that "without the despair of loss, there is no hope". Back in hyper-modern Tokyo, the narrator learns that his mind will soon slip forever into the becalmed seclusion of the Town. In the Town, conversely, he seeks reunion with his "shadow" – that part of the self that carries the weight of the past – and wants to escape back into mortal, messy, dangerous reality (or a futuristic version of it). "It's not the best of all worlds," his shadow admits, "but it is the world where we belong." Our hero falls for loveable librarians in both dimensions. A unicorn's skull, relic of that over-interpreted legendary beast "that can embody any value one wishes", serves as a hinge between the worlds.

On one level, these rival spaces perhaps encode two rival Japans. One is automated, soulless, corporate, an oligarchy where "private enterprise…enlisted state interests"; the other an idealised realm of ritual grace, where only the wistful beauty of changing seasons interrupts "perpetual peace and security". Cherished by readers (especially younger ones) across the planet, Murakami has converted the extreme dislocations of post-war Japanese culture into a fictional architecture where the emotional orphans of urban modernity, whatever their origin, can find a home. "You have doubts, you have contradictions, you have regrets, you are weak," a senior officer of the Town tells the narrator. "Winter is the most dangerous season for you." In the chilly cities of our digitised, scrutinised wonderland, Murakami has woven new myths of enchantment to keep us warm.

Translation: Alfred Birnbaum (1991) switches with zest and poise between the science fiction noir of "Wonderland" and the elegiac dreamland of the Town.

See also: Stendhal, *The Red and the Black* (1830); Sōseki, *The Gate* (1910); Kafka, *The Trial* (1925); Lem, *Solaris* (1961)

Selected works by the same author: *A Wild Sheep Chase* (1982)*;* *Norwegian Wood* (1987)*; The Wind-up Bird Chronicle* (1995)*; Kafka on the Shore* (2002)

95 | SEE UNDER: LOVE (1986) by David Grossman.

Hebrew (Israel)

Translated by Betsy Rosenberg (Vintage Classics)

Much misquoted, the philosopher-critic Theodor Adorno did not decree that writing poetry after Auschwitz was impossible but that to do so was "barbaric". The Israeli writer Shlomo Neuman, the principal narrator and implied author of *See Under: LOVE*, torments himself with precisely that judgment. His lover Ayala treats his proposed "encyclopaedia" of a child's life during the Nazi genocide as "a documentation of your crimes against humanity". David Grossman himself grew up in post-war Israel, surrounded by survivors (much of his own family included). They had escaped the "barbarism" of stories about the Holocaust only to lapse into traumatised silence. His novel wrestles mightily, and in the end triumphantly, with the brazen audacity of its task on every level: emotional, artistic, above all ethical. This is an outstanding work of Holocaust fiction that continuously questions its right to exist. It interrogates the means of its creation, the language of its testimony, and the claims of art to encompass an age of annihilation when reality burst its banks and "seemed to overflow into the realm of imagination". The character who feels that inadequacy is an Armenian magician named Harotian. Through magic of many kinds, above all the spells woven by narrative, Grossman restores this unknowably dark planet to the orbit of the human mind and heart. For Shlomo, as for the other tale-bearers that he chronicles, "there is only the story. Write, then, please."

Against the deadened silence in the aftermath of horror Grossman launches a cascade of stories. The novel channels a torrential dam-burst of memories, fables, histories. The first of its four main sections, each of them distinct in voice and style, evokes the late-1950s world of nine-year-old Shlomo, known as "Momik", in a poor neighbourhood populated by immigrants to Israel. Through the overheard dialogue of his relatives and neighbours, their newly acquired Hebrew spiced with Yiddish imported from the eradicated shtetls of Jewish Europe, Momik glimpses the unspeakable events that took place "Over There". He becomes a junior spy, alert to the "top-secret codes and passwords" that give access to the vile deeds of the "Nazi Beast". A new "grandfather" arrives to join these numbed survivors, who have their camp numbers tattooed indelibly on their arms. He is Anshel Wasserman: also a haunted fugitive but one who, in pre-war Poland, wrote much-loved adventure stories for children.

Wasserman's uplifting tales featured the "Children of the Heart", a multi-ethnic band of young champions of justice who fought "the powers of darkness". Their exploits flow through the novel, a stream of hope that reflects but resists the fires of the inhuman nightmare around it. First, however, Shlomo goes in search of a real (and uniquely gifted) author swallowed by the Holocaust: the Polish Jewish short story writer Bruno Schulz. His only novel, *The Messiah*, vanished along with its maker. Grossman depicts Schulz, whose fabulously original prose he quotes at length, as a reinventor of language itself, a seeker after "pure, crystalline truth". We see Schulz as a sort of aquatic escapee from genocide, a migrating "salmon among men", in one of the soaring leaps of imagination that reveal Grossman's aesthetic kinship not only with Schulz himself but with the "magic realist" wave of Günter Grass, Salman Rushdie and Gabriel García Márquez. In the third part, Shlomo recreates Wasserman's experience in a concentration camp, where the writer became a sort of Jewish Sheherezade. Night by night, he buys his life from the commandant Neigel by recounting adventure stories. Neigel rages against this shabby yarn-peddler who shuffles his characters "like a general moving battalions". All the same, the captive Sheherezade conquers the enemy, tale by suspenseful tale. Wasserman succeeds in "infecting Neigel with humanity" as his stories incorporate more of the hellish truth around them. Eventually, the fanatic Nazi loyalist slides into spiritual crisis. With grotesque, even farcical, episodes to offset their harrowing cruelties, these camp scenes court vulgarity, even absurdity: this anti-world obliterates every standard of taste and decorum. The "sacred unities of time and place" have no role in a vacuum that sucks order, reason and causality into its domain of absolute nothingness.

For Neigel's ears, Wasserman revives the "Children of the Heart" and sends them, as wiser adults, into the war-time Warsaw of ghettos, massacres and deportations. There, in the zoo, they raise a child, Kazik, who in this universe stripped of logic lives an entire lifetime within a day. The concluding "encyclopaedia" of Kazik's accelerated span – under headings that range from "Love and Choice" to "Hitler, Adolf"– dances with a madcap inventiveness. Shlomo, channelling Wasserman, shakes his fist of art against the death machine directed by the "Beast". Little Kazik's protectors pray that, in the juster world of the future that he will never see, "he might end his life knowing nothing of war". But even the highest works of Holocaust art (such as this novel) cannot accomplish that. "Out of the leaven of humanity," Wasserman advises Neigel, "One cannot bake a miracle!". Miracles aside, our storytellers can and must keep up their attritional defence of memory and humanity – whether trail-blazing pioneers such as Schulz, or big-hearted entertainers like Wasserman himself. They are not the accomplices of barbarism but its precious challengers, who wage without respite "a guerrilla war with words".

Translation: Betsy Rosenberg (1989) convincingly finds an English idiom – or rather several idioms – for this polyphonic work, whose original Hebrew is shadowed by the Yiddish, Polish and German past.

See also: Agnon, *Only Yesterday* (1945); Grass, *The Tin Drum* (1959); Singer, *The Slave* (1962); Sebald, *The Emigrants* (1992)

Selected works by the same author: *The Smile of the Lamb* (1983); *The Book of Intimate Grammar* (1991); *Be My Knife* (1998); *To the End of the Land* (2008)

96 | The Black Book (1990) by Orhan Pamuk.

Turkish

Translated by Maureen Freely (Faber & Faber)

On a snowy night in Istanbul, the lawyer Galip climbs the minaret of the great Suleymaniye mosque. As he scans the city of domes and hovels below, gazing across its cracked and frayed expanses of "concrete, stone, tile, wood and Plexiglas", he feels that "he was looking at the surface of a planet that had yet to find its final shape". *The Black Book* maps that unfinished planet in a mood and style of visionary fervour. It contains a detective story crammed with mirrors and labyrinths, a study in memory and mourning, a rhapsodic scavenge through Turkish history and culture, and a tear-stained, ecstatic love letter to Orhan Pamuk's home town. In a time of political strife and personal unease, not long before the Turkish military coup of 1980, Galip's wife Rüya – a cousin from the squabbling clan who grew up together in their gossip-ridden warren of apartments – disappears. Has she fled the marital home with their kinsman Celâl? He is the legendary newspaper columnist who for decades has spellbound his readers with tales of the folklore, the myths, the byways and the occult secrets of Istanbul, convinced that only by telling stories could he "come to know the mystery of the city and the mystery of life itself". Through chilly winter streets, haunted by his own and the city's past, Galip turns "apprentice detective". He navigates a "sea of clues" in search not only of the absconding pair but a key that may let him understand "the thick cloak of melancholy sitting over our people".

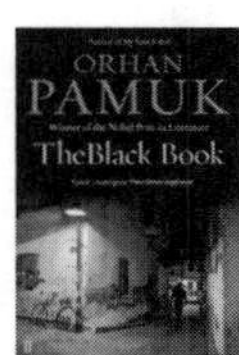

Alternating with Galip's distraught zig-zags from neighbourhood to neighbourhood, enigma to enigma, Pamuk invents Celâl's own columns. Sumptuously woven out of Ottoman history, urban myth and shared nostalgia, they engage in an almost paranoid pursuit of a mysterious "other realm" hidden within the signs, the faces, the bric-à-brac of urban life. These pieces burrow deep into the collective malaise of an era of disguise and masquerade when "we all tried so hard to become someone else". In the aftermath of the Ottoman Empire, in thrall to Western modes and models in fashion, books, ideas and politics, Celâl's – and Pamuk's – Turkey has lost itself in a maze of facsimiles and simulacra, as found in the eerie mannequin museum that Galip visits. The circuitous hunt for missing persons turns into a search, historical and metaphysical, for "life's secret meaning" amid the fog of change. A contact who might hold the key to the couple's fate tells Galip that "To live in an oppressed, defeated country is to be someone else". Yet fables wrenched from the past, individual or national, can never return these vagabond souls to some pristine condition of authenticity. We may peer into "the garden of memories" but its gates stay stoutly shut. Turkey's "Eastern" and Islamic heritage becomes as much of a consolatory illusion here as its "Western" and secular present.

Galip's memory-guided investigations, and Celâl's literary excursions, conjure an Istanbul of the mind. It feels both cinematically precise and poetically elusive. Page by page, Pamuk reanimates every grimy nook, down to the stairwells of backstreet apartment blocks "that stank of sleep, garlic, mildew, lime, coal and cooking-oil". Yet these streets, squares, cafés, clubs and flats also become mystery-laden "extensions of a dream". In this oneiric atmosphere, identities blur and shift. Galip starts to inhabit the life of his quarry. He camps out in Celâl's hideaway in the old family block, and even files columns in the voice of the absent chronicler. His assumption of this other self embodies the novel's suggestion that "What made the world mysterious was the second person that each of us hid inside ourselves, the twin with whom we shared our lives". Beyond the public entanglement of East and West, tradition and modernity, the mystic signs that crowd the frozen streets hint at this universal doubleness. "The carpet store, the pastry shop… the sewing machines, the newspapers" – they all "shimmered with their second meanings" when observed by passers-by who all hid second selves.

In torrents of incident and anecdote, rumour and parable, Sufi mysticism and tabloid sensationalism, Pamuk draws on his "bottomless well of stories" to plumb "the mystery of defeat, misery and ruin". But *The Black Book*, paradoxically, explodes with joyous life. Each episode of mourning, melancholy and nostalgia has such buoyancy and brio that the "muddy concrete forest" of the city becomes an icy, sooty fairyland. Among the list of tips for columnists Celâl gathers from his journalistic cronies, number fifty-nine runs: "Never forget that the secret is love. The key word is love." Galip's pursuit of Celâl and Rüya will end in sorrow, as we always suspect. But stories of love, that "antidote to solitude", thread *The Black Book* together. They range from

Galip's reveries of remembrance, with young Rüya minutely recalled down to the "lone green sock" worn on a cycling trip, to Celâl's enraptured excavations of the city's eccentric past and people. Among them, we encounter the veteran journalist "so enamoured" of Proust (rather like Pamuk himself) that he endlessly re-reads *In Search of Lost Time*. Pamuk's city of loss and mourning is also a metropolis of desire. It is a place that resounds to "the enchanting harmonies, the barely audible music, of longing itself".

Translation: Maureen Freely (2006) crafts an utterly persuasive English voice for Pamuk: thrilling, intimate, tender, mysterious – and comic.

See also: Proust, *In Search of Lost Time* (1913–1927); Cela, *The Hive* (1951); Tanpinar, *The Time Regulation Institute* (1962); Cabrera Infante, *Three Trapped Tigers* (1965)

Selected works by the same author: *The White Castle* (1985); *My Name is Red* (1998); *Snow* (2002); *The Museum of Innocence* (2008)

97 | The Emigrants (1992) by WG Sebald.

German (Germany/United Kingdom)

Translated by Michael Hulse (Vintage)

In the last of the four character studies that make up *The Emigrants*, the narrator visits a spa town in northern Bavaria. There

he sees pieces of wood sculpted by the mineral salts in the water into "the very strangest of petrified or crystalline forms". Those encrusted branches, uncannily suspended between nature and artifice, have much in common with WG Sebald's work. Through the deadpan, lugubrious but drily witty voice of its narrator, *The Emigrants* introduces us to a quartet of characters – all of them exiles from Germany or German culture – who appear to belong to real life. As for our rueful, melancholic guide to their biographies, his personal data seem to match those of WG Sebald: from his birth in May 1944 and his childhood in the Bavarian uplands to his spell as a junior lecturer in Manchester and his permanent settlement away from Germany, amid the "flat expanse" of Norfolk. The evocative, but uncaptioned, period photographs dropped into the text – a ploy mimicked by Sebald's legion of imitators – add to this quasi-documentary tone. This, however, is a novel – a great, and a greatly influential, one. Its own migration between fact and fiction, biography and invention, history and nightmare, mirrors the intrusion of traumatic memory into the present that has shaped, and ruined, all these lives.

Born just before the downfall of the Third Reich, Sebald was raised in an amnesiac Germany. In his East Anglian voluntary exile, he turned the unspoken horrors of yesterday into mournful, but gorgeous, fables for today. His prose – old-fashioned by post-war German standards, but then shepherded with his close oversight into singing, sumptuous English – attends to the unhealed wounds that afflict his characters. When Sebald's narrator closes in on the sources of their trauma, we grasp that these "biographies" compose a litany of suicide, depression and withdrawal. The sheer loveliness of these journeys through lost cities, landscapes and cultures, and the "astounding precision" of these recovered memories, only deepen the prevailing mood of devastation. Max Ferber, the solitary Manchester painter whose story occupies the final, and longest, section, confesses that the "tragedy in my youth" has put forth "evil flowers". They have "spread a poisonous canopy over me" and darkened his days. Those evil flowers diffuse life-blighting toxins through the book.

After his escape to England as a child, Ferber's parents have been murdered in the early stages of the Holocaust. No non-Jewish author in the German language has brought richer literary art, and deeper moral tact, to the endless reckoning with genocide than Sebald. The narrator is "continuously tormented by scruples" about his probing into hidden anguish. Sebald builds those scruples into the oblique and elliptical design of *The Emigrants*. It starts with the elderly Norfolk physician Henry Selwyn: a childhood refugee not from Hitler's Germany but the anti-Semitism of the Tsarist Empire. The recovery of the long-frozen corpse of an Alpine guide whom Selwyn befriended in 1913 first sounds a haunted, elegiac note. This will rise in volume as the stories develop: "And so they are ever returning to us, the dead."

Then comes Paul Bereyter, the narrator's inspirational primary school teacher in Bavaria. Despite his part-Jewish ancestry, he has joined the Wehrmacht and witnessed "more than any eye or heart can bear". His railway-track suicide ("the logistics of railways", those iron facilitators of the Holocaust, often play a part in Sebald's fiction) closes an accursed life. From the advent of the Third Reich, Paul seemed to be "headed for death". In the third section, Ambrose Adelwarth, the narrator's great-uncle, has flourished in Europe and America as a hotel servant and butler to the rich. Above all, he has acted as the companion (perhaps lover) of the vagabond son of a Jewish banking family in New York. His "infallible memory" proves both his salvation and his torment. After Ambrose's descent into depression, ECT sessions will burn every phantom away.

Sebald layers his "biographies" inside and around a host of other stories. The narrator consults documents, interviews relatives, pores over diaries and letters. With Max Ferber, he recalls how conversations with the reclusive artist helped him tolerate his dank sojourn amid the ruined factories and warehouses of 1960s Manchester. The "industrial Jerusalem" of Victorian times, the pioneer manufacturing city now feels like a soot-blackened "necropolis or mausoleum". In this drizzle-soaked urban tomb, itself an "immigrant city" where many German Jews congregated, he uncovers Ferber's lifetime of grief, with its plunges "from one abyss to the next". "Mental suffering," Ferber confides, "is effectively without end". His murdered mother's diaries return us, with exquisite tenderness, to the ordinary Jewish family life of a Bavarian town. Now, we can only reach it across "a wilderness of graves".

Critics make much of Sebaldian melancholia, his art of ruins, as if he was simply striking an aesthetic pose. But fierce rage and despair at the bottomless sufferings of history often break through the jewel-inlaid surface of this prose. So does dry, allusive humour – as in the coded tribute to Vladimir Nabokov, another virtuoso memory-artist, who (unnamed) turns up three times, brandishing his butterfly-catching net. For Nabokov, the butterflies of reminiscence may redeem the ravages of time; for Sebald's figures, their beauty merely aggravates the pain. In the "ghost house" of European history, he lets the spectres speak. However sweet their voices, they tell us of sorrow without measure, and without term.

Translation: Michael Hulse (1996), who collaborated with the author, creates an "English Sebald" thoroughly, and beautifully, steeped in the literary traditions of Sebald's adopted country.

See also: Nabokov, *The Gift* (1938); Grass, *The Tin Drum* (1959); Bassani, *The Garden of the Finzi-Continis* (1962); Grossman, *See Under: LOVE* (1986)

Selected works by the same author: *Vertigo* (1990); *The Rings of Saturn* (1995); *On the Natural History of Destruction* (1999); *Austerlitz* (2001)

98 | The Land of Green Plums (1993) by Herta Müller.

German (Romania/Germany)

Translated by Michael Hofmann (Granta)

Mediocre novels of oppression and resistance give to tyranny a glamour and competence that, in real life, it seldom ever possesses. Their secret policemen are cunning; their bureaucrats sophisticated; their interrogators suave. A streamlined autocracy tracks, probes and crushes its brave rebels with technocratic efficiency. Turn from such fantasies to the run-down, ramshackle, horribly intimate cruelties of Herta Müller's fiction, and the reader experiences not just the force of art but the shock of truth. Born into the German-speaking minority community of Romania, Müller was a child, student and young adult under Ceausescu's dictatorship. She migrated to Germany in 1987. From the torn material of her youth, she fashioned this uniquely sinister work of witness and of vision.

A chillingly lucid testimony from a country where "we had to walk, eat, sleep and love in fear", *The Land of Green Plums* also shows in a language of shattered beauty how the virus of totalitarian terror ravages the minds and bodies of its victims. Its terse, almost documentary precision fuses with poetic subjectivity. In this shambolic realm of falsehood and dread, feelings of self-doubt, even self-hatred, can drive solitary free-thinkers into doing the authorities' dirty work for them. Various exit-routes from this living death beckon: oblivion through sex or drink, passivity, flight – and suicide. The narrator senses that "Death was whistling for me from afar, I needed to sprint to get to him". Only a faltering pulse of courage and integrity – a "heart-beast", the novel's original title in German – will hold her back. In the forest, her fellow student Georg explains, the old men make whistles in order to madden birds, disorient them, and push them to their deaths. Only one species, the "imperturbable" butcher-bird, withstands these torments and "refuses to go crazy".

The Land of Green Plums depicts a group of characters who either draw strength from their own "heart-beast" or succumb to that fatal whistle. We begin in a student dormitory. Six young women under the nosy surveillance of the Party and its minions secretly manufacture mascara out of moistened soot and seek out "whisper-thin nylons" rather than baggy cotton stockings. These are country girls, vulnerable newcomers in the city who wear the look of some "poor province" in their faces. Lola, most deprived of all, will find solace in the arms of rough factory-workers and then – the first of several such escapes – choose suicide.

Apart from its periodic flashbacks to the narrator's rural childhood, Müller's storytelling has the dream-like logic and swift, uncanny poetry of some dark fairy tale. Here, arbitrary power and the urge to resist it come dressed as a Gothic fable: a tale of forests and mirrors, knives and sacks, rabbits and stags, crones and butchers. Those unripe plums, one of several plants or creatures laden with symbolism here, will poison the greedy picker: "you'll swallow your death". Yet the police gather toxic fruit with seeming immunity. The perils and horrors of the Brothers Grimm return as peasant-style Communist despotism. Totalitarian control has infantilised an entire society, locking it into the primitive nightmares of village childhood. "No cities can grow in a dictatorship," we learn, "because everything stays small when it's being watched."

The narrator and her trio of German-Romanian friends, Edgar, Kurt and Georg, furtively whisper their dissent and read banned books: among them, Durkheim's *On Suicide*. Their fathers, as ethnic Germans, have fought as volunteers for Hitler's SS and helped to "make graveyards". In this history-scourged landscape, one vile regime hands the baton of terror to another; the parents' complicity in state violence shadows family life. The students' watcher is Captain Pjele, a wicked uncle of a low-level spook. His regular attentions, aggrieved as often as sadistic, deepen the mood of warped, scuffed domesticity. This security state functions like a low-budget soap opera. In keeping with this stifling climate, the narrator will be betrayed by her beloved, duplicitous friend Tereza. By then, however, "My distrust caused everything close to me to slide away."

While the narrator works, post-university, as a translator of instruction manuals for a factory, Kurt becomes an engineer in a slaughterhouse. In this gory, reeking microcosm of the state, the cattle killers "drink warm blood" from their terrified prey. Dismissed from their posts for "subversive activities", the malcontented quartet slip rapidly towards a final break with their benighted land – or perhaps with life itself. Georg dies, an apparent suicide, soon after he flees to Germany. After her own escape, the narrator receives death threats. For all their shabbiness, the arms of Captain Pjele and his henchmen may be long. As for the treacherous Tereza, a plum-shaped tumour threatens her from within: punishment internalised. Still, the exiled narrator has overcome her desire "never to take another step on this earth". Her "heart-beast" has survived, and broken free.

Translation: Michael Hofmann's version (1996) has the story-book strangeness, the curdled lyricism, and the visceral intensity that Müller's prose demands.

See also: Kafka, *The Trial* (1925); Platonov, *The Foundation Pit* (1930); Kadare, *Chronicle in Stone* (1971); Kundera, *The Book of Laughter and Forgetting* (1978)

Selected works by the same author: *The Passport* (1986); *Travelling on One Leg* (1989); *The Appointment* (1997); *The Hunger Angel* (2009)

99 | A Dictionary of Maqiao (1996) by Han Shaogong.

Chinese

Translated by Julia Lovell (Columbia University Press)

From Gogol's nameless Russian backwater and Eliot's Middlemarch to García Márquez's Macondo, fiction with the highest goals and broadest views has often flourished in small places. Nonetheless, few major works can have sprouted in so harsh a soil as Maqiao: that dirt-poor village of "a few dozen households" between the Luo river and the unforgiving mountains in Hunan province. This spot has "almost dropped off the map". During the chaos and carnage of Mao's Cultural Revolution, the then-teenaged Han Shaogong was sent in 1970 to this remote corner of China as one of the "Educated Youth", ordered to purge the sins of urban privilege in a life of redemptive toil. After six years, Mao died, and China started on its road to reform. The "Educated Youth" returned to civic life. Han would eventually embark on a literary career. Two decades later, he transformed those life-shaping years into a work that ranks among the most original, most powerful and yet most entertaining of the novels that, as the 20th-century ended, sought to dramatise and interpret the drama, and trauma, of China's recent past.

Often, in the work of Han's contemporaries, one feels that the mass and energy of this historical material has, like a river in spate, overwhelmed the genre that seeks to harness it. If Western authors from affluent, stable communities may wither from a dearth of nutrients, their Chinese contemporaries face the opposite challenge. Han's solution is shrewd, bold and, although at first outlandish, deeply satisfying to any reader who shares the skittish, scurrilous but humane spirit of his book. He presents his novel of Maqiao, its people and their turbulent times as a "dictionary". The 110 entries – local stories, legends, character-sketches, notes on dialect, history and folklore – add up to the lexicon of this community: a deprived village fated to withstand history's unending shocks.

This is not an overtly "dissident" novel. Even so, the arbitrary cruelties of the system that exiled Han crowd his tales. He deplores the death-dealing upheavals of the Great Leap Forward and the Cultural

Revolution as "act upon act of bitter farce… far too much human brilliance dissipated into absurdity". His "Dictionary" narrows its focus from the vast canvas of oppression and revolution to the intimate scale of an inter-related group of peasants. They absorb the blows delivered by distant powers, in one "reign of terror" or another, then revert to the customs, the stories and above all the words that mould their way of life. "There is no unified sense of time," the narrator discovers. His spell among the quizzical misfits of the "Educated Youth" in some ways feel likes time travel. If his mishaps as a gauche outsider in this remote nest of myth and gossip bind the book, so do the unfolding relationships between a dozen or so main characters. They include the Party secretary Ma Benyi, the former village head Uncle Luo, the stonemason's tragic wife Shuishui and the unforgettable Ma Ming – a curmudgeonly Daoist eccentric whose free-spirited scorn for convention and conformity allows him to "overpower any authority".

Han's method is to pick a dialect term or phrase that reveals some unique aspect of village mentality, then expand it into a story: ribald, spooky, farcical, poignant, horrific, often all at once. Language matters deeply here, in a book that, anecdote by anecdote, suggests speech can never be "absolutely objective or neutral". Maqiao's lack of "an independent system for female nomenclature", for example, testifies to its women's subordination. "Words," we learn, "have lives of their own." When Maqiao folk reverse the meaning of terms, so that "brutal" signifies skilful, they voice a past in which specialist knowledge carried a "tendency towards violence and terror". Here, people define "cleverness as the enemy, brilliance as treachery". Han balances this almost anthropological investigation into language as the circumference of mind with splendidly robust tales of ghosts and passions, tricks and monsters. These episodes anchor us in the most ancient traditions of Chinese storytelling.

Today, however, the Party seeks to control all narrative, all vocabulary. For the narrator, the remembered jargons and slogans of the Cultural Revolution can provoke "deep, uncontrollable revulsion". Surveying not only his rustic microcosm, but Chinese and global culture, our well-travelled and well-read guide asks if history is "nothing but a war of words… Does grammar chop off arms and heads?". Han shows that it can, and does. Against Party doctrine, rigid meaning and standardised speech, the novel rejoices in slippages, ambiguities, digressions; in "sidelong glances" that break the "main line of cause and effect". So, at one point, Han chooses to write the "biography" of two maple trees that shade the villagers and "provide company for the lonely". Eventually, Party cadres, fearful of the "superstitious" awe the trees command, axe them into furniture. But all who sit on the seats where the ghosts of the "Maple Demons" now languish suffer an uncontrollable itch. As so often in Han's world, the old, the vernacular, the peculiar, has the last laugh (or scratch). Even trees may take revenge on "the murderers who chopped them down".

Translation: Julia Lovell's spirited, ingenious English rendering (2003) keeps pace with a work that treats language as both theme and medium.

See also: Gogol, *Dead Souls* (1842); Laxness, *Independent People* (1934-35); García Márquez, *One Hundred Years of Solitude* (1967); Kadare, *Chronicle in Stone* (1971);

Selected works by the same author: *Pa Pa Pa* (1985); *Woman Woman Woman* (1985); *Homecoming and Other Stories* (1992); *Intimations* (2002).

100 | The Feast of the Goat (2000) by Mario Vargas Llosa.

Spanish (Peru/Spain)

Translated by Edith Grossman (Faber & Faber)

In *The Feast of the Goat,* one of the cronies of President Rafael

Trujillo privately sums up the Dominican Republic as "a small country, a huge hell". From 1930 until his assassination in May 1961, the tyrant Trujillo presided through terror, torture, bribery and fraud over the "grim spectacle" of a people "destroyed, mistreated and deceived", and "the enthronement, through propaganda and violence, of a monstrous lie". By the time that Mario Vargas Llosa published this novel, though, Trujillo had lain in his grave for almost four decades; his grotesque regime in the Caribbean state had drifted into a twilight zone between folklore and history. Since the Argentinian writer-statesman Domingo Sarmiento pioneered the genre with *Facundo* (1845), the "dictator novel" in Latin America had tended to cloak the misdeeds of actual autocrats with fictitious identities, and to push topical critique in the direction of fable or allegory. Deploying, with captivating zest and drive, all the weapons of the modern political thriller, Vargas Llosa chooses to root his dictator story in a specific place and time. He follows the chronology of real events in the Dominican Republic and – apart from one invented family – fills the book with historical figures. Yet this semi-documentary "faction" about the bloody end of a half-forgotten despot turns into a study of corrupted and corrupting power that achieves an authority stretching far beyond Latin America. Trujillo's ravaged fiefdom serves as the testing-ground, the tropical laboratory, for Vargas Llosa's investigation into moral and social "paralysis". He dissects the "numbing of determination, reason and free will" under dictatorship, and reveals the ways in which a poisoned public realm will envenom every human bond. For the author, this was more just than a literary conceit. In 1990, the novelist had rashly run for the Peruvian presidency. For a while, he even looked likely to triumph. The populist demagogue who beat him, Alberto Fujimori, would himself become a milder sort of Andean Trujillo.

The Feast of the Goat traces, in swift-moving, suspenseful chapters that race and swerve with a breathless velocity, the climax of a conspiracy to murder the tyrant after his 30 years of rule as "Benefactor" of his country. He has become one of those "anomalies of history" whom disciples treat as "Forces of Nature, instruments of God, makers of nations". Emboldened by the progressive winds blowing through the Caribbean in the era of both Kennedy and Castro, fortified by the Catholic hierarchy's belated stand against Trujillo's abuses, the plotters have mixed motives and diverse backgrounds. They do succeed in slaying "the Goat" as he drives towards yet another rape of a hand-picked teenager at the Mahogany House: the lair to which the infirm seventy-year-old satyr summons well-born virgins. Then blunders, backslidings and mix-ups stall their plan for a wider coup and the installation of a joint civilian-military government. The ascetic figurehead president, Joaquín Balaguer, emerges as a shrewd and decisive operator who seizes power himself.

The captured conspirators endure atrocious, sustained torture before their inevitable execution. However, the slaughter of the "Beast" has whipped up an irresistible storm of change.

The novel begins and ends not with the plotters but with Urania, a successful New York lawyer and daughter of Senator Agustin Cabral: one of Trujillo's compromised political entourage. As we slowly learn, in the scenes of her reluctant return to the capital, Santo Domingo, in the 1990s to visit her ailing father, she has also been a victim of the Goat. Agustin had agreed to sacrifice her to win back the dictator's favour. Even now, "I'm empty and still full of fear." If the Dominican Republic acts a microcosm for Vargas Llosa's interrogation of the reasons why a people may worship a monster, then Trujillo's serial abuse of terrified girls becomes the ultimate, concentrated proof of his depravity. Now forty seven, and alone, Urania feels that "Papa and His Excellency turned me into a desert".

Vargas Llosa takes care to show us the Goat's charming and charismatic side. Despite his thuggish and rapacious sons, those "operetta buffoons" and his epic embezzlements, he has modernised the republic, renewed its infrastructure. The "Chief" argues with force and guile that the mission to redeem his country from "backwardness, chaos, ignorance and barbarism" justifies the bloodstains (including the xenophobic massacre of thousands of Haitian immigrants in 1937). The devil does play plausible tunes. But, beyond even the plotters' horribly prolonged torture (one of them has to swallow his own testicles after castration with scissors), the novel's form makes the cruelties inflicted on girls and women the final riposte to any apologia for autocracy. Vargas Llosa intercuts the Cabrals' family story with the assassination plot. Urania's solitary fate becomes the clinching indictment of the Goat. For all its Hollywood-style craft and pace, as one action-packed sequence flows into another, *The Feast of the Goat* delivers a commanding analysis of macho politics. It shows how tyranny magnifies intimate violence into mass coercion. Along with most of his fellow tyrants, Trujillo has long departed. Yet the pathologies, both private and public, that Vargas Llosa dramatises still thrive – not only in Latin America. As Urania says, "Something from those times is still in the air." This novel not only thrills and shocks, but warns us to beware of its return.

Translation: With force and finesse, Edith Grossman (2001) conveys both the sheer excitement of the plot, and the cancerous sorrow that the Goat's cruelties have spread.

See also: Kleist, *Michael Kohlhaas* (1810); Fuentes, *The Death of Artemio Cruz* (1962); Kundera, *The Book of Laughter and Forgetting* (1978); Müller, *The Land of Green Plums* (1993)

Selected works by the same author: *The Green House* (1966); *Conversation in the Cathedral* (1969); *Aunt Julia and the Scriptwriter* (1977); *The War of the End of the World* (1981)

INDEX OF AUTHORS

INDEX of BOOK TITLES